Family Mediation

The LAW AND PUBLIC POLICY: PSYCHOLOGY AND THE SOCIAL SCIENCES series includes books in three domains:

Legal Studies—writings by legal scholars about issues of relevance to psychology and the other social sciences, or that employ social science information to advance the legal analysis;

Social Science Studies—writings by scientists from psychology and the other social sciences about issues of relevance to law and public policy; and

Forensic Studies—writings by psychologists and other mental health scientists and professionals about issues relevant to forensic mental health science and practice.

The series is guided by its editor, Bruce D. Sales, PhD, JD, ScD(hc), University of Arizona; and coeditors, Bruce J. Winick, JD, University of Miami; Norman J. Finkel, PhD, Georgetown University; and Stephen J. Ceci, PhD, Cornell University.

* * *

Family Mediation

Facts, Myths, and Future Prospects

Connie J. A. Beck and Bruce D. Sales

American Psychological Association, Washington, DC

Published by
American Psychological Association
750 First Street, NE
Washington, DC 20002

Copies may be ordered from
APA Order Department
P.O. Box 92984
Washington, DC 20090-2984

In the U.K., Europe, Africa, and the Middle East, copies may be ordered from
American Psychological Association
3 Henrietta Street
Covent Garden, London
WC2E 8LU England

Typeset in Goudy by EPS Group Inc., Easton, MD

Printer: United Book Press, Inc., Baltimore, MD
Cover Designer: Naylor Design, Washington, DC
Technical/Production Editor: Jennifer L. Macomber

The opinions and statements published are the responsibility of the authors, and such
opinions and statements do not necessarily represent the policies of the APA.

Library of Congress Cataloging-in-Publication Data
Beck, Connie J. A.
　　Family mediation : facts, myths, and future prospects / Connie J. A. Beck,
　Bruce D. Sales.
　　　　p. cm.—(The law and public policy)
　　Includes bibliographical references and index.
　　ISBN 1-55798-748-3 (alk. paper)
　　　　1. Family mediation—United States.　2. Divorce mediation—United States.
　3. Family psychotherapy.　I. Sales, Bruce Dennis.　II. Title.　III. Series.

KF535 .B43 2001
362.82'86—dc21

00-066507

British Library Cataloguing-in-Publication Data
A CIP record is available from the British Library.

Printed in the United States of America
First Edition

CONTENTS

ACKNOWLEDGMENTS

We thank Robert E. Emery, PhD; A. John Rush, MD; David Gooden, ACSW, CISW; and Fredric F. Mitchell, Jr., PhD, for their helpful comments on an earlier draft of the manuscript. Although we used their recommendations in creating the final draft of this book, we assume full responsibility for any errors.

Some of the material contained in this book previously appeared in the journal *Psychology, Public Policy, and Law*.

I

DIVORCE MEDIATION
PRACTICE
AND SCHOLARSHIP

1

AN INTRODUCTION TO DIVORCE MEDIATION

Mediation is a task-oriented, time-limited, alternative dispute resolution process (an alternative to litigation) wherein the parties, with the assistance of a neutral person or persons, isolate disputed issues in order to consider options and alternatives and to reach *consensual* settlement (J. Folberg & Taylor, 1984). In the literature, it is also stressed that mediation emphasizes the parties' responsibility for making decisions.

Why was mediation perceived as needed? Divorcing parents (Spanier & Anderson, 1979), nonjudicial court personnel (Goerdt, 1992), judges (Burger, 1982; Gerber, 1990), and attorneys (W. L. F. Felstiner & Sarat, 1992) have been, at times, frustrated with litigation as a method of resolving domestic relations cases. At one end of the continuum are those divorcing parents who are basically cooperative and frustrated with the rigid rules and adversarial nature of litigation. They would like a more informal and cooperative, less legalistic, process. At the other end of the spectrum are parents who are frustrated because their spouses exploit the legal process by filing unnecessary legal motions, relitigating minor issues, and often failing to comply with judicial decisions. These spouses wish to harass or punish their co-parent or to delay the legal process in hopes, for example, that the co-parent will reconsider their demands and reconcile (Pearson, Thoennes, & Vanderkooi, 1982).

Judges become frustrated when the parties are unwilling or unable to settle issues among themselves or to comply with court decisions and thus repeatedly return to court, clogging judicial calendars. In the 1980s, more than 40% of divorced individuals in the United States failed to comply with support and custody orders (Kelly, 1990b, 1991). In addition, the legal standard that judges must follow for determining child custody and visitation—the *best interests standard*—is at best problematic and has come under attack (a) for being too vague to be helpful in judicial decision making, (b) for increasing acrimony and producing detrimental psychological effects on parents and children, (c) for increasing litigation because the recommendations from a custody hearing are unpredictable, and (d) for creating limitations in the appellate review because of vagueness (D. G. Brown, 1982; Emery, Shaw, & Jackson, 1987; Emery & Wyer, 1987b; Fineman, 1988; Krauss & Sales, 2000; Mnookin, 1975; Scott, 1992). Although there are other standards proposed (i.e., the *approximation standard* and the *least detrimental alternative*), to date they have not been substituted for the best interests standard (Krauss & Sales, 2000; Scott, 1992). Moreover, judges and court personnel often become frustrated with parents who are unwilling to contain their emotions. In most cases, court professionals are not trained to handle emotionally charged litigants in dealing with very private, family-related matters.

Experienced domestic relations attorneys also express frustration in managing divorce cases. In these cases, an attorney's job is to divide assets and future income; to negotiate custody, support, and visitation; and sometimes to protect the physical safety of a parent and the safety of his or her property (W. L. F. Felstiner & Sarat, 1992). Attorneys must ascertain and then negotiate their clients' desires in relation to these issues. This is not always an easy task.

> Clients may not know what they want or may not want what they ought to want. They may change their minds in unpredictable ways, or they may not change their minds when they ought to do so. . . . Emotionally off-balance, angry, depressed, anxious or agitated, they may have trouble understanding what they are told, believing the information that they get and focusing on the alternatives that are presented to them. (W. L. F. Felstiner & Sarat, 1992, pp. 1459, 1460)

In addition, some clients may wish to strike out at the other spouse, thereby altering the posture of the other side and making goals even more difficult to attain (W. L. F. Felstiner & Sarat, 1992). Unrealistic expectations are common, such as saving the marriage, transforming the spouse, or obtaining all the financial assets (W. L. F. Felstiner & Sarat, 1992). Although most lawyers are trained to manage the legal aspects of a divorce, they are untrained to manage the more emotionally based aspects of a client's behavior (Kallner, 1977).

Finally, mental health practitioners who specialize in resolving family conflicts also express frustration with litigation. The adversarial nature of the litigation process can be at odds with parents cooperatively working toward renegotiating new parenting roles and responsibilities. Mental health practitioners are often better trained than legal professionals to deal with the emotional aspects of a divorce and have supported mediation as an alternative to traditional litigation because it supports their efforts in cooperative parenting. Indeed, conciliation court staff mediators are mostly composed of these specially trained mental health practitioners.

Given the importance of mediation in the law's response to families undergoing divorce, the remainder of this chapter describes the evolution of divorce mediation in the United States, delineates current mediation practices, identifies the argued benefits of mediation, specifies the goals for this book, and presents how the remaining chapters are organized to achieve these goals.

THE EVOLUTION OF DIVORCE MEDIATION IN THE UNITED STATES

Turning to mediation taps into a dispute resolution tradition that dates back for thousands of years. Mediation has existed in other countries such as China and Japan, and in particular religious groups such as Jews and Quakers (D. G. Brown, 1982; J. Folberg, 1983; Kelly, Zlatchin, & Shawn, 1985). Although some probation officers were conducting custody evaluations in the United States as early as the 1930s (Cauble, Thoennes, Pearson, & Appleford, 1985), divorce mediation has a very short history in this country (for a detailed history, see D. G. Brown, 1982).

Divorce or custody mediation essentially began in the 1960s when several probation officers and family division employees within the court system began experimenting with informal methods of dispute resolution, and it gained momentum in the 1970s with the changes in the laws governing divorce from fault-based to a no-fault-based divorce system (D. G. Brown, 1982; Cauble et al., 1985; J. Folberg, 1983; Kelly et al., 1985; Little, Thoennes, Pearson, & Appleford, 1985; Lyon, Thoennes, Pearson, & Appleford, 1985). In a fault-based system, litigation is useful in determining who is at fault or guilty (Kelly et al., 1985). As the theory goes, the transgressor deserves to be punished, whereas the other spouse is considered the innocent victim and deserves sympathy, support, alimony, at times most of the family assets and property, and custody of the children (D. G. Brown, 1982). Alimony, custody of children, and division of property based on a determination of fault for the breakup of the marriage were gradually replaced by considerations of equity, fairness, need, ability to pay, and the best interests of the children (J. Folberg, 1983). The legal basis of a decision to divorce in most states is now if the marriage is irretrievably broken, without reference to the specific behavioral transgressions of either party.[1] These no-fault divorce laws then made it possible to develop a no-fault divorce resolution procedure to settle contested issues between divorcing parties (D. G. Brown, 1982).

The first serendipitous mediators were a cadre of court workers who in the 1960s began experimenting with informal procedures in dispute resolution. For example, in 1964 in Hennepin County, Minnesota, the Domestic Relations Division staff began using an approach to custody studies that focused on families making decisions, referred to as *multiple impact therapy* (Cauble et al., 1985). Although the program was later dropped because it was expensive, the family-centered method of dispute resolution was never totally abandoned and the staff never fully returned to a purely investigative model (Cauble et al., 1985). In Stamford, Connecticut, in 1963, a Domestic Relations Officer developed an informal procedure in which he would meet with the parties and their attorneys to attempt to work out a resolution as opposed to conducting a formal investigation (Lyon et al., 1985). This method became increasingly popular, and by 1967, it was firmly established in that court (Lyon et al., 1985).

In the 1970s, several outspoken and politically influential lawyers took to heart the no-fault basis of divorce legislation and more formally began popularizing mediation as a method of divorce dispute resolution (J. Folberg, 1983). For example, in 1969, Coulson, an attorney and president of the American Arbitration Association, encouraged attorneys to use alternative dispute resolution techniques such as mediation and arbitration to minimize the trauma associated with divorce (D. G. Brown, 1982; Coulson, 1969). In the early 1970s, he convened a meeting of the American Arbitration Association and invited social workers, family therapists, divorce lawyers, and a few family mediators to discuss alternative dispute resolution in divorce cases. In the years following, the American Arbitration Association drafted rules for conducting family mediation and developed training for family mediators. In 1983, Coulson wrote an influential book on the topic.

After going through an emotionally traumatic and expensive divorce process himself, Coogler, an attorney and family counselor, also wrote an influential book devoted to his systematic model of divorce mediation (Coogler, 1978), established the first formal private divorce mediation center in the United States (i.e., the Family Mediation Center in Atlanta, Georgia), and established the first professional organization of mediators, the Family Mediation Association (D. G. Brown, 1982). Coogler's model has served as the basis for training thousands of mediators across the nation. By 1982, more than 500 people had completed his basic 40-hour, 5-day

---

[1] There is currently a movement toward reverting back to a pseudo-fault-based system. Some states have passed legislation allowing couples to choose "covenant marriages," which require certain steps before the marriage can be dissolved (e.g., Arizona, 1998b).

workshop (D. G. Brown, 1982), and his model remains one of the pre-eminent models in the field today.

In the 1970s, several legal scholars began writing about the nature of disputes and dispute processing in general (Danzig, 1973; L. L. Fuller, 1970, 1978; Sander, 1976), and their works have been identified as the "intellectual origins of the modern disputes processing field" (Esser, 1989, p. 504). In 1970, Fuller, a professor at Harvard Law School, wrote an article discussing the uses of mediation including divorce mediation (D. G. Brown, 1982; L. L. Fuller, 1970). In 1973, Danzig offered a systems approach to understanding why governmental institutions fail at handling social problems and recommended that complementary processes be added to adjudication to help with social regulation (Danzig, 1973; Esser, 1989).

Court conciliation staffs were most likely the first to offer mediation services as they exist today (J. Folberg, 1983). In 1974, Irving, a family counselor and member of the faculty of social work at the University of Toronto, Ontario, Canada, developed and began evaluating the use of conciliation counseling as an alternative to divorce litigation (D. G. Brown, 1982; Irving & Benjamin, 1983; Irving, Benjamin, Bohm, & Macdonald, 1981; Irving, Bohm, Macdonald, & Benjamin, 1979; Irving & Irving, 1974). The counseling offered in Irving's work was much like the mediation that is offered today. Folberg was the first to use the term *mediation* in connection with counseling couples in a conciliation court setting and suggested how disputes between couples concerning custody and visitation could be mediated by a conciliation court counselor when it became clear the marriage was irretrievably broken (D. G. Brown, 1982; H. J. Folberg, 1974).

Legislation mandating mediation for certain classes of cases (i.e., custody or visitation disputes) was first passed in Massachusetts and Connecticut in 1980, and California soon followed in 1981 (D. G. Brown, 1982). By 1991, there were at least 205 court-related divorce mediation programs, and in 1997 there were estimated to be at least 2,000 programs, many of which offered divorce mediation (J. Nagle, personal communication, April 14, 1997).

As we write this book, there is a workgroup composed of representatives from several professional associations (e.g., the Family Law Section of the American Bar Association, the Association of Family and Conciliation Courts, the Academy of Family Mediators, the American Bar Association Section on Dispute Resolution, the Conflict Resolution Education Network, the National Association for Community Mediation, the National Conference on Peacemaking and Conflict Resolution, and the Society of Professionals in Dispute Resolution) that has developed draft model standards of practice for divorce and family mediators (Model Standards, 2000). The workgroup hopes that the final version of these standards, which is expected to be published in late 2000 or early 2001, will then be adopted by the participating organizations (Shepard, 2000).

Finally, the family mediation movement was also strongly influenced by the writings of scholars from various disciplines, by practitioners (J. Folberg, 1983), and by empirical researchers. Cultural anthropologists such as Nader studied the dispute resolution practices of different cultures and discussed how these processes play a part in social control in those cultures as well as in U.S. culture (J. Folberg, 1983; Nader, 1990). Deutsch (1969, 1973), a sociologist, examined constructive and destructive processes in dispute settlement and the use of third parties in resolution of conflicts (D. G. Brown, 1982). He made a significant contribution toward encouraging more cooperative dispute resolution procedures generally (D. G. Brown, 1982; J. Folberg, 1983). Social psychologists such as Rubin (1971, 1980; Rubin & Brown, 1975) and Pruitt (1971, 1981; Pruitt & Carnevale, 1982; Pruitt & Drews, 1969; Pruitt & Johnson, 1970) laid the early theoretical groundwork for understanding conflict resolution strategies and techniques of individuals and groups. Legal scholars such as Spencer and Zammit (1976), Mnookin (1975, 1984, 1993; Mnookin & Kornhauser, 1979), Fisher (R. Fisher & Ury, 1981; R. Fisher, Ury, & Patton, 1991), and McEwen and his colleagues (McEwen, Mather, & Maiman, 1994; McEwen, Rogers, & Maiman, 1995; Rogers & McEwen, 1994) then shaped changes in legal procedures and techniques for dispute resolution processes to take place outside the traditional legal procedures (J. Folberg, 1983). Practitioners such as Coogler (1978), Irving (Irving & Benjamin, 1983, 1995, 1992, 1989; Irving et al., 1979, 1981), J. Haynes (1988, 1994; J. M. Haynes, 1981), Johnston (Johnston & Campbell, 1987), Saposnek (1983), and J. Folberg and Taylor (1984) have developed and published models of mediation so that hundreds of others could use these techniques in resolving divorce disputes (J. Folberg, 1983). Researchers such as Felstiner and Sarat (W. F. Felstiner, 1974, 1975; W. L. F. Felstiner & Sarat, 1992; W. L. F. Felstiner & Williams, 1978, 1980; Sarat & Felstiner, 1986, 1989, 1995), Irving (Benjamin & Irving, 1995; Irving et al., 1979, 1981; Irving & Benjamin, 1983, 1992, 1995; Irving & Irving, 1974), Kressel (1985; Kressel, Frontera, Florenza, Butler, & Fish, 1994; Kressel & Hochberg, 1987; Kressel, Jaffee, Tuchman, Watson, & Deutsch, 1980), Pearson and Thoennes (1982, 1984a, 1984b, 1985a, 1985b, 1986, 1988a, 1988b, 1988c, 1989; see also Pearson, 1993, 1994; Pearson, Ring, & Milne, 1983; Pearson et al., 1982; Thoennes & Pearson, 1985; Thoennes, Pearson, & Bell; 1991; Thoennes, Salem, & Pearson, 1995), Kelly (1983, 1989, 1990a, 1990b, 1991, 1993, 1995, 1996; Kelly & Duryee, 1992; Kelly & Gigy, 1989; Kelly, Gigy, & Hausman, 1988; Kelly et al., 1985), Emery (1990, 1994; Dillon & Emery, 1996; Emery & Jackson, 1989; Emery, Matthews, & Kitzmann, 1991; Emery, Matthews, & Wyer, 1991; Emery, Shaw, & Jackson, 1987; Emery & Wyer, 1987a, 1987b; Kitzmann & Emery, 1993, 1994), Bickerdike

(1998), and Bickerdike and Littlefield (in press) have evaluated many mediation programs and provided invaluable information concerning its process, practice, clients, and effectiveness.

CURRENT MEDIATION PRACTICES

Mediation does not refer to just one process. The current practice of mediation varies along several dimensions, which we discuss in the following sections.

Models of Mediation

There are several models of mediation, which make different assumptions about the techniques that facilitate couples reaching an agreement on disputed issues (A. I. Schwebel, Gately, Renner, & Milburn, 1994): the legal model (Coogler, 1978), the labor management model (J. M. Haynes, 1981), the therapeutic model (Emery et al., 1987; Irving & Benjamin, 1989, 1995; A. I. Schwebel, Gately, Milburn, & Renner, 1993; R. Schwebel & Schwebel, 1985), and the communication and information model (Black & Joffee, 1978). Although these are not all of the models available to guide mediation practice (e.g., transformative mediation model), they are the ones that were developed specifically for divorce mediation.

Legal Model

This model assumes that parties are rational and will commit to a cooperative process if it is mandated and if they sign an agreement to do so (Coogler, 1978; A. I. Schwebel et al., 1994). The structure of the mediation sessions is argued to be responsible for enabling parties to work together and to produce mutually acceptable agreements by discouraging discussion of emotional issues, which are believed to threaten cooperative problem-solving (Coogler, 1978; A. I. Schwebel et al., 1994). Parties are encouraged to pay in advance for the cost of 10 hours to further encourage commitment to the process. Although this limit of 10 hours is somewhat flexible, clients are encouraged to develop an agreement within this time frame.

All disputed issues are to be resolved in mediation (i.e., division of property, spousal support, child support, and custody and visitation), and the mediator is to address them in a particular order (Coogler, 1978; A. I. Schwebel et al., 1994). Usually one mediator directs the mediation process and is encouraged to offer options, discuss advantages and disadvantages of certain options, and control the decision-making process by retaining sole power to open and close negotiations on each issue (Coogler, 1978; A. I.

Schwebel et al., 1994). Mediators, however, are not encouraged to advocate for, or educate parents about, the interests of the child or children, nor are they encouraged to recommend to the disputants that an agreement be drafted until such time as a sound agreement is reached.

Finally, clients are required to agree to use an impartial advisory attorney who will prepare the negotiated agreement once one is reached. Parties also must agree that if they fail to reach an agreement on all issues, they will submit their case to an arbitrator (Coogler, 1978; A. I. Schwebel et al., 1994).

Labor Management Model

The labor management model (J. M. Haynes, 1981) assumes that give-and-take bargaining on the part of equals representing their own interests will produce a mutually acceptable solution. Adequate agreements are defined to meet eight criteria: full disclosure of economic assets, equitable division of assets, no victims, open and direct channels of communication between parents, protected parental roles, assured access to children for both parents, an explicit process for making future decisions, and assured access to important relatives for the child or children (A. I. Schwebel et al., 1994). Mediators will not draft agreements for couples unwilling to meet these criteria (A. I. Schwebel et al., 1994). Once an agreement is reached, the clients are encouraged to submit the draft mediation agreement to their lawyers.

In this model, mediators are seen as educators and active problem solvers. They primarily teach bargaining skills. But they also take an active position and suggest options; assess whether there is a power disparity between the couple, balance it if there is, and protect the needs of the child or children; define what is reasonable; encourage compromises; hold private caucuses with litigants; selectively summarize the content of the sessions; and stress the unfavorable consequences of failing to reach an agreement (Bickerdike, 1998; J. M. Haynes, 1981; A. I. Schwebel et al., 1994).

In his original model, Haynes also required mediators to assume a therapeutic role if emotional blocks were seen as impeding the progress of the negotiations (Bickerdike, 1998; J. M. Haynes, 1981). More recently, Haynes (J. M. Haynes & Charlesworth, 1996) has changed his position and now argues against mediators assuming this role. He states that his original position was in error. Over the years, he found that combining these roles confuses the clients and the mediator and prevents them from concentrating on ending the dispute by reaching an adequate agreement (Bickerdike, 1998; J. M. Haynes & Charlesworth, 1996).

Therapeutic Model

Proponents of the therapeutic model argue that other models have paid too little attention to the relational processes that disrupt mediation

(Bickerdike, 1998) and that interpersonal or intrapersonal factors often block a couple's attempts at effective problem-solving, rendering the couple incapable of negotiating an agreement (Benjamin & Irving, 1992; Bickerdike, 1998; Bienenfeld, 1983; Campbell & Johnston, 1986; Emery et al., 1987; Irving & Benjamin, 1995; Milne, 1978; Saposnek, 1983; A. I. Schwebel et al., 1993). Thus, the overall goals of therapeutic mediation are to address and resolve emotional issues, develop an equitable agreement that will address the needs of the couple over the long term, and focus on meeting the needs of the children (A. I. Schwebel et al., 1994).

Typically, under this model, mediators (a) take active, directive roles and often serve as educators to inform the clients concerning the needs of the child or children; (b) cover only issues of custody and visitation and assume that splitting these issues apart from the financial issues reduces the chance the child or children will be used as pawns in the financial settlement; (c) often require attorneys to have a limited role (but see Emery et al., 1987); (d) often require clients to sign agreements that they will not see a lawyer while in mediation (e.g., Saposnek, 1983), will not subpoena the mediators to appear at any future divorce-related litigation (Emery et al., 1987), and will not use the content of the mediation sessions in such litigation (A. I. Schwebel et al., 1994); (e) require and provide many more hours of service, when compared with other models of mediation, because of the therapeutic focus of the mediation (Irving & Benjamin, 1995; A. I. Schwebel et al., 1994); and (f) recommend using only one mediator (although some argue that male–female mediator teams are advisable and reduce the possibility of unbalanced alliance between the clients and the mediator(s); Emery et al., 1987). Despite the defining characteristics of this model, it encompasses a wide range of intervention approaches based on different theoretical perspectives (e.g., humanistic, cognitive–behavioral, family systems, organizational development; A. I. Schwebel et al., 1994). This makes it difficult to define the therapeutic model as a single entity (Bickerdike, 1998).

Communication and Information Model

This model assumes that the most efficient way to assist divorcing parents is to provide a lawyer–therapist mediator team approach to solving disputes (Black & Joffee, 1978; A. I. Schwebel et al., 1994). The lawyer-mediator provides parties with legal advice, assists in problem-solving, drafts the agreement, and focuses on the specific details of the settlement (Black & Joffee, 1978). The therapist-mediator provides the parties with information regarding what to expect in the future, educates the clients about the needs of their child or children, teaches communication skills to assist in problem-solving during the negotiations, and focuses on how the couple will negotiate the disputed issues (Black & Joffee, 1978; A. I. Schwebel et al., 1994).

The model used by Black and Joffee (1978), like Irving and Benjamin's (1995), begins with an assessment phase to ensure the couple are ready to negotiate. If the couple are not deemed ready, they are seen by the therapist-mediator for 5 to 10 sessions to help them assess their relationship. Once ready, all issues are discussed separately during the negotiation phase, to provide a clear structure for negotiation (Black & Joffee, 1978). Once an agreement is reached, the lawyer-mediator drafts the agreements and handles the court proceedings (Black & Joffee, 1978). The couples are provided with lists of community resources and relevant books and articles about divorce to provide a framework for understanding their personal experiences during the transition (Black & Joffee, 1978).

Hybrid Models and Programs

There are also hybrid mediation models and programs. These combine mediation and arbitration or some other combination of programs and resources (e.g., using lawyers more fully and effectively in mediation) but have not been clearly articulated in the literature.

Means By Which Cases Are Referred

In some states, mediation is mandatory (e.g., California, 1999); in other states, judges have the discretion to assign cases to mediation (e.g., Colorado Revised Statutes, 1998; Illinois, 1999). In yet other states, participation is voluntary such that the courts need only mention the possibility of mediation to litigants (e.g., Michigan, 1999; New Hampshire, 1999). Although some states do not have statutes explicitly providing for mediation, individual jurisdictions within those states often choose to enact local rules to use mediation (McCrory, 1987; S. Myers, Gallas, Hanson, & Keilitz, 1988; Thoennes et al., 1991).

Criteria to Exclude Cases

Some states allow a waiver from mediation for cases involving domestic violence (hereinafter used synonymously with the phrase *spousal abuse*; e.g., North Carolina, 1999; Oregon Revised Statutes, 1997). Most state statutes, however, do not address the availability of mediation for cases in which there are allegations of spousal abuse (Thoennes et al., 1995). In several states where the court is responsible for making referrals to mediation (as opposed to it being categorically mandated or voluntary), litigants cannot be ordered to mediate in cases of domestic violence (e.g., Louisiana, 1999; Montana Code Annotated, 1998). In at least one state, it is the mediator who is responsible for considering domestic violence issues and is required by law to terminate the sessions if there is evidence of such violence (e.g., Wisconsin Statutes, 1998). One state requires participation in all contested custody and visitation matters, regardless of whether spousal abuse is present, but allows separate mediation sessions for clients when there has been spousal abuse (e.g., California, 1999). There are no guidelines in any of the state statutes for identifying spousal abuse or guidelines for determining the level of spousal abuse that should trigger the exclusion of a case.

Issues to be Settled

Issues range from combinations of custody, visitation, and child support (Keilitz, Daley, & Hanson, 1992) to the entire divorce settlement, including spousal support and division of property (Kelly, 1990a, 1990b, 1991). One jurisdiction has instituted mandatory mediation for any contested issue, whether or not the clients have children (i.e., Minnesota, 1999b).

Behavioral Commitments Imposed on Clients

A few states require that the participants put forth a good faith effort in mediation. What constitutes this effort is not specified in these statutes. One state (Maine, 1998) allows the court to impose a sanction, determined at the court's discretion, upon a party's failure to appear for mediation. This is an important issue for several reasons. Without the threat of sanctions, attendance in even mandatory mediation jurisdictions is in effect voluntary (Thoennes et al., 1991; Trost & Braver, 1987). This creates problems for the courts that will later need to decide what to do next with the case, creates problems for the mediation program in attempting to schedule mediation sessions, and burdens the clients who choose to attend only to have their efforts stymied because the other party is not available to negotiate.

Confidentiality of the Mediation Sessions

In many states the contents of the sessions are both confidential and privileged (e.g., New Hampshire, 1999; South Dakota, 1999). Other states specifically define instances in which information can be divulged, for example, when ethical violations of the mediator occur; both parties consent to a waiver; child abuse is raised; threats of physical violence occur in session; past, ongoing, or future crimes are divulged; or one of the parties commits perjury during the sessions (e.g., Kansas, 1999; New Hampshire, 1999; North Carolina, 1999).

Setting and the Number of Mediation Sessions Offered

Mediation can be conducted by programs within the court (Emery, Matthews, & Wyer, 1991; Emery & Wyer, 1987a, 1987b; Pearson & Thoennes, 1988c) or through private mediators (Kelly, 1991). Research has consistently found that whether the service is free or fee-for-service had great bearing on how many sessions are provided. Private, fee-for-service mediation programs tend to offer many more sessions than are allowed in court-based programs, with the number of mediation sessions ranging from 2 or 3 sessions to as many as 20 (Emery, Matthews, & Wyer, 1991; Kelly, 1991). Even within the court-based programs, the number of sessions or hours devoted to each case varies from court to court (Pearson & Thoennes, 1988c).

Qualifications of the Mediator

Some jurisdictions require specialized training (e.g., South Dakota, 1999) and continuing education (e.g., Louisiana, 1999; South Dakota, 1999) in family mediation and a college or professional degree to conduct mediation (e.g., Louisiana, 1999), whereas other jurisdictions have no training or educational requirements for mediation practitioners (e.g., Kansas, 1999; Mississippi Court Rules, 1998). In addition, whereas some programs require paid professional mediators (e.g., Minnesota, 1999a), others use unpaid volunteers with varied levels of qualifications (McEwen et al., 1995; Singer, 1992). In a 1988 survey, over one third of responding mediation programs reported using unpaid volunteers to mediate divorce and custody cases (Singer, 1992).

Presence or Extent of Lawyer Involvement

Two states require the mediator to advise clients to obtain legal advice (i.e., Louisiana, 1999; Kansas, 1999). In other states, however, mediators are allowed to exclude lawyers (e.g., Montana Code Annotated, 1998; South Dakota, 1999; Wisconsin Statutes, 1998).

Similarities Across Programs

Not all aspects of programs vary as widely as those issues noted above. There are some similarities among court-sponsored, mandatory mediation programs focusing only on custody and visitation issues that are conducted by mental health counselors. This limited range of mediation programs processes the vast majority of clients seen in mediation historically (Pearson et al., 1983) and today, and the programs follow a fairly routine procedure. After contacting the mediation service for an appointment, parents receive a packet of information, including a description of mediation and a questionnaire, which requests general information about the contested issues and specific information about domestic violence. The parents are asked to bring this questionnaire to the initial session. In addition to obtaining this self-report questionnaire, many jurisdictions allow the mediation service to request the parents' divorce file from the courts. The information on the questionnaire and in the file allows the mediators to assess whether the case is best handled by a mediation team. Long-term contentiousness or serious domestic violence necessitates special arrangements, such as the use of a combination male–female mediator team. Many mediation services also provide alternative procedures for those cases with a history of domestic violence (e.g., "shuttle mediation" in which parents come in on separate days or are located in separate rooms on the same day).

The initial portion of the first meeting typically includes an orientation session, which explains in detail the process and goals of mediation. In many (although not all) jurisdictions, the parents are then seen individually to more specifically screen for domestic violence issues that may not have been discussed in the court file or expressed on the questionnaire. This individual assessment also helps to identify other potentially problematic issues, such as mental health, drug or alcohol problems, extreme levels of conflict between the couple, or other specific issues of concern for the client in negotiating a settlement. The couple is then brought together, and the more formal portion of mediation begins. Issues to be considered are enumerated, and the spouses are given the opportunity to present their positions and negotiate. After the presentation and negotiation of the issues, the mediator drafts an agreement reflecting any decisions that are reached. If the parents have attorneys, this draft agreement is then sent to the attorneys, and one of the parties' attorney is asked to file the agreement with the court once approved by both attorneys. If there are no attorneys involved, the parties sign the agreement, and the mediation service files it with the court.

The Growth of Mediation in the United States

The reason for the growth of mediation programs throughout the United States is partially due to the political success that mediation advocates have had in influencing social policy. By 1991, there were at least 205 court-related mediation programs for domestic relations cases: 75 categorically mandated participation, 75 permitted judges to decide mandatory referrals on a case-by-case basis, and the remaining 55 allowed initiation by one or both parties (McEwen et al., 1995). There is no indication that this trend has changed significantly in the last decade. The National Center for State Courts' personnel estimate that there are now at least 2,000 alternative dispute resolution programs, many including mediation programs for domestic relations cases (J. Nagle, personal communication, April 14, 1997). In addition, the American Bar Association Standing Committee on Dispute Resolution estimates that 4,500 separate jurisdictions mandate mediation in contested custody and visitation disputes (Melamed, 1989). In terms of issues to be mediated, 109 of the above-mentioned 205 court-related programs focused exclusively on custody or visitation conflicts, and the other 96 also undertook spousal support and property division issues (McEwen et al., 1995).

THE BENEFITS OF MEDIATION

Mediation has grown extensively because of presumed wide-ranging benefits of the mediation process. Through this process, benefits can flow to the litigants and the legal system. For litigants, benefits of mediation are argued to be empowerment and self-determination (D. G. Brown, 1982; Dukes, 1993; Engram & Markowitz, 1985; Marlow & Sauber, 1990; Newmark, Harrell, & Salem, 1995; Yellott, 1990; see also Cobb, 1993), which are accomplished in numerous ways, such as when mediators (a) assist parties to settle their conflict and teach cooperative dispute resolution skills; (b) allow each party the opportunity to completely air grievances while the other parent listens, which is rarely allowed in litigation; (c) provide a less adversarial forum than a courtroom setting; (d) focus the parents on the needs of the children and thereby limit the psychological damage to the children and the parents' relationship reportedly caused by the litigation process and its focus on discrediting the other party's position to obtain a better bargaining position; and (e) develop agreements that are more satisfying to both parties, thereby increasing the likelihood that the parents will comply with them over time (D. G. Brown, 1982; E. M. Brown, 1988; Camplair & Stolberg, 1990; Elson, 1988; Emery et al., 1987; Emery & Wyer, 1987a, 1987b; J. Folberg & Milne, 1988; J. Folberg & Taylor, 1984; Kelly, 1989; Melamed, 1989; Newmark et al., 1995; Pearson, 1994; Pearson & Thoennes, 1985a, 1985b, 1986, 1988a, 1989; A. Taylor, 1988).

Benefits for the legal system include referral of emotionally charged and difficult cases out of the traditional court processes to another agency with specialized processes and personnel specifically trained to manage them (Gerber, 1990). Mediation is generally conducted by either mental health professionals or other professionals with specific training in family conflict and dispute resolution skills, whereas in the courtroom disputes are argued by attorneys and monitored by judges, most of whom have no training in mental health issues, family conflict, or alternative dispute resolution methods. Mediation is also argued to be quicker, less expensive, and private. It increases child support payments, enhances the adjustment of both the parents and the children, teaches parents how to use problem-solving skills in the future to address issues, and is better able to deal with the root causes of problems and conflicts (Benjamin & Irving, 1995; Cavanaugh & Rhode, 1976; Gerber, 1990; Kelly, 1990a, 1990b, 1996; Mnookin & Kornhauser, 1979; Pearson, 1994; Pearson & Thoennes, 1984a, 1984b, 1985a, 1985b, 1986, 1988a, 1989; Pearson et al., 1982).

GOALS OF THE BOOK

Because of the importance of the above-argued benefits of divorce mediation, we decided to critically assess the validity of these claims in this volume. By doing so, this book provides opportunities for mental health professionals to improve the mediation and litigation process for divorcing couples. Although mediation programs are extremely variable within and across jurisdictions, making it difficult to conduct research or to compare program results (Kelly, 1996; Ricci, Depner, & Cannata, 1991), these programs can be evaluated against themselves. Where mediation exists, its argued benefits were used as the basis for drafting statutes or local court rules authorizing its use. These benefits become visible by identifying the goals of these new laws. For example, two state statutes and several scholars define the goals as follows:

> (1) To reduce any acrimony that exists between the parties to a dispute involving custody or visitation of a minor child; (2) [To develop] custody and visitation agreements that are in the child's best interest; (3) To provide the parties with informed choices and, where possible, to give the parties the responsibility for making decisions about child custody and visitation; (4) To provide a structured, confidential, non-adversarial setting that will facilitate the cooperative resolution of custody and visitation disputes and minimize the stress and anxiety to which the parties, and especially the child, are subjected; and (5) To reduce the relitigation of custody and visitation disputes. (North Carolina, 1999)
>
> The purpose of a mediation proceeding is to reduce acrimony that may exist between the parties and to develop an agreement that is supportive of the best interests of a child involved in the proceeding. (Montana Code Annotated, 1998)

Scholars and mediation practitioners have also published statements of the goals of mediation:

> While mediation's goals of decreasing relitigation and increasing compliance are particularly appealing to legal professionals, mediation is also hypothesized to increase communication between parents, decrease bitterness and tension, and clarify the best interests of the chil-

dren. Given the strong emotions and animosity associated with the divorce process, it can be argued that an adversarial method of dispute resolution such as the traditional litigation process can serve to fuel the hostility of the divorcing parents. Mediation's focus on the emotional needs of the family contributes to its popularity among both legal and mental health professionals. (Dillon & Emery, 1996, p. 132)

In contrast to the competitive bargaining model, divorce mediation introduced different elements and potential into the conflict resolution process: direct contact and communication between disputants (reduced distortion in perception and communication), a safe environment and managed conflict (reduced fear, minimized retaliatory actions and conflict spiral), identification of shared as well as individual goals (incentive to cooperate), focused problem-solving (minimized recrimination and accusation, promoted efficiency of process), active participation in the process (better knowledge of facts, higher likelihood of ownership of solutions and agreements), integration of issues (encouraged tradeoffs and meeting individual needs), interest-based negotiations (more likely to produce more satisfactory agreements), and control over and mutual agreement on all issues (more satisfaction, greater likelihood of compliance). (Kelly, 1990b, p. 5)

Enthusiastic claims have been made on behalf of the divorce mediation process by its practitioners and supporters. In particular, mediation is thought by many to reduce hostility and stress, improve the communication and cooperation of the participants, accelerate the psychological adjustment to divorce, result in higher levels of satisfaction with the result, lead to greater compliance with the agreements and after divorce, and reduce the cost and time necessary to obtain final divorce. Few research studies have addressed these claims. (Kelly et al., 1988, p. 453)

Mediation reduces hostility by encouraging direct communications between the participants. This facilitates the permanence of a settlement agreement and reduces the likelihood of future conflict. Mediation tends to diffuse hostilities by promoting cooperation through a structured process. In contrast, litigation tends to focus hostilities and harden the disputants' anger into more rigidly polarized positions. The adversarial process, with its dependence upon attorneys who communicate on behalf of clients, tends to deny the parties the opportunity of taking control of their own situation and increases their dependency on outside authority. Feelings of esteem and competence are important by-products of the mediation process, which also help to provide self-direction and lessen the need for participants to continue the fight between themselves. (J. Folberg & Milne, 1988, p. 9)

Most of these goals can be grouped into the following categories: allow disputants to fully discuss and air their concerns; provide a neutral third party as a mediator; reduce adversarialness to increase the emotional stability of the parents; increase the satisfaction of disputants with legal procedures and outcomes; increase their compliance with court orders; and decrease divorce processing costs. By assessing whether these goals and intended benefits have been achieved and whether unintended consequences have ensued, we can then evaluate whether mediation has fulfilled its promise and potential (Sales, 1983).[2]

In evaluating the implications of the mediation research, we often refer to research that compares mediation with divorce litigation because many of the mediation researchers make this direct comparison by using litigation clients as a comparison group. Because our goal in this volume is to understand mediation, we do not exhaustively review all research addressing divorce litigation. We only review that which is relevant to understanding divorce mediation. Thus, the conclusions we draw in this book are about the goals and benefits of mediation and not about the goals and benefits of divorce litigation. This is an important distinction because future scholarship will need to address this latter topic, using the same evidence-based approach that we apply in this book to mediation. So why did we tackle mediation first? For us, the answer is fairly straightforward. Mediation proponents make evidence-based assertions about its goals and benefits that are rarely, if ever, asserted in regard to divorce litigation.

ORGANIZATION OF THE BOOK

To achieve our goal of assessing mediation's presumed benefits in these areas, Part II of the book evaluates the existing mediation research relevant to the above goals and benefits of mediation. For Part II to be understandable, however, it is first important that the reader understand the methodological limits in the existing scholarship. Thus, chapter 2 considers this issue. Our subsequent analysis in Part II leads us to conclude that mediation diverts many cases from overcongested courts, that it can be satisfying for some disputants, and that it provides some time-limited benefits in regard to cooperative co-parenting. We also conclude that the goals of divorce mediation are confounded and thus lead to research conclusions that are at times equivocal and contradictory. In addition, the research that exists clearly suggests that mediation proponents have overpromised what mediation can accomplish and have failed to confront unintended consequences that can negatively affect disputants and the legal system.

So what direction should mediation advocates and scholars take in

---

[2] We do not address in this book the special concerns presented by individuals who choose to pursue a divorce without having attorney representation. Although this class of disputants is increasing (Sales, Beck, & Haan, 1993a, 1993b), research focusing on them is almost nonexistent. For further discussion of the issues presented by this group for mediation, see Beck and Sales (2000).

the future? We believe that pursuing a true theoretical approach to understanding divorce mediation and then designing methodologically sound programs of research based on that theory (i.e., matching the theoretically driven research question asked with the most appropriate empirical design to answer it) is the first and most important task for developing mediation policies and practices that will meet its intended goals and achieve its presumed benefits. Toward this end, the book concludes in Part III by arguing for the application of new methodologies to mediation research and by outlining the fundamental fabric for how a theory of mediation should develop. It is our hope that the analyses and recommendations contained in this volume will provide the stimulus for the next generation of mediation research and theory that will substantially improve mediation policies and practices.

2

METHODOLOGICAL LIMITS IN MEDIATION RESEARCH

Before we turn our attention to an analysis of the goals and benefits of mediation, it is important to understand the methodological limits in the research that has addressed these issues. This chapter summarizes these methodological concerns, while in Part II, we elaborate on them, citing specific examples of the issues summarized in this chapter.

SUMMARY OF METHODOLOGICAL LIMITS

Taken as a whole, mediation research has been marked by numerous methodological problems. Common problems in nearly all studies include the following: small sample sizes, nonrandom samples and nonrandom assignment to dispute resolution methods, nonequal comparison groups or (more often) no comparison groups, confounding of the dispute resolution process with issues resolved by that process, few actual sessions recorded, and few sufficiently detailed manuals of the model of mediation used. Thus, replication of any study by independent research groups is nearly impossible. Common problems that occur across studies that make comparisons between the studies extremely difficult include differences in the models of mediation used; the issues to be mediated; the physical setting where mediation occurs (i.e., court-connected or private setting); the clients' socioeconomic status, ethnicity, and degree of acculturation; the clients' level of cooperation before entering the dispute resolution process; the number of sessions offered; the outcome measures; and when the data were collected in relation to when the final divorce decree was issued by the court.

At a more fundamental level, mediation programs were created to solve myriad problems associated with the litigation process. Interestingly, other than statistics concerning the enforcement of child support orders and the number of cases that reach trial, there is a glaring lack of comparison data that document these problems. How many parents abuse the legal system to harass their co-parent? In how many cases do attorneys find that the clients are unrealistic in their demands? How many parents are unable to contain their emotions in court hearings? In how many cases do lawyers create significant acrimony between the spouses, and how do lawyers do this (see, e.g., Beck, Sales, & Benjamin, 1996)? There are also no empirically sound studies of lawyer conduct in which random samples of lawyers and client sessions are videotaped or audiotaped so that the true conduct of lawyers can be evaluated, coded, analyzed, and then generalized to the population of all lawyers.

In addition, there are no investigations of the work of lawyers or courts in negotiating divorce settlements that come close to the scope or level of detail found in mediation studies (Dingwall & Eekelaar, 1988; Kressel, 1985). The studies of lawyer negotiations that do exist are qualitative and use nonrepresentative samples of lawyers, so that it is unclear if the findings of these studies would generalize to the greater population of all divorce lawyers (W. L. F. Felstiner & Sarat, 1992). And although research indicates that it is the court hearing itself that litigants find most aversive about the litigation process, there have been no investigations altering elements of court hearings to ascertain if the hearing could be modified to increase user satisfaction with traditional court processes or compliance rates once the case is concluded.

Although there are more studies on mediation than there are on litigation, research on the process of mediation is in its infancy. Few studies have moment-to-moment data from actual mediation sessions giving a clear picture of both mediator and client behaviors (Kelly, 1996; A. Taylor, 1997). Most research on mediator and litigant behaviors relies on self-reports by mediators or disputants, or observations and qualitative analysis by another party (Slaikeu, Culler, Pearson, & Thoennes, 1985; Slaikeu, Pearson, Luckett, & Myers, 1985). And it is not clear how well these self-reports would correlate with objective ratings of mediator and client behaviors, such as those coded and analyzed from audiotaped or videotaped sessions (Thoennes & Pearson, 1985). In addition, the units of behavior from self-reports are not uniform, and investigators have frequently been forced to make assumptions about the intent of observable behaviors (Slaikeu, Culler, et al., 1985; Slaikeu, Pearson, et al., 1985). To date, there are only seven distinct samples of audiotaped or videotaped mediation sessions that have been collected (Bickerdike, 1998; Cobb & Rifkin, 1991b; Dingwall, 1988; Kandel, 1994; Kressel et al., 1994; Pearson & Thoennes, 1982; Thoennes et al., 1991). Several of these samples have been used by different teams of researchers to answer different research questions (Kelly, 1996). For example, the data from Pearson and Thoennes (1984b, 1985a, 1985b) were used by Slaikeu and his colleagues (Slaikeu, Culler, et al., 1985; Slaikeu, Pearson, et al., 1985), Jones (1985, 1988), and Donohue (1991) and his colleagues (Donohue, Allen, & Burrell, 1985; Donohue, Drake, & Roberto, 1994; Donohue, Lyles, & Rogan, 1989; Donohue & Weider-Hatfield, 1988). In addition, all of the samples include several of the methodological limits noted earlier: self-selected samples of clients and mediators, only few mediation sessions of this self-selected sample recorded, nonrandom assignment of clients to intervention, and no manual of treatment provided. Consequently, we do not understand well what actually occurs in mediation sessions; the true differences in behaviors of mediators, lawyers, and judges; or what actually occurs in sessions between attorneys, sessions with attorneys and clients, or sessions with any combination of attorneys, clients, and mediators.

It is critical to note that applied research within the legal system, which is both empirically sophisticated yet inexpensive enough to complete, is extremely difficult to conduct (Levy, 1984). Research is limited by practical and ethical considerations that have generally limited experimenters' control over the research designs used in their studies. Practical considerations are that judges and program administrators are cautious against having their courtroom business, court calendars, or scheduling of clients dictated by the needs of empirically sound research; they have other interests that they view as more important in implementing programs under their direction (Esser, 1989). In addition, clients are extremely mobile and difficult to locate for follow-up, and at times they view discussing highly personal and emotional issues as an invasion of their privacy. Clients can be reticent to have their negotiations videotaped or audiotaped for concerns that the tapes will become evidence in court should their case go to trial. These valid concerns could be minimized and empirically sound research conducted if the administrators of the courts, presiding domestic relations judges, and mediation program directors nationwide understand the benefits and drawbacks of mediation and litigation and agree that it is time to test the veracity of mediation (see Esser, 1989).

Court administrators and presiding judges have the powers necessary to require that certain procedures be followed, and these procedures could make allowances for empirically sound data to be collected and for clients' confidentiality to be protected. Mediation program directors can require that mediators follow the directives given by court administrators and domestic relations judges so that meaningful data can be collected and analyzed (e.g., videotaped sessions; random assignment of mediation clients to different mediation groups). There is some precedent for detailed, empirically sound research including audiotaped and videotaped sessions being allowed in the courtroom. Criminologists have scrutinized the criminal court process using videotaped and audiotaped sessions for at least the last half century (Irving & Benjamin, 1995). It is curious that similar research has not been allowed in the family court arena (Irving & Benjamin, 1995).

CONCLUSION

Collectively, what do these methodological considerations teach us? The answer is that assertions have been made, and questions have been asked, that often cannot be answered with confidence. Indeed, the most obvious conclusion that can be drawn from the research and analysis to date is that it is difficult to assess the success of mediation given the limitations in both methodology and research designs found in much of the published literature (Emery & Wyer, 1987b; Kerbeshian, 1994).

Although we are critical of the mediation research and scholarship, we strongly believe that mediation researchers to date have done an invaluable job of conducting studies in extremely difficult situations. Courts are typically reticent to support, and disputants are hesitant to comply with, empirically sound mediation research design. Thus, despite our concerns with the existing literature, it provides substantial information that is essential to understand and address if we wish to evaluate mediation as a legal approach to dispute resolution for divorcing couples and improve mediation policy and practice. We turn to a critical consideration of this scholarship in Part II.

II

ASSESSING THE GOALS AND BENEFITS OF THE MEDIATION PROCESS

3

FULL DISCUSSION OF CONCERNS

At the heart of mediation is the goal of using nonadversarial procedures to resolve disputes to achieve several benefits for the participants and the legal system—benefits that are argued to be unavailable in the litigation process: the opportunity for each parent (a) to completely air her or his concerns while the other parent listens, (b) to do so in front of a neutral third party, and (c) to do so in a less adversarial forum than a courtroom. Flowing from these procedures are assumed benefits to the litigant and legal system. This chapter addresses the first of these procedural goals: airing concerns. The other two procedural goals are addressed in chapters 4 and 5, respectively.

AIRING CONCERNS

Generally, parents seem to agree that mediation provides an opportunity to discuss their concerns in detail and that this provides some benefit to them. Indeed, studies have shown that one of the major reasons parents are satisfied with mediation, as opposed to litigation, is because they are able to discuss their concerns. For example, in one study 70% to 80% of the respondents agreed that the opportunity to air grievances was extremely important for them (Pearson & Thoennes, 1985b, 1986).

Not everyone agrees that mediation provides ample opportunity to air concerns, however. Some parents feel that the mediation process is rushed and that they were given assembly-line treatment (Pearson & Thoennes, 1985b, 1986, 1988a, 1989). This perception is not surprising given that in some counties mediation is limited to only one session (Delaware; see Pearson, 1993), even though in other counties it can include up to 10 sessions (Dillon & Emery, 1996). Thus, some programs may provide more of an opportunity for airing concerns than others.

In addition, there is a growing literature concerning specific instances when airing concerns face-to-face in mediation can be extremely detrimental to one or both of the parties and to their children (Bryan, 1992; Fischer, Vidmar, & Ellis, 1993; Grillo, 1991; Treuthart, 1993). Cases that include spousal abuse that are characterized by a "culture of violence" provide one example. Culture of violence relationships include three main characteristics. First, a pattern of abuse is present, which can include physical, emotional, familial (e.g., abuse to children and/or extended family), sexual, or financial abuse (e.g., abuser controls all money and financial resources) or a combination of these. Second, a pattern of domination and control is present wherein the abuser maintains control over every aspect of the abused person's life. The abuser makes the rules for the family and enforces them by threats of future violence against the abused person as well as the person's children or extended family and friends. Emotional abuse and social isolation are common and eventually lead the abused person to feel depressed, alone, and fearful that no one will support her[1] or help her if she leaves. Eventually, the abused person is led to feel responsible for the abuse because of minor violations of the rules, even though the rules are seldom explicit and may change from day to day. Third, culture of violence relationships include a pattern of denial and minimization of the abuse. Even when questioned, the abused spouse will deny the abuse or make excuses for why it must be her fault. Ellis (1990) explained that the family is regarded socially as a "private domain" where outsiders are extremely hesitant to intervene in disturbances within the family or come to the aid of even an assaulted wife or partner. In addition, privacy norms governing family relations dictate that observers' or victims' reporting spousal abuse is a deviation from these norms or "snitching." Thus, privacy norms surrounding families support and encourage abused spouses to keep the abuse a secret.

There is also empirical support in other disciplines for the notion that there are different types of marital violence. For example, in the psychotherapy literature researchers have found one type includes mild to moderate physical violence and may be relatively common (Holtzworth-Munroe, Smutzler, & Stuart, 1998); it has been labeled *common couple violence* by Johnson (1995) or *physical aggression* by O'Leary (1993). The

---

[1] Although it is theoretically possible for the abused spouse to be male, it is much more common for the abused spouse to be female.

second type is characterized by more severe husband violence and more pervasive husband control (Holtzworth-Munroe et al., 1998) and has been labeled *patriarchal terrorism* (Johnson, 1995) or *severe violence* by O'Leary (1993). In this second type of marital violence scenario, women are most in danger when attempting to divorce their abusive husbands.

The notion that there are different types of marital violence and that these couples find their way into mediation is also supported in the mediation research. In a study of clients mandated to mediation for custody/visitation in Portland, Oregon, the researchers divided abuse into several categories: intimidation (e.g., threats, stalking, or telephone harassment); physical abuse (i.e., slapping, grabbing, shoving, kicking, or punching); severe abuse (e.g., beating or choking); and use of a weapon to threaten or injure (Newmark et al., 1995). Using an inclusive criteria of "abused" to be those reporting any occurrence of physical abuse, severe physical abuse, or use of weapons or two or more incidents of intimidation, Newmark et al. classified 80% of the total sample of women (and 72% of the men) as abused. The most common type of abuse was intimidation (74% of the women and 61% of the men). Physical abuse was reported by 68% of the women and 55% of the men. Severe abuse was reported by an alarming 38% of the women and 20% of the men. And threats with a weapon were reported by 18% of the women and 15% of the men. The abused women in the study also scored significantly lower than the women who were not abused on measures of empowerment (both personal and in relation to working with the court system). Abused men scored significantly lower than nonabused men in personal empowerment but not in terms of working with the court system. In another study of mediated divorces, about 50% of the women reported that there was violence in the marriage and that the violence impaired their ability to communicate with the ex-spouse on an equal basis (Pearson, 1991, 1993). Of this 50%, approximately 33% of these women also reported that they felt they had less bargaining power in mediation (Pearson, 1991, 1993). The Alaska Judicial Council conducted a study in 1992 concerning visitation mediation and found that 68% of the parents who requested mediation were ineligible because of a statutory requirement that excludes all cases involving domestic violence (Alaska Judicial Council, 1992). It is not known how these categories would map onto Fischer et al.'s (1993) culture of violence couples or whether they would appear at all in the prevalence statistics noted above, because women from culture of violence relationships are not likely to reveal the violence to anyone. But it is reasonable to suggest that estimates of abusive litigants vastly underestimate the problem.

Fischer et al. (1993) argued that relationships characterized by a culture of violence are qualitatively different from relationships with isolated acts of violence. The degree of power imbalances and long-term consequences that occur in relationships characterized by the culture of violence are often absent in relationships with isolated acts of violence (Fischer et al., 1993). For the abused spouses, the pattern of abuse and pattern of domination and control are long-lasting, leave them in a state of emotional exhaustion, and perpetuate fear for their own lives as well as the lives of their children, friends, and extended family. Thus, for these abused spouses, several factors indicate that meeting face-to-face and airing concerns is extremely detrimental.

First, one of the most dangerous times for abused spouses is once they have separated from their abuser (Ellis, 1987, 1990; Fischer et al., 1993; Mahoney, 1991). Contrary to the popular assumption that separation will reduce the amount of relationship violence, the abuser's fear of abandonment from his spouse/partner (Dutton & Browning, 1988) or actual separation tends to increase, not decrease, the violence, with women who are separated from their partners disproportionally assaulted, raped, and murdered (Ellis, 1990; Fischer et al., 1993). Separation limits the abuser's ability to dominate and control the partner (Fischer et al., 1993). Therefore, some abusers will pursue court action including court-mandated mediation because it offers an opportunity for the abuser to see the spouse face-to-face (Fischer et al., 1993). In Newmark et al.'s (1995) study noted above, the researchers found that 45% of the abused women thought physical harm was somewhat or very likely compared with 5% for nonabused women (9% of the abused women reported that it was very likely their spouse would physically hurt them in the next 6 months; 28% thought it was somewhat likely). In addition, abused women were significantly more likely than their nonabused counterparts to report that they were afraid of openly disagreeing with their abuser for fear he might hurt them or their children and were significantly more likely to report that their abuser had gotten back at them in the past for times when they had gotten their way (Newmark et al., 1995). Hence, attending and representing their interests at mediated sessions may be dangerous for abused spouses. Indeed, there are documented cases in which several abused women have been killed by their estranged abusers as the women arrived at a courthouse for a hearing (Fischer et al., 1993; "Lawyers See Rise in Anger," 1996).

There are also documented security problems found at mediation program sites. Of the 56 court-mandated mediation programs in California, 33 reported that security problems or incidents had occurred in mediation sessions or related family court services ranging from physical violence directed toward spouses and other family members to violence toward attorneys and mediators (Ricci et al., 1991). Although 14 of these programs reported having both bailiffs nearby to intervene in the event of violence or other security measures in place, 15 of these 33 had no provisions for security (e.g., no bailiff nearby or beepers to signal for assistance). The programs reporting security problems also noted that they commonly confiscated weapons brought into their offices (Ricci et al., 1991).

The second reason why meeting face-to-face may be extremely detrimental is the actual communication pattern of the couple. Fischer et al. (1993) argued that all couples develop idiosyncratic modes of communication. Single words, facial expressions, gestures, or tones of voice go unnoticed by outsiders but convey clear meaning to the couple. An abuser, therefore, is able to intimidate and control the abused person through hidden symbols that even the most astute mediator may not identify (Fischer et al., 1993). Such illicit communication stymies all meaningful airing of concerns.

Some argue that mediation programs can screen for these types of relationships and offer the abused spouse alternative procedures, for example, meeting with the mediator on separate days, meeting in separate rooms, and offering to have someone walk the abused spouse to her car (Duryee, 1995; Erickson & McKnight, 1990; Girdner, 1990; Landau, 1995; Magana & Taylor, 1993; Marthaler, 1989; Newmark et al., 1995; Vincent, 1995; Yellott, 1990). All of these measures *assume* that the abuse will be identified. As noted above, Fischer et al. (1993) argued that abused spouses involved in culture of violence relationships will often not identify the abuse even when directly questioned because of embarrassment or fear of future violence against themselves, their children, and their extended family or friends. Mediators, like everyone, are incapable of identifying abusers' hidden signals; thus current screening procedures are useless for this population of abused women. At best, these screening procedures give legislators, program administrators, and mediators a sense of security that spousal abuse victims will be identified, and these procedures probably do identify a number of women who are willing to disclose their abuse. At worst, the screening fails to identify a number of abused women—the women who are at most risk of future violence. Therefore, the culture of violence victim is placed in a no-win situation. Identify the abuse and risk heightened future violence; refuse to identify the abuse and place herself in danger by simply attending a court-mandated, face-to-face session; or not respond or not attend the mediation sessions and risk contempt charges and possible sanctions for failing to appear at the sessions.

It is not only mediators who fail to identify abuse. Domestic violence, at least in its milder forms, is commonly found in couples seeking therapy. Nonetheless, detailed pretreatment assessments by therapists likewise often miss the presence of abuse (O'Leary, Vivian, & Malone, 1991). O'Leary et al. showed that therapists are treating violence in many couple therapy sessions without realizing it. If trained mental health professionals fail to detect abuse, it is unlikely that mediators untrained in mental health issues will detect it. And even if spousal abuse is detected, there is another imposing problem. There are currently no legal or empirically derived criteria that specify the level or type of abuse that would preclude a couple from mediating their case. The mediator is thus put in an extremely difficult position of first trying to assess for domestic violence, which in some cases will not be effective. Then, if it is found, the mediator has to try to decide how to proceed without the benefit of any research findings or established guidelines.

Abused spouses are not the only ones who may find meeting face-to-face to air concerns harmful. One type of family, characterized by a particular pattern of enmeshed interaction, has been identified by many researchers as making mediation extremely harmful (Isaacs, Montalvo, & Abelsohn, 1986; Johnston & Campbell, 1987; Kressel et al., 1980; Mathis & Yingling, 1990; McIsaac, 1987; Ricci, 1980, 1989; Saposnek, 1983; J. A. Walker, 1986). Although much of the above-cited research is anecdotal, found in extremely small sample sizes or in studies in which no control group is used, it does appear to be a pattern consistently identified in article after article. Given different labels by different researchers, Mathis and Yingling (1990) provided a summary of the different terms and descriptions of the pattern (i.e., disorganized structure, negative intimacy, frequent and direct fighters, impasse, fused, chaotic, incompatible spousal strategies, structurally coupled, pas-de-deux). Essentially the couples become stuck in endless negotiation and "dispute for the sake of disputing, negotiate and renegotiate interminably, derive little benefit from it and ultimately achieve no settlement" (Mathis & Yingling, 1990, p. 125). Ricci (1980) argued that the couple has no sincere desire to resolve substantive issues but to continue to fight to maintain a level of intimacy in the relationship. In essence, the couple have a tacit understanding; they "agree to disagree," and they agree to act out this understanding by rigidly holding opposing positions (Jones, 1994). Additionally, if allowed, the couple will fight until both are financially and emotionally drained (Isaacs et al., 1986).

Kressel et al. (1980) described one variant of the enmeshed relationships noted above. These couples tend to have extremely high levels of conflict, frequent communication, and extreme ambivalence about the decision to divorce. They often continue to live in the same residence, sleep in the same bed, and have sexual relations. Most times one or both come to mediation grudgingly. Negotiations are long, acrimonious, and get bogged down in squabbling over minutiae. Airing concerns then becomes a vehicle to continue the enmeshed relationship rather than end it.

In the second type of relationship identified by Kressel et al. (1980), autistic relationships, communication and overt conflict about the possibility of divorce are almost entirely absent. There is, however, an undercurrent of anger, hurt, and anxiety about discussing the issues to be settled in mediation. Negotiations are described as one parent acquiescing without offering opinions or ideas. The acquiescing parent will then sporadically make demands and not allow any negotiation of the terms of the demands. The couple has an extremely difficult time communicating, and informed negotiations never occur. Because of the lack of mutuality of decision making, the authors contend that these settlements may break down over time.

Both patterns of relationships (i.e., enmeshed and autistic) share the same underlying inability of the spouses to engage each other in constructively identifying areas of conflict and then resolving them (Kressel et al., 1980). The opportunity to air concerns tends to recapitulate the major dynamics of the relationship in a capsulized form (Kressel et al., 1980). For these two types of couples, airing concerns is not helpful. It may be that there is a basic incongruence between the goal of the mediator and the goal of the clients. Whereas the goal of the mediator is to engage the couple in cooperative and constructive problem-solving, the unstated goal of the clients is either to maintain the conflicted relationship (enmeshed couples) or to avoid open discussion of the problems (autistic couples). This basic incongruence between goals of the respective parties then makes it extremely difficult for mediation to succeed in producing an agreement.

While illuminating, the studies from which these couple types arise are limited in that the sample size is extremely small (14 couples) and there are no data offered on prevalence of any of these couple types in mediation or litigation. Therefore, it is unclear how many of each type are divorcing and how many of each type are involved in mediation and litigation. Further research to replicate these patterns is essential.

Beyond the mediation literature, the clinical literature also identifies a pattern of couple interaction that is not conducive to airing concerns. In the "demand–withdraw" pattern of couple interaction (DWI), one partner is very critical and demands behavioral changes from the partner, whereas the partner defends his or her behavior, avoids directly talking about the issues, or withdraws completely (Christensen, 1987, 1988; Shoham, Rohrbaugh, Stickle, & Jacob, 1998). This pattern is commonly found in couples in which the husband has a problem with alcohol (Bepko & Krestan, 1985; Shoham et al., 1998; Treadway, 1989). In these relationships, the wife criticizes and demands changes from her alcoholic husband. The husband then withdraws or defends himself. This response leads to more demands on the part of the wife. This pattern repeats itself, both partners playing integral parts in keeping the cycle going (Shoham et al., 1998). Shoham and her colleagues conducted a study with couples high and low on DWI and tested two therapeutic interventions, one which places a high level of demand on the drinker for abstinence and change (cognitive–behavioral), and one which takes a more permissive stance toward abstinence and adjusts itself to the drinker's readiness to change (family systems). The researchers hypothesized that therapeutic intervention that mimicked the family communication pattern currently operating would be seriously compromised. The researchers reasoned that the high-demand therapy would recapitulate the unhealthy pattern of interaction that the couple currently have (i.e., the therapist demanding change and the husband withdrawing, defending). They further reasoned that for the couples to change and break this ineffectual pattern, the intervention would need (a) to be more fluid with less demands for change in a specified time frame and allow for setbacks without punishment and (b) to reduce the demands of the wife. The results indicate extremely high dropout rates for high DWI couples enrolled in the cognitive–behavioral intervention, the therapy that mimicked the current relationship. These dropout rates were much higher than for those couples enrolled in the family systems intervention, the one which did not mimic the ineffectual relationship interaction pattern. A similar pattern of results was obtained for abstinence rates.

Extrapolating these results to the mediation context, it may well be that there is a Treatment × Couple interaction. Divorcing couples high on DWI who attempt to resolve their contested issues with a mediator using a model of mediation high on demand and directiveness (i.e., structured mediation, see Coogler, 1978; labor management model, see J. M. Haynes, 1981) may well find that the airing of concerns is harmful and mimics the currently operating family interaction process. The "demander" will monopolize the speaking time, criticize, and make demands, and the "withdrawer" will defend his or her position, which leads to more demands, and so on.

If the mediator attempts to control the interactions by placing demands on the husband to respond to the wife's concerns, to produce counterproposals and negotiate directly, the relationship created between the husband and the mediator recapitulates the relationship between the husband and wife.

The DWI variable has also been found to differentiate domestically violent couples (Holtzworth-Munroe et al., 1998). Using observational measures of couple interactions, these researchers found the husband/demand wife/withdraw pattern in a sample of domestically violent and distressed couples. In this pattern, the husband makes the demands (i.e., pressures, nags) while the wife withdraws (i.e., becomes silent or refuses to discuss the issue further). The researchers found that the husband/demand wife/withdraw pattern was more common among couples in which the husband displayed higher levels of violence and distress and less common among the less violent and nondistressed couples. In other words, the husband/demand wife/withdraw pattern may be uniquely related to couples with high levels of marital violence and distress (i.e., culture of violence couples wherein the wife files for a divorce). Other researchers have also found that violent distressed couples are more likely to self-report high levels of negative behaviors (Lloyd, 1990).

Holtzworth-Munroe et al. (1998) found elevated levels of contempt in violent distressed couples during discussions in which the wife was requesting a change in the dynamics of the marital relationship or changes in specific behaviors of her spouse. These researchers suggest that this finding may reflect other coercive and abusive behaviors and raises questions about whether the wife is truly free to request relationship changes in therapy. A parallel concern could be made for negotiations in mediation for these wives; wives in these relationships may not be free to negotiate for their respective interests. Taken together, these findings indicate that there are potentially important differences in the communication patterns of domestically violent couples that may interfere with an ability to mediate differences in a divorce. In particular, if the wife wants the divorce, and there is a husband/demand wife/withdraw pattern of communication between the couple, airing of concerns and negotiating equitably will be difficult if not impossible for the wife.

As Holtzworth-Munroe et al. (1998) noted, national data indicate that approximately 2 million women are severely assaulted by their husbands each year (Straus & Gelles, 1990). Many of these woman will divorce their husbands and be mandated to attend mediation. This, coupled with the findings that violent men in distressed relationships are particularly likely to respond violently to situations in which they perceive their wives to be abandoning them (Dutton & Browning, 1988; Holtzworth-Munroe et al., 1998), abused women are significantly more afraid than their nonabused counterparts of openly disagreeing with their husbands because they fear he may hurt them or their children, and abused women are significantly more likely to perceive their abuser to have greater decision-making power, makes for a serious situation for these women in mediation. At present there are no criteria for determining when or if mediation is appropriate with domestically violent or abusive couples. It may be that the DWI variable can shed some light on when wives in these couples are possibly unable to participate meaningfully in mediation. In addition, careful and detailed research studies of the type initiated by Newmark et al. (1995) wherein the researchers attempt to determine the types of violent episodes, how often these events occur, and how the different types of violence relate to women's fears and feelings of empowerment both with the court system and personally take a giant step forward in understanding this important issue. Recommendations for managing divorce cases for couples with abuse in their backgrounds offered by Newmark et al. (1995, pp. 58–59) are reasonable and prudent and include the following:

1. All court personnel, including judges, court commissioners, mediators, and evaluators, should be trained in the dynamics of domestic abuse.
2. Effective screening protocols should be incorporated into all family court dispute resolution services, including those contracted out to private providers. Screening should include the

opportunity for each parent, without the other parent present, to discuss concerns about safety or intimidation prior to any joint negotiation or decision making.

3. Screening questions should be specific and ask about prior abuse, decision-making procedures, conflict resolution practices, and concerns about safety.

4. Options that allow parents to avoid face-to-face contact should be made available to anyone who has concerns about joint sessions. This may include custody evaluations with separate sessions exclusively, shuttle mediation, and so on.

5. Parents should have the option of bringing a support person and/or legal counsel to assist them in any process that is intended to include negotiations over custody or visitation.

6. All court-connected services should have information on resources within the community (e.g., shelters, anger-management programs, and counselors) for clients.

Although these recommendations are important, it also must be acknowledged that they may still fail to identify the women from culture of violence relationships—those most at risk for future violence—because they rely on the women to identify the abuse.[2]

Obviously, not all couples are likely to have problems airing their concerns in mediation. Mediation is likely to be helpful in some cases, even though it is harmful in others. For example, Kressel et al. (1980) identified two additional relationship types that are quite compatible with airing concerns: direct-conflict and disengaged types. The direct-conflict relationships have high levels of overt conflict but frequent and open communication. Most have seen therapists and have worked through the more emotional aspects of the divorce. The conflicts are mainly focused on realistic fears of dividing scarce financial resources. Disengaged relationships have little communication and conflict, but through lack of interest, as opposed to anxiety in the autistic types of couples discussed earlier. Both members of the disengaged couples only wish to complete negotiations and are basically fair to each other as well as the children. For these couples (i.e., direct conflict and disengaged), there is an overall congruence between the mediator's goals and those of the couple, and both wish an even-handed, directive intervention to arrive at an equitable settlement. It is interesting that although disengaged couples do well in mediation (Kressel et al., 1980), research has found that these couples do not do well in behavioral couple therapy (Jacobson & Addis, 1993). There may be less

[2] The mediation process might be improved if alternative procedures (e.g., non–face-to-face sessions) were offered to *all* couples, not just those identified as having domestic violence as a factor. In this way, women can more safely participate in mediation without having to specifically identify their abuse or abuser.

congruence between the goals of the couple and the goals of the therapist in this situation (i.e., disengagement vs. active engagement).

Beyond the couple-level variables, several researchers argue that there are also individual-level variables that are important to consider in mediation (Bickerdike, 1998; Bickerdike & Littlefield, in press; Campbell & Johnston, 1986; Kressel, Pruitt, & Associates, 1989). In some cases, these individual-level variables might make airing concerns face-to-face in mediation unproductive and detrimental. Kressel et al. argued that there has been a historically strong focus on family systems theories, or the "equal blame" perspective, in mediation which postulates that each part of the family system is simultaneously a cause and an effect for the current couple dynamics. The researchers postulated that in this way, mediators can more easily fulfill the demands of the philosophy of mediation that they remain impartial. Because all members are equally culpable, impartiality is reasoned to be appropriate. While this is attractive in theory, Kressel et al. argued that there are also individual-level variables that must be acknowledged as extremely detrimental to the mediation process and eventual settlement. Kressel and his colleagues conducted an in-depth case study of 12 cases with high levels of parental conflict and found three such individual-level variables: the interpersonally dysfunctional parent (IDP), the bad faith negotiating style, and the unresolved marital attachment.

The IDP exhibited five characteristics (Kressel et al., 1989, p. 59):

1. A narcissistic preoccupation with own needs and inability to perceive needs of other parent or children.
2. A disparaging, dismissive, or irresponsible attitude toward other parent, particularly around child-care arrangements.
3. An open or covert encouragement of the children to be disrespectful of the other parent.
4. Irresponsible or destructive behavior during mediation.
5. An incapacity to acknowledge any genuine responsibility for one's own role in the conflict.

Kressel et al. stated that although having an IDP parent in mediation was not necessarily "fatal" to mediation, there were several predictable negative consequences, including the other parent becoming withdrawn or uncooperative. In addition, the mediators had an extremely difficult time generating any productive efforts at joint problem-solving, and often mediation would come to a grinding halt. In essence, the presence of this single disruptive negotiator made problem-solving difficult, even in the presence of the mediator (Bickerdike, 1998; Bickerdike & Littlefield, in press), and made any airing of concerns impossible.

In the case of the bad faith negotiator style, these negotiators failed to keep appointments or appeared very late for sessions. They also revised positions when old demands had been met, postured without serious efforts to negotiate, and introduced new sets of demands when agreements were nearing completion (Kressel et al., 1989). These negotiators again made any meaningful airing of concerns unproductive because no true problem-solving occurred.

In the case of unresolved marital attachment, one or both of the spouses remained ambivalently attached. One or both spouses indicated that they still wished to go for marital counseling or were deeply upset by the breakup. Or, at times, the attachment was inferred by a preoccupation with the other's postdivorce relationships or activities. The results of having one or both spouses attached in this manner in mediation attempting to negotiate a divorce agreement were punitive or rigid stances, or sometimes total noncommunication in negotiations, an inability to clearly articulate needs, or refusal to approve a settlement agreement that had been just worked out in detail in mediation. Although Kressel et al.'s (1989) work on the individual-difference variable is fascinating, it needs to be replicated with a larger sample. With only 12 cases, it is difficult to extrapolate these findings to the larger population of divorcing couples. For example, it is unclear how many of each type of individual noted above are involved in mediation and litigation.

Another researcher also found an important individual-difference variable. Bickerdike (1998) and Bickerdike and Littlefield (in press) found that high levels of disparity in attachment between the couple were negatively associated with problem-solving and settlement in mediation. He reasoned that this high disparity is probably indicative of both an individual-level variable (i.e., that one spouse is more attached than the other) and a couple-level variable. At the individual level, high attachment disparity indicates that the resulting negotiating behavior is that one person is obstructing settlement by not participating in effective problem-solving. Bickerdike reasoned along the lines of Emery's (1994) model of the cyclic nature of the divorce process. At the couple level, the movement of an individual along his or her emotional path is extricably tied to that of the partner. While the attached party is obstructing negotiations, the unattached party is probably responding angrily and with contentious behavior. Bickerdike stated that the cause-and-effect relationship between these two variables is not clear. Bickerdike also indicated that polarized couples may have difficulty agreeing about what should be discussed such that the unattached initiator of the divorce may wish to discuss practical and substantive issues, whereas the attached responding party wants to discuss emotional issues surrounding the relationship.

In addition, Bickerdike (1998) and Bickerdike and Littlefield (in press) also found that both at the couple and individual levels, high levels of anger prior to entering mediation were associated with less problem-solving behaviors, higher levels of contentious behaviors, and poorer mediation outcomes. Bickerdike suggested that for some couples even the interventions of skilled mediators are unable to overcome the detrimental effects of preexisting levels of anger. He also reiterated that several researchers have argued that conflict can be exacerbated by facilitating face-to-face communications between these angry couples (Kressel et al., 1989; Rubin, 1985; Rubin, Pruitt, & Kim, 1994). The couples take the opportunity to abuse and attack each other, thus increasing the conflict rather than dampening it.

CONCLUSION

In summary, face-to-face airing of concerns is a particularly complex phenomenon, one that cannot be adequately addressed by a sweeping philosophy that regards airing concerns in this manner as a much more effective method of dispute resolution for everyone involved in a dispute. As the research discussed in this chapter indicates, mediators must pay close attention to both couple- and individual-level variables that affect face-to-face negotiations. It is also important to acknowledge that at present the state of the art in assessing the suitability of couples for this form of dispute resolution is insufficient for mediators to fully recognize and screen out clients whose characteristics indicate that face-to-face airing of concerns is unproductive, detrimental, or potentially physically dangerous. These concerns are particularly poignant in programs driven by state-level mediation statutes or local court rules mandating clients to attend mediation for certain disputes.

4

A NEUTRAL THIRD PARTY
AS MEDIATOR

Some argue that mediation is distinct and stands apart from the traditional adversarial litigation (hereinafter "litigation") system in that it returns control to the parties for decisions concerning the conditions of their divorce (J. Folberg & Milne, 1988; J. M. Haynes, 1981; Irving & Benjamin, 1995). For jurisdictions that accept this argument, it will be reflected as one of the goals within their mediation statutes or local court rules. In support of this goal, these state statutes may define the role of a mediator as *neutral facilitator* and give the clients the right to determine the terms of the final agreements. This chapter addresses whether the neutral facilitator position can be achieved and under what conditions.

NEUTRALITY-AS-IMPARTIALITY

Cobb and Rifkin (1991b) demonstrated that there are two separate and competing conceptions of neutrality used in the mediation literature: neutrality-as-impartiality and neutrality-as-equidistancing (cf. Feer, 1992). Neither conception is clearly defined, nor are the practice implications of each conception ever fully explored empirically or theoretically in the mediation literature. When Cobb and Rifkin examined possible scenarios for how mediators could meet these competing directives, they found that it was impossible to attain both types of neutrality simultaneously. As a result, it is impossible to create mediator neutrality and adequate ethical and practice guidelines for mediators.

Neutrality-as-impartiality is defined as an absence of bias on the part of the mediator. Mediators are to separate their own private attitudes and values from the mediation process to avoid having these personal attitudes influence the negotiation process or the content of mediation agreements. Impartiality is the result of a mediator monitoring her or his internal psychological processes and guarding "against psychological processes that may favor either disputant" (Cobb & Rifkin, 1991b, p. 44). Mediator bias is thus bad and to be avoided (Cobb & Rifkin, 1991b). But an obvious question is, can mediators set aside all personal biases (developed through attitudes and values) in their decision making and be truly impartial?

To answer this question, we need to examine the relevant social psychology literature. Verbal interactions are always somewhat ambiguous and frequently have multiple meanings. As a result, some degree of interpretation on the part of the individual receiving the information is required (Fazio, 1986; D. G. Myers, 1996). The filter through which people interpret these communications is to an important extent composed of their attitudes and values (D. G. Myers, 1996). Research suggests that attitudes include several components and that, under certain circumstances, attitudes and values serve as a guide for behavior (Fazio, 1986; Kraus, 1995). Thus, the notion of impartiality implied in the mediation literature includes impartiality in the initial *perception of information*. But more importantly, impartiality also involves the mediator's judgment and *use of information*.

Attitudes comprise three sources of information: affective, behavioral, and cognitive (the "ABCs" of attitudes). Information from these sources is then used to categorize a stimulus or piece of information along an evaluative dimension (Zanna & Rempel, 1988). It is generally agreed that the affective component is defined as all positive or negative emotions toward the object (S. E. Taylor, Peplau, & Sears, 1997). The *cognitive component* is defined as the thoughts, facts, knowledge, and beliefs the person has about the particular object, whereas the *behavioral component* refers to a tendency to act regarding an object (S. E. Taylor et al., 1997). Attitudes facilitate quick access to relevant information and other related attitudes, because they provide important linkages among information held in memory. Thus, preexisting values and attitudes facilitate quick perception and categorization of information (Judd, Drake, Downing, & Krosnick, 1991), which in turn facilitates rapid decision making (Fazio, 1986).

Applying this information to the mediation context, mediators have preexisting affects, behaviors, and cognitions (the "ABCs") regarding the mediation clients, preexisting beliefs about appropriate models and strategies for conducting divorce mediation, and preexisting beliefs about the appropriate terms for divorce agreements. The As, Bs, and Cs then serve as the filter through which information from a particular couple is perceived. In other words, to be truly impartial, mediators would need to have no preexisting positive or negative feelings concerning divorce mediation or the specifics of divorce agreements (the affective component). Mediators would also need to have no preexisting knowledge so the new information processed would not be biased (the cognitive component). And the mediators would need to have had no previous experience with the mediation process to act truly freely, without influence of previous experience (the behavioral component). Of course, none of these three contingencies hold true. Mediators do have previous experience, or (one hopes) at least some training, and thus have preexisting negative or positive feelings, thoughts, facts, knowledge, and beliefs about mediation clients, mediation agreements, and appropriate models and strategies for conducting mediation sessions. It should not be surprising, therefore, that researchers have shown that mediators do not separate their attitudes and values from the mediation process and that these attitudes and values have a profound impact on the process of mediation and the agreements that are ultimately produced (e.g., Dingwall & Greatbatch, 1991; Folger & Bernard, 1985).

The second issue regarding impartiality is how people act on or use information as a result of their biased perceptions—the B portion of the ABCs of attitudes. There is a long tradition of social psychology research investigating the connection between attitudes and behavior (Kraus, 1995). Although there is some controversy concerning the specific conditions under which attitudes guide behavior, it is now generally agreed that under certain circumstances there is considerable consistency between an individual's attitudes and behavior.

> It now appears that stable attitudes, important attitudes, easily accessed attitudes, attitudes formed through direct experience, attitudes about which people are certain, and attitudes that show a high degree of consistency between cognition and affect are most likely to predict behavior. (Kraus, 1995, cited in S. E. Taylor et al., 1997, p. 166)

At least in the court-sponsored mediation context, in which much of the mediation is practiced today, most of these conditions are met. For example, in court-sponsored mediation programs, mediators work with clients every day and thus have a good deal of direct exposure to their attitude objects (e.g., litigants and the mediation process generally). It is well established that attitude–behavior consistency is greater when direct experiences with the attitude objects occur than when attitude objects are only heard or read about (Fazio, 1986; Kraus, 1995).

Frequently expressed attitudes are very accessible (S. E. Taylor et al., 1997), and those attitudes that are more accessible in memory influence behavior more strongly. Again, court-sponsored mediators are working with clients on a daily basis and are accessing and expressing their attitudes frequently. In court-sponsored mediation programs, a mediator must explain to clients the mediation process and how it will be applied to them. In doing so, the mediator must frequently express his or her attitudes. Attitudes often become more extreme when they are expressed frequently (Downing, Judd, & Brauer, 1992). It is therefore likely that mediators will become more extreme in their attitudes because they express them on a daily basis. In addition, highly accessible attitudes heavily influence behavior because they are automatically activated at the mere presence or mention of the object (Kraus, 1995; S. E. Taylor et al., 1997). It may be that mediators' attitudes are activated when they see the clients or when they start thinking about work. Recent research suggests that even less accessible attitudes may automatically become active when the attitude object is present (Bargh, Chaiken, Govender, & Pratto, 1992)—in the mediators' case, when clients are present.

Moreover, much of one's behavior is guided by one's attitudes and values, albeit often without one's awareness or intention (S. E. Taylor et al., 1997). Thus, it seems exceedingly unlikely that a mediator will be able to monitor internal and automatic cognitive processing of information without their personal attitudes affecting their judgment and behavior (Cobb & Rifkin, 1991b).

Values are similar to attitudes and are defined as central principles around which an individual's goals and behavior can be integrated (e.g., freedom, justice; Reber, 1985) or as personal convictions about what is desirable and how people ought to behave (D. G. Myers, 1996). Research has shown that for most individuals values also have a profound influence on attitudes and behavior (Mellema & Bassili, 1995). In the mediation context, mediators' values appear to have significant impact on their behavior. Those mediators who hold self-determination to be an important value would allow parents to make their own decisions, even if it meant allowing them to reach an agreement with which the mediator did not ethically agree (Folger & Bernard, 1985). Those mediators who hold justice as a value, however, would intervene to shape agreements to their own sense of justice and, for example, try to favorably balance the interests of weaker parties (Folger & Bernard, 1985). It appears from Folger and Bernard's study that the values mediators hold could strongly influence their decisions concerning when and how to intervene in the mediation process. Empirical research in practice settings of actual mediator behavior is needed to confirm this finding.

Information perception, and often behavior, are biased by attitudes and values. As A. Taylor (1997, p. 220) stated: "There is no such thing as total impartiality, neutrality, or lack of bias when working with people, even though as practitioners they may strive for such ideals." Taylor then went on to define ethical practices along a continuum from "strict" to "expanded" neutrality (A. Taylor, 1997). Whereas the strict neutrality anchor represents mediators who do not balance power, do not use private caucuses with individual clients to deal with emotional or intrapersonal conflict, and stay mainly within a narrow definition of neutrality, the expanded neutrality anchor includes mediators who actively use power-balancing techniques, intervene to help clients bargain, and use private caucuses with individual clients to strategize and train a client to be a better negotiator and allow the client to vent emotions (A. Taylor, 1997). The use of the term *expanded* neutrality to define this second anchor epitomizes the current conundrum of defining acceptable mediator practices while still using the word *neutrality* as a descriptor. What is described is anything but neutral. A more literal definition of the expanded neutrality anchor would be described as active, directive, and therapeutic intervention. Defining expanded neutrality as neutral only masks mediator practices behind a guise of neutrality that no longer exists for many mediators.

The Family Law Section of the American Bar Association (ABA) also seems to acknowledge that information perception and subsequent behavior are biased by attitudes and values but maintains the use of the term *neutrality*. The ABA *Divorce and Family: Mediation Standards of Practice* (1986), although not official ABA policy, instructs mediators to disclose to their clients their biases and strongly held views on issues to be discussed in mediation (Standard IIIb). Standard III states that by doing so the mediator discloses information concerning when his or her "judgement might influence the participant's decision making." The clients are therefore informed that the information they provide to the mediator will be perceived through the filter of the mediator's stated biases and strong views. It is reasonable to assume that for the drafters of the ABA Standards, biases and strong views are the result of what the social psychology researchers define as values and attitudes. Thus, it appears that the ABA Standards de facto recognizes that it is impossible to perceive information totally independently of these values and attitudes. The ABA Standards clearly recognizes that these biases may strongly affect mediators' judgments and the advice they give, which in turn influences their clients' decision making. Unfortunately, the ABA Standards still retain the directive for mediators to be impartial even though other portions of the Standard clearly recognize that impartiality is impossible and require mediators to identify their biases.

ALTERNATIVES TO IMPARTIALITY

It is interesting to note that several mediation researchers have abandoned the notion of impartiality altogether. These researchers strongly advocate against mediators adopting an impartial style, arguing that a more active, directive, and investigative style will produce more durable agreements and more satisfied clients (e.g., J. M. Haynes, 1981; Kressel et al., 1994; Maxwell, 1992). In support of this view is a study that identified two distinct mediator styles: maintaining impartiality (settlement-oriented) and investigating underlying causes of conflicts and directing discussions of options (problem-solving; Kressel et al., 1994). Settlement-oriented mediators mainly strive for obtaining an agreement. They do not probe the clients for background information concerning their conflict, circumstances, or needs. If the parents do not wish to address the underlying causes for conflict, then these issues are left unaddressed. Settlement-oriented mediators place great weight on maintaining impartiality, leaving the primary responsibility for resolving conflicts with the parents. They also do not strategically direct the negotiations to reach a particular result. A problem-solving mediator, on the other hand,

> attaches greater importance to sound problem solving than to settlement per se, subordinates "neutrality" to the task of correctly identifying the relevant sources of conflict, and acts in a manner suggesting that leadership of the problem-solving rests with the mediator rather than the parties. (Kressel et al., 1994, p. 77)

Because of the active, investigative role that problem-solving mediators play, the researchers argue that problem-solving mediators are better able to present the parties with integrative proposals for breaking impasses (Kressel et al., 1994). As a result, problem-solving mediators often decide the terms of the agreement, as well as directly control the process.

In terms of case outcomes, Kressel et al. (1994) found that settlement-oriented mediator cases settled less often and had more postmediation court action, indicating less durable agreements. These researchers theorized that because the underlying reasons for the conflicts are not addressed at the time the tentative agreements are reached, the agreements fall apart and the couple resumes the conflict. It also appears that clients of problem-solving mediators are more satisfied than clients of settlement-oriented mediators. Problem-solving mediation clients who reached agreements were much more willing to be interviewed 18 months after mediation was completed than were settlement-oriented clients (57% vs. 28%, respectively), and they had more positive feelings toward mediation.

Kressel et al. (1994) concluded that a problem-solving mediation model thus produces a more focused, structured, and vigorous approach during mediation; more frequent and durable settlements; and a generally more favorable attitude toward the mediation experience. Thus, they argued that impartial mediators do their clients a disservice and that, in fact, mediators should not strive to be impartial (Kressel et al., 1994). In this view, mediators should strive to use the problem-solving style, which is much more active, investigative, and directive than the neutrality-as-impartiality position would advocate.

It may well be that the needs of the clients dictate how a mediator must proceed. The style of the mediator may need to vary depending on the quality of the relationship between the parties. Pruitt (1995) argued that when there is a positive relationship between the parties, the couple can generally negotiate a solution and third parties should stay away from the controversy and let the parties negotiate on their own. When the relationship is not heavily conflicted but the spouses have reached an impasse on some issues, Pruitt suggested that a third party may be useful to overcome minor problems in the perception of the other party's position and move beyond bargaining postures to actually resolving issues. An impartial mediator may be effective in this situation. When there are negative feelings on both sides, Pruitt suggested that there may need to be a significant amount of relationship therapy before mediation or negotiation can be effective. The more escalated the battle between the couple, the more effort needs to be put into building a relationship before the couple will actually be able to resolve their differences (Pruitt, 1995). This type of mediation does not necessarily fit well with the neutrality-as-impartiality model. Relationship therapy requires active intervention on the part of the mediator and willing parties.

In addition, long-term success in mediation (compliance, improved relationship, and satisfaction with the agreement in the long term) was not related to either short-term success (whether an agreement was reached) or initial satisfaction with the agreement (Pruitt, 1995). Long-term success was related to the degree of joint problem-solving during the session and may be related to practicing a skill that is useful in the future (Pruitt, 1995). Both the relationship type of the couple and the desire for long-term success of any agreement reached may necessitate different intervention styles that move well beyond neutrality-as-impartiality for some couples.

NEUTRALITY-AS-EQUIDISTANCE

A second conception of neutrality in the mediation literature is equidistancing (Cobb & Rifkin, 1991b). By this definition, mediators are required to prevent parties from coercing each other, and they do so by balancing power between the parties when it is appropriate. Neutrality-as-equidistance is seen as a relational process between the parties and the mediator rather than a psychological process internal to the mediator, as was the case with neutrality-as-impartiality. "The notion is that mediators may, at a given moment, favor one side or the other, but unbiased settlement is the 'summative outcome' of this process" (Cobb & Rifkin, 1991b,

p. 44). Bias is thus used as both a negative psychological characteristic that should be avoided and a positive strategy that should be used to attain balanced negotiations (Cobb & Rifkin, 1991b). Unfortunately, there are no clear criteria for determining what a power difference is and when it is occurring, so it is left to individual mediators to make this determination. As Brodsky (1990) noted, the vaguer the goals or criteria are for any given task, the more likely it is that the person making the decisions will use her or his own biases or values.

> In other words, if mediators are equidistant, they cannot be impartial, and if they are impartial, they cannot be equidistant. . . . The presence of these two competing notions of bias (bias as a negative psychological phenomenon and bias as a proximate relationship) makes it difficult, if not impossible, for mediators to assess their own practices: there are no criteria for differentiating these two notions of bias. . . . The discontinuity between these two definitions of "neutrality" and the competing definitions of "bias" contributes to the absence of any coherent or concrete guidelines for the practice of neutrality and leads to paradoxical dilemmas for mediators. (Cobb & Rifkin, 1991b, p. 45)

In addition, there is considerable disagreement in the literature about whether, and how, a mediator should attempt to balance power (Bryan, 1992, 1994; Ellis, 1990; Forester & Stitzel, 1989; Grillo, 1991; Kelly et al., 1985; Marlow & Sauber, 1990; Singer, 1992). Both Mnookin (1984) and J. Haynes (1988) defined elements of power and indicated that if these elements are possessed by spouses in unequal amounts it would constitute a power imbalance. Mnookin (1984) discussed five elements of power:

1. legal endowments (i.e., What are the legal rules governing distribution of marital property, alimony, and child support?);
2. personal preferences (i.e., How do the parties evaluate alternative outcomes?);
3. attitudes about risk (i.e., What is the level of risk each party is comfortable with?);
4. transaction costs (i.e., Are the parties able to wait, pay lawyers or other professionals, and negotiate?); and
5. strategic behavior (i.e., How able are the parties to bluff, support their positions, deceive, or manipulate each other or make power plays to gain the advantage?).

Identification of these five elements of power is an important initial step toward recognizing potential power imbalances. What is now important is to operationalize these five concepts and empirically test whether imbalances in them cause differential assessments of power by the clients, differential assessments of power by the mediators, or differential outcomes of cases containing such imbalances in mediation or litigation forums.

J. M. Haynes (1981; see also J. Haynes, 1988) developed two methods for assessing power imbalances. In one method, J. Haynes (1988) adopted for the divorce context French and Raven's (1959) five areas of social influence and argued that the following are critical components of power: informational influence (i.e., ability to persuade), referent influence (i.e., desire to maintain approval of an individual or group), legitimate influence (i.e., rights given a specific person in a specific role), expert influence (i.e., superior knowledge or ability of one spouse acknowledged by the other spouse), and coercive and reward influence (i.e., ability of one spouse to coerce the other by offering or retracting rewards). From these areas, J. Haynes (1988) developed a rating instrument—the Relative Power Relationship Assessment Form—which sets out each of the five areas of power listed above and can be used to rate both the husband and wife on six different areas important in any divorce where power could be exercised: money, assets, employment (i.e., determination of employment possibilities of each spouse), children, skills (i.e., problem-solving and negotiating skills), and rejection (i.e., which partner initiated the divorce and the extent to which the other partner agreed to or opposed the decision). Future scholarship needs to operationalize these five elements of power and the six assessment areas. Research then should assess the validity or reliability of J. Haynes's (1988) instrument to support differential outcomes for cases in which the framework and instrument were and were not used.

In the second method, J. M. Haynes (1981, pp. 127–128) developed a series of eight guidelines that he used in his practice to determine if balance has been achieved and the divorce mediation has been successful:

1. There has been full disclosure of all the economic assets of the marriage.
2. The economic division of the assets and the necessary support payments are essentially equitable and designed to meet the joint needs of the family and the individual needs of each member.
3. There are no victims as a result of the agreement.
4. The channels of communication between the ex-spouses are open and direct; the mediator will have helped the couple organize a direct way to make decisions about the children.
5. The couple relate to their children as parents, not as spouses, through the acceptance of the permanence of their parental roles in the context of the ending of their spouse roles.
6. The children are able to develop and maintain an ongoing relationship with both parents; thus, the agreement must provide for direct communication with both parents along with an appropriate range of access options regarding both parents.
7. The couple are empowered to make decisions and given the

skills during mediation to continue the decision-making process in their respective futures.

8. The extended families, particularly blood relatives, are protected in their relationships with the children, and the children enjoy the same open access to them as to their parents.

These guidelines now need to be operationalized and research conducted to support their validity and reliability.

Some argue that mediators can balance power by ending mediation themselves or by using various tactics, such as providing pertinent information, organizing material so the weaker party may make his or her case more effectively, forbidding discussion of certain issues, advising a party who seems to be at an economic disadvantage to seek a financial counselor, or advising clients to obtain an attorney to discuss legal options or who can provide a review of the agreement before it is signed (Emery, 1994; Grillo, 1991; Kelly et al., 1985). None of these tactics has been empirically tested, and all are predicated on the premise that a mediator can recognize true power disparities when they occur and can either intervene to lessen their impact (Grillo, 1991) or end the session (Emery, 1994).

There is research that indicates mediators may not be able to "read" power imbalances as well as some would like to believe. In an experimental study, Morrill and Facciola (1992) found that mediators did not form impressions about disputant credibility, socioeconomic class, education, and blameworthiness on the basis of the disputants' speech styles or particular language proficiency, whereas a sample of undergraduates and to a lesser extent superior court judges did so. The authors suggested that the results could be interpreted in two ways. On one hand, mediators could be less swayed by initial impressions because they are trained to draw their inferences about disputants on the basis of sustained interactions as opposed to speech style. On the other hand, because mediators are trained to be tolerant of multiple types of disputant abilities (including language proficiency), they could unintentionally miss important language clues to disputants' relative social power or abilities to represent their own interests. Unfortunately, there are no empirical investigations of differential power and status between disputants, mediator behavior in these cases, and case actual outcomes (Morrill & Facciola, 1992).

Other research in the communications literature supports this view. For example, Singer (1992) noted that in studies of conversations between men and women who know each other, masculine control of male–female dialogues through such techniques as monopolization of speaking time and interruption is so commonplace that even trained mediators may not recognize the power imbalances they so seek to correct.

It may be prudent to hire a legal advisor to attend the sessions. Lawyers are both trained and ethically bound to strongly advocate for their clients. In doing so, they automatically perceive the other party as either having or engaging in activities that will give them a power advantage and a greater chance of achieving a more desirable outcome for their side. This perspective makes lawyers particularly sensitive to potential power imbalances. It may not be economically feasible, however, for a majority of the divorcing couples to use legal counsel (Sales et al., 1993a, 1993b), nor may it be allowed by state statute or local court rule.

ACCOUNTABILITY

There is a distressing dilemma in mediation concerning how to preserve its private, informal nature while providing adequate safeguards for clients against incompetent or unethical practices by mediators. For example, there is a strong desire to maintain the private, informal nature of the mediation process and to balance the power between the parties so the clients can negotiate without coercion and resolve exceedingly emotional and difficult issues out of public view and without the fear that the content of the mediation sessions will be used against any of the parties in the adversarial forum. To a large extent, mediation and mediator practices are purposely designed to be confidential to facilitate negotiations between the parties and to allow the mediator as much flexibility as possible. The focus of those who support private, informal mediation is on *accountability of the result postnegotiation* (e.g., agreements and continuing relationships) and not on *accountability within the process of negotiating* (or mediator strategies in conducting negotiations).

This focus on keeping mediation private and informal can be problematic, however. A substantial portion of mediation is carried out by court-sponsored programs, with heavy system pressures on the mediators to settle cases and settle them quickly to provide relief to the judicial calendars, save the costs of expensive litigation (Gerber, 1990; Kressel et al., 1994), and justify the existence of the mediation program. In addition, private mediators have economic interests that may bias their judgment about whether mediation is appropriate for any given couple. Ellis (1990) noted that in a survey of private mediators, nearly all indicated they would mediate cases of all couples *who could pay them*, presumably without regard for whether the clients and the specifics of their cases were appropriate for mediation. Within this context, it is essential to provide adequate safeguards to protect clients from possible negative results of systemic or economic pressures on mediators that encourage the following: acceptance of inappropriate clients in mediation, misconceived imbalances of power between the parties and thus inappropriate mediator strategies to balance power, mediator pressure for clients to reach agreements, and mediator pressure to dictate the terms of such agreements.

In addition, clients may misconstrue the relationship between themselves and the mediator. There are no formal physical or emotional distancing mechanisms between mediators and parties to the mediation (Grillo, 1991). Mediators may sit close to the parties, frequently see the parties separately without confiding the information to the other party, and often make little attempt to limit the type of personal information considered in mediation, resulting in very emotional and intimate material being discussed (Grillo, 1991). Grillo (p. 1589) concluded that mediators establish a "risky relationship of informality and apparent intimacy with the parties," particularly when the mediator is a mental health professional and not particularly well trained in the important differences between therapy and mediation (Kelly, 1983). Mediation clients may also misconstrue the mediator's role as more that of a therapist than that of a mediator because mediation resembles the therapeutic setting in many ways (Grillo, 1991). For example, both are settings in which the personal problems of the clients are discussed and resolved through talking, intense emotions occur, and therapist-mediators provide active listening, sympathy, and guidance in problem-solving (Grillo, 1991).

Probably the most important aspect of mediation that results in a lack of oversight and external control is that the process is absolutely private in most states (Singer, 1992). There are no records kept of the process, and in most cases mediators are not allowed by statute to submit recommendations to the court or testify in court regarding the content of the negotiations (see Ricci et al., 1991). It can be argued that this flexibility (or unaccountability) is the strength of mediation. The process can be tailored to the needs of the particular litigants and the facts of the case, without worry that the information presented in mediation will be used against either litigant. In the majority of cases in which mediators function ethically, this flexible, private process is one that is probably fair and meets the needs of the litigants. This flexibility has its weakness, however. If the mediator accepts clients who are inappropriate for mediation, misconstrues the balance of power between the parties, applies heavy pressure for the clients to reach agreement, dictates many of the terms of the agreement, or uses other inappropriate intervention strategies, there is little a litigant can do after the fact.

Mediators have tremendous influence over the process of mediation and the content of agreements merely by the manner in which they interact with the clients in session. For example, the order in which the litigants tell their stories has been found to have a profound impact on the process of mediation (Cobb, 1994a; Cobb & Rifkin, 1991a; R. M. Fuller, Kimsey, & McKinney, 1992). The first story told becomes the dominant narrative, and without some positive intervention on the part of the mediator, the second story takes a subordinate position as opposed to a truly alternative position (Cobb, 1994a; Cobb & Rifkin, 1991a). In addition, the process of *selective facilitation* occurs when a mediator's framing of a previous statement of a party seriously constrains a future statement or position of that party and thus leaves the perspective effectively unexplored (Greatbatch & Dingwall, 1989). These problems have not gone unnoticed by the mediation scholars. According to Folger and Bush (1994, p. 5),

> the fundamental flaw is that, because of its lack of formality and structure, mediation cannot adequately regulate their party interventions and even tends to encourage abuse. Without rules of law guiding mediators' response to parties' issues, mediators can alter the very terms of disputes that the parties themselves have framed. Without formal rules of evidence and procedure, less skillful or powerful parties are likely to be at a serious disadvantage during the process. Moreover, without public scrutiny of or accountability for what goes on in the privacy of mediation sessions, there is no way to monitor or limit the kind of abuses just mentioned. As a consequence, when conflicts are mediated, social justice issues can be suppressed, power imbalances can be ignored (or reinforced), and outcomes can in fact be determined by covertly imposed third-party values despite the rhetoric of "mutually acceptable settlement" (Abel, 1982, 1988 [sic]; Fineman, 1988).

Unless the litigant can stop the process and terminate the mediation, there is little recourse. McEwen et al. (1995) noted that one of the benefits of having lawyers present in mediation is to provide a check on mediator behavior. Lawyers can intervene or advise their clients to terminate mediation if inappropriate strategies or pressures are being applied by the mediator. In addition, McEwen et al. noted that in mediation sessions there is a "tumbling-toward-agreement" dynamic that occurs, even when it may be in the clients' best interest to slow down and take time to think about the terms to which they are agreeing. Mediation can be an intense, exhausting experience, and clients may unwisely push for quick resolution to alleviate the need for additional sessions (Bryan, 1994). This, coupled with the excitement of the mediator to draft an agreement, propels clients forward when it may be in their interests to first discuss these issues with their respective attorneys.

There are no empirical studies concerning the number or types of cases in which litigants have questioned, after the mediation was completed, the mediator's impartiality or equidistancing. Several feminist legal scholars have, however, presented anecdotal evidence and case studies of severe abuses of power by mediators (Bryan, 1994; Grillo, 1991; cf. Kelly & Duryee, 1992). This is not surprising. Although a majority of divorce mediators state that they hold neutrality as a goal, in practice it is highly unlikely that they consistently attain this complex goal. Mediators report that they try to consummate only "win-win" (R. Fisher & Ury, 1981) or fair settlements, to balance power between the parties by empowering the weaker party (Kelly et al., 1985), and to protect the interests of the children or other third parties (i.e., grandparents). Neither power balancing nor protecting third parties is consistent with impartiality. In addition, research involving recorded sessions indicates that the interests of the child are rarely mentioned (Dingwall & Greatbatch, 1991). When the interests of the children are mentioned, they are used as a means of applying moral pressure to accept or reject a particular option as opposed to urging parents to consider the well-being of their children (Dingwall & Greatbatch, 1991). Although the profession clearly expects its members to be more than mere process monitors or scribes for any decision the parties might reach, there is no consensus in the literature, and the profession offers no guidelines, regarding when or how to move beyond what Cobb and Rifkin (1991b) defined as neutrality-as-impartiality (Kolb & Kressel, 1994; Kressel et al., 1994). Individual mediators are therefore free to choose their own perspective and apply their own philosophy in each case (Folger & Bernard, 1985). As a result, mediation is to a large degree carried out in an idiosyncratic manner based on the individual values and attitudes of the mediators.

CONCLUSION

Several researchers have suggested that rather than arguing about whether mediators can be neutral, mediators should develop clear statements of their values and list preferred outcomes so that couples are aware that they will be steered in particular directions (Dingwall & Greatbatch, 1991; Maxwell, 1992; Menkel-Meadow, 1993). As already noted, the ABA Standards (1986) adhered to this suggestion to some extent and included the recommendation that mediators inform the parties of any biases or strong views concerning issues to be negotiated. This strategy allows the couple to retain some control over the influence exerted by the mediator (Bernard, Folger, Weingarten, & Sumeta, 1984) and respects the couple's desire to choose a mediator with values matching their own (Menkel-Meadow, 1993). Obviously, the ABA Standards are a model produced by a professional association and not a state statute (see ABA Standard IIIb, 1986).

Other authors have argued that mediation professionals should take it a step further and stop stating that they function as a neutral third party (Forester & Stitzel, 1989). These authors stated that the neutral label presents an image of the mediator that actually obscures issues of power and representation, as well as the mediator's own active influence on the outcomes that might be achieved.[1] It is not clear, however, that such an ap-

---

[1] As noted earlier, it has been argued that to solve the issue of mediator neutrality, attorneys should be involved in the mediation process to help guide outcomes for their clients (McEwen et al., 1995). This, of course, assumes that the litigants are represented and that attorney involvement actually aids neutrality. Unfortunately, attorney representation cannot be assumed.

proach will be helpful in many cases. Court-connected mediation programs do not provide clients with a list of staff mediators from which the client can choose a mediator. And, for those states that use private mediators, mediators are usually assigned to the case, leaving the client little choice. Thus, learning of a mediator's biases, without providing an opportunity to seek a different mediator, may only create or exacerbate frustrations with the mediation process.

Many clients obtain divorces without any legal advice (Beck & Sales, 2000). In addition, there is a range of roles attorneys can provide clients in divorce cases (see p. 63, chapter 5). It is likely that only when taking more active roles are lawyers likely to assist clients in assuring that mediators are neutral. Finally, this solution may merely replace the value-driven influence of the mediator with that of the attorney. But because litigants have a right to select their own attorney, they presumably are comfortable with their attorney's attitudes and values. This assumption is indirectly supported by the fact that, in one study, the clients were active shoppers and contacted an average of 2.3 attorneys before deciding on the one to hire (Sales et al., 1993a, 1993b).

5

REDUCED ADVERSARIALNESS AND EMOTIONAL STABILITY OF PARENTS

The third goal of mediation is to make it less adversarial than litigation, thereby increasing the emotional stability of parents and improving their parenting skills. The adversarial nature of traditional negotiations between lawyers is argued to be a major factor in creating acrimony between parents (Coogler, 1978; Ellis, 1990; Emery et al., 1987; Gerber, 1990; Marlow & Sauber, 1990; Mnookin, 1975; Rich, 1980; Schlissel, 1992) and in creating lasting psychological distress (Bloom, Asher, & White, 1978). Mediation advocates argue that providing parents with a much less adversarial process for resolving divorce disputes will lessen these negative effects (Coogler, 1978; Ellis, 1990; Emery et al., 1987; Gerber, 1990; Kelly, 1990a, 1991, 1996; Marlow & Sauber, 1990; Pearson & Thoennes, 1985b, 1989; Rich, 1980). In this chapter, we consider the sources of adversarialness and its effect on the disputants.

SOURCES OF ADVERSARIALNESS

Adversarial feelings are thought to spring from three sources: (a) the parents' negotiating through intermediaries, as opposed to doing so through direct communication between parties; (b) the very basis of litigation, that is, the presentation of competing positions from which a "truth" or "justice" will emerge, as opposed to cooperation in the development of a solution; and (c) the notion that the lawyers, as opposed to the parents, are in charge of defining the solution. These are all issues that mediation was developed to address. Negotiations in mediation are conducted by the parents, in the presence of a mediator or mediators, and sessions are based on the assumption of cooperation and parent-centered decision making (Emery & Wyer, 1987a).

Concerning the first point, that intermediaries negotiate as opposed to parents, misunderstandings or misinterpretations can occur if a message sent from one spouse is passed through two attorneys before reaching the intended receiver of that information, the other spouse. Social psychological research suggests that information passed through several sources can change significantly as it is passed from one party to another (Allport & Postman, 1975). Yet, no research addresses whether and how this occurs in the adversarial process, and if it does, whether it has a negative impact on clients.

Some attorneys could also cause adversarialness because of their obnoxious negotiation strategies or a desire to prolong cases to increase fees (Mnookin, 1993). Qualitative research from interviews with divorce lawyers indicates that at least some lawyers are argumentative in negotiations and thus could create conflict and animosity. Divorce lawyers in Maine, for example, indicated that it is much easier for them to be obnoxious or aggressive during telephone conversations with opposing counsel or in documents traded back and forth with opposing counsel than in face-to-face meetings with the parents present (McEwen et al., 1995). Unfortunately, there is no empirical research to confirm that *most* lawyers are aggressively adversarial in their negotiating strategies and thus are responsible for creating acrimony between the divorcing parties. Qualitative studies of lawyer conduct, however, indicate that obnoxious, argumentative lawyers are in the minority (W. L. F. Felstiner & Sarat, 1992; Griffiths, 1986; McEwen et al., 1995; Sarat & Felstiner, 1986, 1989, 1995). For example, McEwen et al. (1995) found that the professional norm among the divorce attorneys they interviewed was that of the "reasonable lawyer" who "limits client expectations, resists identifying emotionally with the client, avoids substantially inflating demands, understands the likely legal outcome, asserts the client's interests, responds to new information, and seeks to reach a divorce settlement" (p. 1364).

Sarat and Felstiner (1986) also found in their sample of lawyers that very few encourage angry clients to put forth unrealistic demands without encouraging them to settle and informing them of the risks and likely outcomes of such demands. In fact, research indicates that the major role of the attorney is to limit client expectations and overcome the resistance of angry clients to settle, often called *cooling out* the client (Levy, 1984; McEwen et al., 1995). Indeed, lawyers, like mediators, accommodate their behavior and style to the demands of the case and the parents (Levy, 1984). There is nothing inherent in negotiation that bars lawyers from making attempts to become more sensitive to the client's emotional needs or to learn dispute resolution methods and use them (Ellis, 1990). There is also nothing to bar clients from attending and participating in negotiation sessions between lawyers (Bryan, 1994; Grillo, 1991).

Concerning the second point, that the basis of litigation is the presentation of competing positions thereby creating adversarialness, McEwen et al. (1995) found, in interviews with lawyers, that many clients expect that the lawyer will fight for whatever the client wishes, regardless of the lawyer's perception of the reasonableness of the position. Pearson and Thoennes (1985a) found that, at times, parents wanted their lawyers to be more aggressive and flamboyant. Unfortunately, there are no empirical studies that focus on what lawyers see as their goal in a divorce or that indicate the number and percentage of divorce lawyers who focus on presenting competing positions, and the number and percentage of divorce lawyers who refuse to amicably settle for what is fair. This information is important because, as just noted, the qualitative research has shown that both nationally (Bryan, 1994; W. L. F. Felstiner & Sarat, 1992; McEwen et al., 1995; Sarat & Felstiner, 1986, 1989, 1995) and internationally (Griffiths, 1986), the objective of most lawyers is a "reasonable divorce."

Concerning the third point, that lawyers as opposed to clients define the solution and this in turn creates adversarialness, research indicates that negotiations between clients and their attorneys are complex, and control over decision making is not as straightforward as might be expected (W. L. F. Felstiner & Sarat, 1992; Levy, 1984).

> Interactions between lawyers and clients involve as much drift and uncertainty as they do direction and clarity of purpose. It may be difficult, at any one moment, to determine who, if anyone is defining the objectives, determining the strategy, or devising tactics. (W. L. F. Felstiner & Sarat, 1992, p. 1456)

There are several sources of control in attorney–client relationships that make decision making complex. For example, whereas the attorney has the expertise in determining legal entitlements, the client has the expertise in estimating the other spouse's reaction to offers and demands (W. L. F. Felstiner & Sarat, 1992). Thus, the attorney and client together must negotiate specific terms to maximize the chance of obtaining them.

Divorce attorneys who have clients of diverse social and economic status also are less able to develop firm patterns of domination and control as compared with attorneys whose social position is more consistent with that of their clients (i.e., public defenders and legal aid attorneys; W. L. F. Felstiner & Sarat, 1992). Thus, in some cases divorce attorneys must essentially take orders from high-status, high-power clients and attempt to obtain the directives of the clients as opposed to pursuing their own directives. On the other hand, attorneys may be more directive with clients of similar or lower status and economic power or clients who are emotionally distraught and unable to negotiate effectively or make considered decisions about the future.

W. L. F. Felstiner and Sarat (1992) found that lawyers are intensely concerned that clients adopt "reasonable goals" while giving clients a wide latitude to make decisions. If clients are unreasonable in their desires, there are several methods lawyers use to attempt to persuade clients to reach a more reasonable agreement. For example, one strategy is the "yes . . . but" strategy. Here the lawyers appear to endorse a client's objective only to remind them of the variety of negative consequences associated with it (Sarat & Felstiner, 1986). Procrastination is also used as a strategy when lawyers disagree with their client's agenda or wish to delay the proceedings until the client is more emotionally stable or less angry (W. L. F. Felstiner & Sarat, 1992; Levy, 1984). Given that lawyers' goals can differ from clients' expectations, it is not surprising that lawyers in one study generally espoused an ideology of shared responsibility for decision making, although it was often difficult for both the client and lawyer to determine who was responsible for decisions at any given time (W. L. F. Felstiner & Sarat, 1992).

The conclusions drawn about the attorneys' desires for reasonable outcomes is unfortunately suspect because of the sample that Sarat and Felstiner used. They acknowledged that the lawyers chosen were not randomly selected and that their sample did not match the composition of the population of male and female attorneys or the population of male and female lawyers specializing in divorce. In addition, the samples did not include many lawyers high in income, experience, or status. Finally, the lawyers studied attended less prestigious law schools than would characterize the top divorce lawyers in the two geographic areas studied. Ironically, despite these limitations, the samples may indeed reflect the attorneys who are handling the vast majority of divorce cases in the United States. The vast majority of divorce clients in the United States are not being represented by those top divorce lawyers. Thus, the conclusions may be limited in that they do not apply to a small segment of the divorce attorney population (i.e., the top attorneys).

Another concern with interpreting this research is that the definition of *reasonable goals* is actually quite broad and creates difficulties in generalizing from research on divorce attorneys to research on mediators. Specifically, for some of the studies (e.g., Griffiths, 1986), *reasonable* refers to "a mutually acceptable settlement reached out of court" (p. 169), whereas in other studies (e.g., W. L. F. Felstiner & Sarat, 1992), *reasonable* refers to specifying realistic goals that the lawyer believes the client might be able to obtain. The outcomes achieved according to these definitions might be quite different. Future research will need to carefully focus on understanding what it is divorce lawyers want to achieve for their clients, what it is clients want to achieve for themselves, and how this differs from using mediation as the vehicle to achieve one's goals.

In comparing attorney decision making in litigation with decision making found in mediation, mediators are encouraged to take (and do take) an active, directive role in both controlling the process of mediation and controlling the terms of the agreements that are reached in mediation (Cobb, 1993, 1994a; Cobb & Rifkin, 1991a, 1991b; Dingwall & Greatbatch, 1991; Greatbatch & Dingwall, 1989; Kressel et al., 1994; Pearson & Thoennes, 1988c; Rifkin, Millen, & Cobb, 1991; Silbey, 1993). And these pressures from the mediator appear in reports of both mandatory and voluntary mediation programs (Pearson & Thoennes, 1989). Even though the philosophy of mediation stresses client-centered decision making, Pearson and Thoennes (1989) found evidence in their multisite samples of clients that most mediators were active and directive, structuring both the process of mediation and often the terms of the agreements produced. Yet the pressures to settle as well as the mediators' control of discussions can be more subtle. Although discussions may be presented in terms of client-centered decision making, in fact the mediator has substantial control over both the negotiation process and content of divorce agreements (Cobb, 1994a; Cobb & Rifkin, 1991a; Folger & Bush, 1994; Fuller et al., 1992). Thus, it is unclear under which process, litigation or mediation, clients are actually given more authority in dictating the terms of their agreements. Interestingly, with the lawyers present, parents in litigation may not feel like they have actually made the decisions.

Moreover, to date, much of the theoretical and conceptual work on adversarialness in mediation has been based on idealized and polarized conceptions of the mediation versus the litigation process (McEwen et al., 1994). It is interesting that Felstiner and his colleagues made this same observation about idealized comparisons between litigation and mediation some two decades ago (W. L. F. Felstiner & Williams, 1980). Unfortunately, simplistic comparisons between these two complex systems are still carried out in research today, and criticisms are still presented in black-and-white terms (Ellis, 1990; Levy, 1984). Lawyers and the litigation process are portrayed as contentious and argumentative. Lawyers are said to argue for a client's position regardless of its merit or the client's underlying motivation for it (Kelly et al., 1985). They create issues with little substance to achieve an advantageous bargaining position (Kelly et al., 1985). Instead of working toward a settlement and being sensitive to the parents' feelings and needs, lawyers are seen as wanting to prolong the negotiations, increase time spent on the case to increase fees, go to trial, and win at all costs. Mediators, on the other hand, are portrayed as sensitive, caring, neutral, and clearly able to identify and control the balance of power and empower parents to reach mutual decisions, which will then be complied with over time.

Neither of these polarized visions reflects reality. It is possible in litigation for lawyers to advocate for their clients in an effective manner without becoming unnecessarily contentious and argumentative. Again, qualitative research indicates that this is the goal of most divorce attorneys (Bryan, 1994; Griffiths, 1986; McEwen et al., 1995; Sarat & Felstiner, 1995). Kressel (1985) stated that lawyers attempt to dampen conflict rather than inflame it and that there is also reason to suspect that mediators can be more coercive and directive than is generally realized (Folger & Bush, 1994; Greatbatch & Dingwall, 1989). Sarat and Felstiner (1989) found that divorce lawyers were overwhelmingly prosettlement as opposed to protrial for resolving issues. And Pearson and Thoennes (1985b, 1986, 1988a, 1988c 1989) found that even when using mental health professionals as mediators, mediation clients reported that the sessions were "tension-filled and unpleasant" and that they felt angry (46%–57%) and defensive (44%–47%) during much of the session.

It is ironic, therefore, that some mediation advocates argue that mediation is inconsistent with lawyer advocacy and not so subtly discourage clients from seeking any assistance from lawyers (Marlow & Sauber, 1990). These authors contend that lawyers will only spoil the mediation process by advising the clients that they have "given too much and gotten too little," thus creating adversarialness in the mediation sessions and difficulties in reaching settlements. It is true that some lawyers resent the concept of mediated negotiations and encourage their clients to advocate for their own interests in mediation (Gerber, 1990). But, as Bryan (1994) pointed out, these mediation proponents may be confusing legal advocacy and adversarialness.

Protection of client interests in the context of mediation can be accomplished with dignity, without excessive adversarialness, and without unnecessary provocation of the mediator or spouse (Bryan, 1994; Leick, 1989). Whereas mediators claim that litigation focuses too much on legal entitlements, proponents of litigation claim that mediation focuses on the cost-effectiveness of the intervention and the importance of the continuing relationship between the parties to the exclusion of a client's legal rights and entitlements (Bryan, 1994; Grillo, 1991). Some qualitative research has supported the view that lawyer participation in mediation can be helpful. McEwen et al. (1995) evaluated the effect of a Maine mediation statute that requires lawyers to attend mediation sessions with their clients. Results indicated that settlement rates are comparable with mediation sessions conducted without attorneys. And 85% of the Maine lawyers interviewed request mediation even in cases not involving children. These lawyers believe that mediation focuses the lawyers and the parties on settlement earlier than would otherwise occur. Furthermore, the combination of having clients present, a mediator present, and the mediation process itself demands a higher sense of decorum than do private interchanges between lawyers and clients. The authors concluded that mediation with lawyers present is the best-case scenario. The clients are fully informed and can negotiate face-to-face, while lawyers provide a quality assurance check on mediator conduct. It will be important to corroborate these results using appropriate experimental research methods and an adequate sample of mediators, lawyers, and clients.

Not all agree with such an approach. According to Griffiths (1986), the most desirable divorce process is one in which the couples decide whether to hire attorneys and in what capacity. For example, they may decide not to hire attorneys; they may hire attorneys as legal advisors; they may hire attorneys only to answer specific questions; or they may hire attorneys to help gather and analyze certain information. For couples who can cooperate and negotiate, these options allow clients to select the alternative that is least costly for them, provides the most information, and is the most efficient use of an attorney's time (if needed at all). For example, a couple could choose to hire an attorney or attorneys to provide information while retaining the power to reach a settlement themselves and control the terms of their divorce. Another option might better suit couples who are not able to cooperate and negotiate. For contested cases, it might be that a combination of attorney representation and mediation will best serve these clients. Each client's attorney would be responsible for conducting comprehensive discovery and then explaining options to the client so that the clients enter negotiations well informed and fully capable of representing their own interests. The clients would then take the lead in negotiations and thus have a good deal of responsibility for any agreement produced. The attorney would attend the mediation session to provide a check on the mediator's methods and behavior, would be available to the client to spell out legal ramifications of particular proposals, and would ensure that the clients remember to discuss all important issues.

THE EFFECT OF ADVERSARIALNESS ON DISPUTANTS

Choosing a dispute resolution method without understanding the psychological functioning and levels and types of conflict within and between spouses is unlikely to lead to the successful outcomes that state legislatures, attorneys, judges, mediators, mediation program administrators, and disputants seek. For example, mediation proponents argue that the inherent competitiveness of litigation increases conflict between the divorcing parents (Emery & Jackson, 1989; Gerber, 1990; Johnston & Campbell, 1988; Saposnek, 1983). It does so by relying on a process that focuses on placing the interests, needs, and desires of the individual parties in competition, as opposed to relying on a process that focuses on joint problem-solving to meet the interests, needs, and desires of the family collectively (Dillon & Emery, 1996; Kitzmann & Emery, 1994). According to this argument, competitiveness promotes, among other things, hostile negotiations concerning custody, visitation, property, and division of future income (Maccoby, Buchanan, Mnookin, & Dornbusch, 1993; Somary & Emery, 1991). And this conflict is likely to continue after the divorce (Emery, Matthews, & Kitzmann, 1991).

It is also suggested that mediation has a less detrimental impact on parents' psychological well-being (Emery & Wyer, 1987b) because it is a consensus-building process as opposed to a competitive process. Competition over who is in a better position to meet the "best interests of the child," or who deserves a larger share of the marital assets, fosters anger, depression, frustration, and worry for the parents. With these feelings, parents focus on the conflict itself and less on taking care of themselves emotionally. The emotional stability of divorcing parents then depends on (a) the degree of conflict between the parents surrounding the divorce broadly, (b) the legal process used to divorce, and (c) the psychological functioning of each parent individually.

Conflict Between Parents

The relationship between divorcing parents does not begin with the divorce. Most parents enter mediation continuing many of the same marital behavior patterns and marital themes that existed during the marriage (see also Bryan, 1994). In fact, several researchers have identified typologies of relationship patterns in marriage (Akister, 1993; Fitzpatrick, 1988; L. Fisher, 1995; Fowers, 1996; Gottman, 1993; Lavee, 1993), and many of the typologies are clearly similar. For example, Gottman (1993) developed five relationship types based on a couple's style of discussing a problem area in the relationship. He asked the couples to engage in a 15-minute conversation regarding a problem area of continuing disagreement and then coded the tape-recorded interactions between the couple. Gottman (1993) analyzed the data and then defined three relationship types that are predictive of reasonably stable marriages (i.e., "validators," "volatiles," and "avoiders") and two that are predictive of relatively unstable marriages ("hostile" and "hostile/detached." As defined by Gottman, 1993, *stable* refers to couples that generally stay married as opposed to defining a necessarily tranquil emotional state of the relationship.)

"Validating" couples express emotion, but with a lot of ease and calm. One spouse usually validates the other's description of a problem by verbally or nonverbally indicating that she or he understands and accepts the expressed feelings as valid. There is a sense that the couples are working together, although in the disagreement portion of the interaction there is a good deal of contentious argument by each person in support of his or her position.

"Volatile" couples express a high level of both positive and negative affect—there is a lot of negativity but also a lot of humor and affection—but both parties are very engaged in the process. There appears to be a premium placed on arguing, particularly in defense of individuality and separateness. Many communications between the couple say, in effect, "Your feelings are wrong." The couples attempt to persuade each other from the beginning of the discussion without really listening to one another.

The "avoider" couples do not have specific strategies for resolving conflict. There is an emphasis on common ground rather than on differences. Once each person has stated her or his case, the couple tends to see the discussion as close to an end. There is little give and take and little attempt to persuade the other, and very little positive or negative emotion. The passage of time is what often resolves the problems for these couples.

"Hostile" couples are very negative and engage in a great deal of direct conflict. Blaming and judgmental exchanges are common. Conversations are marked by defensiveness, verbal contempt, and disgust. "Hostile/detached" couples are emotionally uninvolved with one another and are far less engaged as listeners. They do, however, go into brief periods of attack and defensiveness over trivial matters. They are even more negative and less positive than hostile couples.

Gottman's (1993) marital interaction patterns are very similar to those found by Fitzpatrick (1988). Fitzpatrick collected four separate samples of couples (i.e., a convenience sample, a stratified sample, and two community samples) and administered to each of 700 spouses a 74-item questionnaire concerning communications between the spouses. She then conducted a cluster analysis with the responses to these questionnaires and developed three types of married couple types: "traditionals," "independents," and "separates." Gottman agreed that Fitzpatrick's types correspond to his three stable couple patterns: validator = traditional, volatile = independent, and avoider = separate (Gottman, 1993). Thus, there is some consistency among marital interaction researchers on the definitions for marital communication patterns.

Several other researchers have identified typologies of divorced couples (Ahrons, 1994; Ahrons & Rodgers, 1987; Maccoby et al., 1993). On the basis of lengthy face-to-face interviews with a large sample of divorced families, Maccoby et al. identified three types of divorced couples: "cooperative," "hostile," and "disengaged." "Cooperative" couples talk with each other frequently about the children, argue infrequently, try not to undermine each other's parenting, and usually attempt to coordinate rules between their two households. "Hostile" couples argue frequently, challenge the parenting competence or standards of each other, and try to sabotage visitation with the other parent by making last-minute changes likely to irritate a former spouse and disappoint the children. "Disengaged" parents hardly communicate, and some actively avoid communication with the other parent. Avoidance is often played out by exchanging children at a day-care center, the baby-sitter's house, or a relative's house. This pattern also often occurs between parents whose children are older because the children can have some control of visitation arrangements.

Ahrons and Rodgers (1987; Ahrons, 1994) interviewed a sample of 98 ex-spouse pairs at approximately 1 year, 2 years, and 5 years postdivorce. Any new partners acquired postdivorce were interviewed at 3- and 5-year collection points. They found five types of relationships: "perfect pals," "cooperative colleagues," "angry associates," "fiery foes," and "dissolved duos." Ahrons and Rodgers's "perfect pals" are couples who have established a relationship that is cooperative and friendly. Often there is a sense of mutuality in the decision to divorce and feelings of mutual respect. They often spend holidays together, keep relationships with each other's extended families, and share decision making and child rearing much as they did in marriage. "Cooperative colleagues" are much like "perfect pals" and remain cooperative but do not maintain the friendship with the ex-spouses or extended families.

"Angry associates" retain bitter and resentful feelings about their past marriage and resentment about the divorce process. Often these couples have long battles over financial matters and over custody and visitation. For these couples, anger with each other is still an integral part of their divorce relationship, and they continue to do battle. Although the ex-spouses are still able to co-parent their children, the children often get caught in the middle of their parents' struggles. "Fiery foes" are similar to angry associates, although the major distinction is that they are unable to co-parent. The ex-spouses are unable to accept each other's parenting rights, and the nonresidential parent's visits usually decline. The divorces are extremely litigious and legal battles continue for years. "Dissolved duos" completely sever contact with each other. Often one of the partners leaves the geographical area and actually disappears.

The Legal Process Used to Divorce

The couple relationship types described above may interact with the legal procedure used to divorce. For example, it may well be that the cooperative types (i.e., "cooperative," "perfect pals," or "cooperative colleagues") are couples who can participate amicably in a decision-making process, and if they are either referred or choose to use the services of a mediator can benefit from this private, informal, consensus-building process. There is some support for this notion in that Kressel et al. (1980) found direct-conflict couples, which are similar to Gottman's (1993) "validator," Fitzpatrick's (1988) "traditional" Maccoby et al.'s (1993) "cooperative," and Ahrons and Rodgers's (1987) "cooperative colleagues" or "perfect pals," do well in mediation. More often, however, the couples who have a long history of conflict and communication problems are the ones who appear in mediation. Most mediation referrals are for only those cases in which custody, visitation, or financial issues are contested; conflictual relations are much more likely in these cases. The marital themes of these clients are emotionally charged, contentious, and ingrained, and often the couples do not care if their present actions have long-term negative consequences (Irving & Benjamin, 1995). These couples are probably more similar to Gottman's "volatile," Fitzpatrick's "independent," Ahrons and Rodgers's "angry associates" or "fiery foes," or Maccoby et al.'s "hostile" or "disengaged" couple types. Again, there is some support for this notion in that Kressel et al. (1980) found that enmeshed couples, similar to Gottman and Maccoby et al.'s "hostile" and Ahrons and Rodgers's "angry associates" or "fiery foes," do not do well in mediation. For example, the parties remained bitter toward each other and dissatisfied with the settlement, the children of these couples experienced significant adjustment problems, and the parties continued the conflict by initiating lawsuits postmediation (Kressel et al., 1980; see also Bickerdike, 1998).

Moreover, the vast majority of studies indicate that mediation has a limited ability to alter these basic relationship patterns or promote cooperation between divorcing parties (Emery & Wyer, 1987b; Keilitz et al., 1992; Pearson & Thoennes, 1985b). The respondents in one study did not agree that participation in mediation helped them communicate more effectively with their ex-spouse (Keilitz et al., 1992). Johnston, Campbell, and Tall (1985) also found that among more contentious couples there was some reduction in co-parental conflict and hostility; however, 40% of the couples showed no obvious improvement and another 15% of the relationships had deteriorated (Irving & Benjamin, 1995). Unfortunately, there was no control group of litigation clients in this study; thus, the meaning and generalizability of these statistics are unclear.

Indeed, at 3 months postmediation, 15% of the clients in one study reported that the court system helped improve their relationship with an ex-spouse, whereas 40% indicated that it had a detrimental effect (Pearson & Thoennes, 1985a). The remainder said it had no impact. Interestingly, at 12–15 months follow-up the numbers had changed: 25% (as opposed to 15%) said the court system had improved their relationship, and 25% (as opposed to 40%) said it had a detrimental effect on their relationship. It seems that the respondents were regressing toward a similar mean (25% say it hurt the relationship; 25% said it helped).

Another measure of conflict is the number of problems surrounding visitation (Pearson & Thoennes, 1988c). Pearson and Thoennes (1988c, 1989) found that for those couples mediating and litigating their disputes, the percentage of respondents with multiple problems surrounding visitation 12–15 months postdivorce were nearly identical (30%–40%). The respondents reporting the least troubled relationships were those who never contested custody. The last measure of conflict assessed in the literature is reports of ability to cooperate with an ex-spouse (Pearson & Thoennes, 1988c). By 12–15 months postdivorce, 60% of successful mediation clients *and* 60% of those who did not contest custody were able to have some cooperation with their ex-spouse. Thus, the rates are equal for those who are able to produce an agreement in mediation and those who are not contesting custody in the litigation system. Of those who did not settle in mediation, only 10% reported that some cooperation is possible, and 30% of the litigation group who contested custody reported that cooperation is possible (Pearson & Thoennes, 1988c). There are no indications as to which comparisons are statistically significantly different. Thus, for example, it is unclear if the successful mediation clients rates are statistically significantly different from the reports of the litigation clients who contested custody.

In summary, claims concerning the ability of mediation to reduce conflict or change basic relationship patterns between divorcing parents are not supported by the majority of research directly testing this claim. But not all studies agree. A few studies report evidence that mediation improved ex-spousal relationships (Bautz & Hill, 1989; Irving & Benjamin, 1995; Kelly, 1990b, 1991; Pearson, 1994; Pearson & Thoennes, 1984b). One frequently cited study examined the evidence concerning the claim that litigation increases clients' anger while mediation dampens it. Kelly (1991) found that in comparing clients of mediation with those in litigation, the latter are more likely to report at final divorce that the divorce proceedings intensified or increased their anger. In addition, these respondents reported higher scores on questionnaire items regarding wishes for revenge, desires to punish the other parent, beliefs that the other parent is to blame for the destruction of the relationship, and a belief that the other spouse does not deserve happiness. Although there was no difference between mediation and litigation groups on measures of anger at the beginning of the divorce process, there were differences in other important and related variables. There were differences in the clients' initial perceptions of their spouse reported at the time they entered the divorce process and differences in their psychological responses to the divorce reported after the divorce (Kelly & Gigy, 1989; Kelly et al., 1988). Initial differences in the perceptions of spouses reported at the time the clients entered the divorce process indicated that mediation couples viewed their spouses as more honest, flexible, fair-minded, and better able to cooperate regarding the children after the divorce, and they rated the other parent as more able and competent than did the litigation couples. Mediation respondents were also less likely to report that their spouses took advantage of them during their marriage (Kelly et al., 1988). It is interesting that mediation couples also expressed more guilt and depression over the breakup of the marriage, which Kelly et al. argued may indicate some understanding of joint responsibility for the breakup. Litigation couples were, therefore, less trusting of their spouse's honesty and integrity, more likely to see their spouse as rigid or unfair, less able to cooperate regarding the children after the divorce, and less capable of cooperating from the beginning of the divorce proceedings, so it is not surprising that they were more angry at the end of the proceedings.

Unfortunately, it may be that Kelly and colleagues' (1988) findings reflect a strong sample bias, as opposed to indicating something about the dispute resolution process itself. Kelly's sample consisted of well-educated, upper-middle-class professionals who voluntarily attended and paid for a comprehensive (i.e., all issues settled), private mediation program (Kelly, 1990a, 1990b; Kelly et al., 1988). Therefore, as Kelly (1990a, 1990b) suggested, it is difficult to generalize the results to the vast majority of mediation clients who are mandated to attend court-sponsored programs that focus only on custody and visitation issues (Kelly, 1990a, 1990b). The court-sponsored clients tended to be in lower socioeconomic groups (Emery & Wyer, 1987a) or at least did not include the more affluent groups (Depner, Cannata, & Ricci, 1995) and can be more interpersonally contentious (Emery & Jackson, 1989; Irving & Benjamin, 1995). Kelly's sample was also an example of the most pure types of groups found in the literature —those who use a mediator exclusively for negotiations and those who use a lawyer exclusively for negotiations. The mediation group also was able to afford consultations with lawyers, accountants, and other professionals when it was deemed necessary. For most clients who attend court-sponsored mediation, they neither are well-educated, upper-middle-class professionals, nor are they able to afford consultations with outside professionals as needed. And, because court-sponsored mediation generally resolves only issues of custody and visitation, these clients must simultaneously use both the litigation and mediation systems. Interaction with each system may affect clients' views of the other system and thus confound the research in which pure types are not used as comparison groups. Unfortunately, there is no research comparing a mediation group that simultaneously uses the litigation processes with a group that uses only the litigation process (Kelly, 1991). Also needed is research comparing clients mandated to attend court-sponsored mediation who cannot afford outside consults and those who can afford such consults, with the same two types of groups engaged in voluntary mediation. Consultation in mediation may severely alter adversarialness because when differences of opinion occur between the spouses, the advice of a professional may clarify the matter. These complications in obtaining samples have led one researcher to conclude that because those couples who self-select mediation are fundamentally different from those who use litigation, it would be nearly impossible to create a matched sample of litigation and mediation couples (Pearson, 1991).

In another study, Irving and Benjamin (1992) found that 60% to 70% of their respondents reported improvement in ex-spousal relations, including decreased conflict, improved communication, and a reduction in number of problems judged "serious." Furthermore, parents indicated that mediation was the main reason for these changes. These studies are similar in important ways and can be contrasted with the studies noted above that do not find a reduction in conflict between the couples. For example, Kelly (1990b, 1991) and Irving and Benjamin (1995) evaluated private, voluntary, fee-for-service programs and found that these programs allow for many more sessions to resolve the conflicts than do court-sponsored programs. Clients who attend these programs also tend to be more cooperative, better educated, and of a higher socioeconomic status than the vast majority of clients who are referred to court-sponsored programs in states where they are mandated to attend (Emery & Wyer, 1987a; Irving & Benjamin, 1995; Kelly, 1990b; Pearson & Thoennes, 1984b). In addition, Irving and Benjamin (1995) used a therapeutic model of mediation, which specifically addresses conflict between the couple. It is understandable, therefore, why these researchers find positive results in this area. Yet, in relation to litigation, the meaning and generalizability of these findings are unclear.

Although Bautz and Hill's (1989) study found positive effects of mediation on postdivorce relationships, it is unclear how the researchers did so. Table 4 of Bautz and Hill's article, which details the analysis for the postdivorce relationship variables, indicated a total sample size for the litigation group of 71 and a total sample size for the mediated group of 41. Interestingly, in the Method section of the article, the researchers indicated that the entire litigation sample was 52 and the mediation sample size was 68. There was no explanation as to why the litigation group in this analysis had 19 more participants than were enlisted in the study originally and the mediation group had 27 fewer. In fact, the numbers of participants for the litigation and mediated samples varied from analysis to analysis without any explanation. Thus, unless further clarification of the sample sizes becomes available, the results of this study are unclear.

After finding that clients, immediately postmediation, reported a positive change in their interpersonal relationship, both Pearson (1994) and Kelly (1990b, 1991) later found that the positive change was no longer reported. Both researchers found that when interviewing clients 2 to 5 years postmediation, the mediation couples did not differ from the litigation couples in terms of positive changes in interpersonal relationship reportedly associated with the dispute-resolution method in obtaining their divorce. Kelly's research (1989, 1990b, 1991, 1996) with couples involved in a fee-for-service, private mediation program found that during the 6 months prior to divorce and at divorce, mediation parents reported less conflict than did litigation parents, even after controlling predivorce levels of cooperation. One year postdivorce, litigation parents reported more conflict than did mediation parents. Interestingly, 2 years after divorce, all differences regarding conflict evident at final divorce and 1 year postdivorce had vanished (Kelly, 1990b, 1991). Thus, it is important to know when the data were gathered from parents to fully understand the research findings being presented.

Pearson and Thoennes (1985a, 1985b, 1986, 1988a, 1989) suggested several reasons why mediation appears to have had only a modest effect on reducing conflict and promoting long-term cooperation between disputants. First, mediation, at least in court settings, is a brief intervention. Often the mediator meets with the parents for only a few short hours. And mediation often involves parties with long-established behavioral patterns who have lengthy, intimate, and problem-ridden histories (Pearson & Thoennes, 1985b, 1988a, 1989). Mediation, at least in court settings, cannot deal with the underlying psychological problems of families but can only assist families develop custody and visitation plans (Pearson & Thoennes, 1988a). Contested as opposed to noncontested cases involve more anger between spouses, often more violence during the marriage, less initial cooperation, and poorer communication patterns. Family therapy research indicates that changing basic relationship patterns is difficult even when a therapist has willing participants for as many sessions as is required (Jacobson & Addis, 1993). Under the best conditions, all therapy models that have been empirically tested leave many couples unimproved or at least still somewhat distressed. For example, Jacobson and Addis found that 60%–65% of the couples either remained somewhat distressed or remained unchanged during treatment. And follow-up studies indicate that treatment gains are not generally maintained over time (Gottman, 1994). For example, a 2-year follow-up study found that approximately 30% of the couples who made treatment gains in therapy had relapsed (Jacobson, Schmaling, & Holtzworth-Munroe, 1987). Without couples actively pursuing changed relations on an ongoing basis, it is easy for couples to slip back into ingrained behavior patterns. Furthermore, divorcing parents are not always willing or desiring a relationship change but are instead focused on breaking ties with the ex-spouse. Thus, there is less to motivate the divorcing parties to work together.

Second, although some models of therapy have been refined and treatment manuals developed so that the models could be empirically compared for effectiveness, for therapist adherence to the treatment model, and for replication, few such comparable steps have been taken for models of mediation (Kelly, 1996). Although there are several mediation researchers who have described the mediation model used in their research or practice (Benjamin & Irving, 1992; Coogler, 1978; Emery et al., 1987; J. M. Haynes, 1981; Kelly, 1983; Irving & Benjamin, 1995), and one details a session-by-session analysis of content to be covered (Emery et al., 1987), these descriptions do not rise to the level of a step-by-step treatment manual. This may partially account for why there have been very few studies of actual mediator behavior and mediator compliance with the mediation model, and why none of the models has been systematically studied, with results replicated, by an independent research team.

The general tone of mediation advocates' claims has been to the effect that to study the mediation process in controlled, empirically sound ways would destroy the "art" of the mediation process and not substantially increase one's understanding of it. This is similar to arguments presented by some psychotherapists that psychotherapy is an artistic endeavor that is much too rich to be adequately defined, operationalized, and tested by current research methodologies (Fensterheim & Raw, 1996; Shoham & Rohrbaugh, 1996) and that treatment manuals may stifle sensitivity and creativity in delivering appropriate treatments (Davison & Lazarus, 1995; Shoham & Rohrbaugh, 1996). We disagree. It is critical to apply evolving scientific standards to proposed mediation models and practices in order to gain a deeper understanding of what is going to be effective under the myriad of mediation approaches, client types and needs, and court rules and procedures.

Those who do believe that empirically sound, controlled studies are important, however, have found it extremely difficult to secure ongoing funding or secure the cooperation of court administrators and presiding domestic relations judges (Dingwall & Eekelaar, 1988; Emery, 1994; Thoennes et al., 1991). Court administrators and presiding domestic relations judges are extremely hesitant to require random assignment of litigants to specific conditions (i.e., litigation vs. mediation) primarily for fear of violating the clients' due process rights, but also for fear of complicating an already complex set of procedures for court personnel, mediators, and judges.[1]

Finally, the only mediation programs that are likely to create changes in conflictual relations are those that (a) use a therapeutic model of mediation that focuses on such changes in relationship quality between the spouses, (b) allow a greater number of sessions to work through a conflict-ridden history and change ingrained behavior patterns (Irving & Benjamin, 1995), and (c) require follow-up telephone calls to the clients by the mediator and/or follow-up or "booster" sessions with the mediator so that any problems that arise in the first several months can be dealt with quickly (W. L. F. Felstiner & Williams, 1980; Kitzmann & Emery, 1994). One study found that, for parents who reported problems that developed postmediation, these problems began within the first 3 months following completion of mediation (Saposnek, Hamburg, Delano, & Michaelsen, 1984). For cases

---

[1] See chapter 9, Footnote 1, for an argument supporting randomization of clients in the courts.

in which the mediators believe the clients may have trouble complying with the terms of the agreement, in which additional social services are needed, or in which dispute resolution skills were not learned well, active and persistent follow-up on the part of the mediator should be the rule (W. L. F. Felstiner & Williams, 1980). Follow-up should be completed by the mediators and not the staff because the mediators have developed a sense of the case and developed rapport with the clients (W. L. F. Felstiner & Williams, 1980). If the goal is to ensure that clients successfully comply with the terms of their agreements and amicably negotiate further disputes rather than merely produce agreements to justify program funding, then sustained support to the clients is critical (W. L. F. Felstiner & Williams, 1980).

There are many opportunities for conflict and noncompliance with the terms of agreements in postdivorce relations (Pearson & Thoennes, 1985b, 1986, 1988a, 1989). Child support, visitation, decisions concerning education, religious practices, and conflicts over the role of new partners are merely a few areas in which noncompliance or arguments can erupt (Pearson & Thoennes, 1989). In addition, myriad factors contribute to conflict in a couple's relationship (Kressel, 1985). To isolate just one factor, such as the divorce dispute resolution process, and attempt to determine differences in client relationships based on that one factor seems foolhardy. It may be that research has to take a more complex view and isolate several factors in conjunction to make any headway in predicting outcomes of divorce mediation and reducing future conflict between couples. It is likely that the outcomes in divorce mediation are determined by myriad factors, and attempting to measure only a few is likely to be confounded by the influence of other intervening variables (Bickerdike, 1998). It may also be that the determinants of constructive agreements may well be the same whether used by lawyers or mediators (Kressel, 1985). A good case can be made for designing research that assesses the qualities that produce long-lasting agreements in each forum as opposed to pitting one type of intervention against another without regard to the enormous variations within the modes of intervention and widely varying circumstances that exist among the litigants (Kressel, 1985).

INDIVIDUAL PSYCHOLOGICAL FUNCTIONING

The impact of the legal process chosen to resolve the divorcing couple's dispute (i.e., mediation or litigation) also needs to be looked at in light of the psychological functioning of each disputant. As already noted, anger, depression, frustration, worry, and a continued attachment to one's former spouse have been linked to participants in the divorce process. In assessing levels of anger in a sample of upper socioeconomic status clients, one group who litigated their divorce and a second who voluntarily sought private, fee-for-service mediation, Kelly et al. (1988) found that a majority (nearly 60%) of the clients were moderately to extremely angry at their spouse. Of the total sample, 28% reported high/extreme levels of anger and 30% reported moderate levels of anger at their spouse. Only 40% reported mild to no anger. Anger was also highly correlated with stress, poor cooperation between the spouses, and higher marital conflict and tension, and the clients rated their spouses lower on a measure of fair-mindedness (Kelly et al., 1988). In fact, these researchers found that those reporting high levels of anger also reported that they perceived that their spouse was also very angry.

Emery (1990) suggested that anger is both an asset and liability for divorcing couples. The major asset is that it creates the needed emotional distance to ward off depression about loss of the relationship and ideals; liabilities, as noted by Kelly et al. (1988), include increased levels of stress and marital conflict and lower levels of cooperation. The key may be to feel anger but to behave cooperatively (Emery, 1990). As already noted, there is little evidence, however, that mediation has a significant positive impact on lowering the levels of anger for highly angry couples (Dillon & Emery, 1996).

Unfortunately, there is also little evidence that mediation is associated with decreases in other psychological variables as well (e.g., depression or unresolved attachment feelings to the former spouse, either at the time of settlement or 1 year later; Kitzmann & Emery, 1994). An initial report indicated that mothers who mediated were more depressed than mothers who litigated (Emery & Wyer, 1987a), but this finding was not replicated in a second study (Emery, Matthews, & Wyer, 1991). At the 1-year follow-up, both mediation and litigation mothers' levels of depression declined substantially, but there were still no differences between groups (Emery, Matthews, & Kitzmann, 1991). Furthermore, no differences were found between mothers' or fathers' acceptance of the end of the marriage or fathers' levels of depression for any of the groups at any point (Emery, 1994). In general, mediation has not been found to significantly influence the psychological adjustment of the parents involved (Emery & Wyer, 1987a; Kelly, 1990b; Kelly et al., 1988; Kitzmann & Emery, 1994).

Emery (1994) suggested that there are several possible reasons for this failure to find differences in depression specifically, and differences in psychological functioning more generally, between mediation and litigation samples. First, few studies have assessed psychological functioning, and those that have done so have measured only a few domains of functioning (e.g., depression, anger, and attachment to former spouse). Clearly, there are many areas in which these people are experiencing distress (e.g., anxiety, cognitive impairments) that have not been adequately measured.

Second, although parents and children report considerable psychological distress related to divorce, the respondents do not always score significantly higher than a normal population on traditional measures of psychopathology (Emery, 1994; cf. Kelly, 1990b). Emery (1994) did not find a difference, whereas Kelly (1990b) did. The instruments used to assess distress in the first study may be the problem. Traditional measures of psychopathology are designed for psychiatric populations and not for relatively normal people who are experiencing an emotionally difficult period in their lives. Kelly (1990b) used a different standardized instrument, which measured nine symptom dimensions (e.g., depression, anger, anxiety, paranoia, somaticism, hostility) with two separate norm samples (Hopkins Symptom Checklist–90 or SCL-90; Derogatis, 1977). She found that although there was a significant reduction in psychological symptoms from the beginning of the divorce to final divorce, the parents nevertheless scored significantly higher than a nonpatient norm group but significantly lower than a psychiatric population norm group on several subscales of the instrument (Kelly et al., 1988). Researchers may need to develop more innovative measures that are capable of assessing subtle psychological processes in a normal divorce population, rather than relying on existing measures designed for psychiatric populations (Emery, 1994).

Third, although Kelly (1990b) found a difference between beginning and final divorce on reports of psychological distress, a repeated measures analysis indicated that the decrease in reported symptoms that occurred was attributable to the passage of time and was not a function of the mediation or litigation process. Thus, the passage of time alone is a significant factor in reported psychological symptoms and must be accounted for in any measure of psychological distress.

Fourth, mediation is only a short-term intervention directed toward negotiating agreements and generally is not directed toward improving the mental health of individual participants. It may be that the mental health of participants will be promoted only by more direct and intensive interventions focused specifically on these issues (Emery, 1994).

CONCLUSION

One of the most interesting findings in the literature is that approximately one third of the parents who reached agreements in mediation still maintained that they made little or no progress in their case (Pearson & Thoennes, 1985b). This result suggests that a signed agreement is not synonymous with what parents view as a solution or a successful emotional resolution to their dispute. Although a signed agreement signifies successful resolution of the legal divorce, it signifies nothing about the resolution of emotional issues. Resolution of emotional issues is a long process and can take the active intervention of a mental health professional and a substantial amount of work on the parent's part.

It is not surprising then that researchers find that regardless of the method of dispute resolution, in a majority of families whose children had reached age 18, the emotional and practical effects of the separation continued to have an impact on the functioning of the families 9 years later (Dillon & Emery, 1996). Respondents reported conflicts concerning the amount of time children spent with the noncustodial parent, arguments concerning the role of new spouses, conflicts surrounding a parent wanting to relocate to a different state, and general feelings of anger and frustration related to coping with single parenthood (Dillon & Emery, 1996). These problems and feelings persisted for years and may possibly never be resolved (Dillon & Emery, 1996). Whether mediated or litigated, divorces appear to have a severe psychological effect on many people for many years (Dillon & Emery, 1996).

6

INCREASED SATISFACTION OF DISPUTANTS WITH LEGAL PROCEDURES AND OUTCOMES

One of the important goals of mediation is to increase the satisfaction of disputants with the legal procedures used to achieve the divorce settlement and the settlement itself. Mediation advocates argue that clients who use mediation in resolving their divorce dispute are much more satisfied than litigants who use the traditional court process (Bautz & Hill, 1989; Benjamin & Irving, 1995; Emery, Matthews, & Kitzmann, 1991; Emery & Wyer, 1987a, 1987b; J. Folberg & Milne, 1988; Irving & Benjamin, 1995; Kelly & Duryee, 1992; Kelly & Gigy, 1989; Kressel, 1985; Kressel et al., 1994; Marlow & Sauber, 1990; Pearson, 1994; Pearson & Thoennes, 1982, 1985b, 1988a, 1989). Anywhere between 60% and 80% of the mediation clients report being satisfied (76% in Pearson & Thoennes, 1982; 78% for men and 72% for women in Kelly & Gigy, 1989; 59% in Kelly, 1989). Only a couple of studies report rates outside this range (90% in Pearson & Thoennes, 1984b; 33%–50% in Irving & Benjamin, 1992). Conversely, only 30%–50% of litigants felt satisfied with their court experiences (42% in Pearson & Thoennes, 1982; 30% in Pearson & Thoennes, 1989; 47% in Kelly, 1989). Although those who reached agreement were more enthusiastic, 30%–60% of the clients who did not reach agreement in mediation reported they were satisfied (40%–82% in Pearson & Thoennes, 1986;

33% in Kressel et al., 1994). These patterns do not differ for users of mandatory or voluntary mediation programs (Pearson, 1994). Thus, mediation appears to be much more satisfactory than litigation for divorcing clients.

Although these findings are intriguing, a complex set of methodological questions need to be considered: What are the rates of satisfaction and reasons for dissatisfaction with traditional court processes? What are the appropriate comparison groups? What points in time since divorce are the assessments of satisfaction/dissatisfaction gathered? What are the specific questions asked regarding satisfaction/dissatisfaction? Are there gender differences in the findings? This chapter addresses these issues. As we argue below, when the research is scrutinized in light of these questions, the satisfaction rates are equivocal. At a more fundamental level, questions can be raised about what satisfaction rates actually mean in terms of the strength or adequacy of a program (Gutek, 1978).

SATISFACTION AND DISSATISFACTION

Although mediation proponents have found in their studies that litigation couples are much less satisfied than mediation couples, the degree of difference in satisfaction rates varies widely from study to study. In fact, evidence suggests that most people are satisfied with the divorce process they choose, irrespective of whether it was mediation or litigation (Keilitz et al., 1992; Pearson, 1994). For example, one study defined different elements of the legal process and compared rates of satisfaction between mediating and litigating couples in four different states (Keilitz et al., 1992). Researchers found that the majority of litigants in both mediation and litigation felt that they participated in a fair process that provided satisfactory results. Clients felt that their rights were protected (mediation 75%, litigation 60%); the process was fair (mediation 73%, litigation 55%); they got enough of the most important things (mediation 74%, litigation 69%); and they were satisfied with the agreement (mediation 70%, litigation 52%; see Keilitz et al., 1992). There were, however, significant differences between the groups in terms of assessments about the process, which generally favored mediation. Mediation litigants felt less pressure to agree to things they did not want, felt less pressure to agree quickly, were more satisfied with the fairness of the process, and were less intimidated by their spouse (Keilitz et al., 1992). These findings are significant but, as we discuss in the second half of this chapter, need to be replicated using empirically sound research methods.

In another study, an attempt was made to distinguish litigation cases into those in which custody or visitation was contested, those cases that underwent custody evaluations, and those cases in which custody or visitation was not contested (Pearson & Thoennes, 1985a). It is reported that

50%–60% of litigants who dispute custody are dissatisfied. What is not reported is how many of these clients are satisfied or are neutral about the process (Pearson & Thoennes, 1985a). Likewise, Pearson and Thoennes (1985a) reported that 40%–50% of those clients who undergo a custody evaluation are dissatisfied, but again we do not see results concerning how many of these clients are satisfied. It could be that 50%–60% of these couples are satisfied (Pearson & Thoennes, 1985a). And finally, it is reported that 40% of those who do not dispute custody are dissatisfied. Again, it may be that 60% of these litigants are then satisfied with the process (Pearson & Thoennes, 1985a; see also Irving & Benjamin, 1995). These results imply that roughly half of all the litigants in each category, and maybe more in the uncontested category, may be satisfied with their treatment in the litigation system. In fact, Pearson and Thoennes (1988a) indicated that there are similar rates of dissatisfaction with court experiences and mediation.

Moreover, although the majority of people are satisfied with the divorce process, some mediation clients, particularly those who reach agreement, may be more so in some important ways. The litigation group figures are somewhat lower than those for the mediation clients who reach an agreement but very similar to the mediation clients who do not reach agreement in mediation. If the mediation clients were lumped together as the litigation clients are into one category (i.e., no division between those reaching agreement, partial agreements, and no agreement), the upper limit of the satisfaction interval would be lower and thus closer to rates of satisfaction for litigation. As noted below in the section discussing comparison groups, it is important to compare groups that are similar on critical characteristics (e.g., compare mediated agreements with lawyer-negotiated agreements).

Although measuring satisfaction accurately is complex, mediation proponents have argued that there are some common themes that run through many of the parent satisfaction evaluations: (a) Litigants believe mediation helped them to focus on the needs of the children (60%–80%); (b) litigants believed mediation provided them an opportunity to air grievances (70%–80%); and (c) litigants believed mediation kept the discussions on track (70%–80%; see Lyon et al., 1985; Pearson & Thoennes, 1985b, 1986, 1988a). These results are surprising. In empirical analyses of actual tapes of mediation sessions, researchers have found, first, that the interests of the child are rarely mentioned (Dingwall & Greatbatch, 1991). When they are mentioned, the children's interests are used as a means of applying moral pressure to accept or reject a particular option, as opposed to urging parents to consider the well-being of their children (Dingwall & Greatbatch, 1991). Second, airing grievances can be extremely helpful for some couples while extremely detrimental to others (e.g., abusive relationships; Fischer et al., 1993). Third, an analysis of taped mediation sessions has found that mediators do much more than keep discussions on track (Donohue et al., 1985). They actively direct conversations and, at times, heavily influence the terms of the agreements produced.

Because mediation is not widely understood by laypeople, mediators need to indoctrinate clients regarding the process and potential outcomes. In doing so, mediators often state that their function is to consider the needs of the children, assist the parties in airing grievances, offer a less adversarial forum, and keep the discussions on track. The combination of findings outlined above suggests that it is unclear if the satisfied parties are merely reiterating this rhetoric or whether the mediation sessions of these satisfied clients are very different from those involved in the sessions taped and analyzed by Donohue et al. (1985) and Dingwall and Greatbatch (1991). This is an empirical question that should be fully explored.

Finally, one important finding in this regard is that under all circumstances programs that severely restrict the number of sessions available to mediation clients may do so at the expense of client satisfaction and a fully understandable process. For instance, satisfaction was found to be the lowest at a mediation site where the intervention was one 45-minute session that was devoted exclusively to calculating the child support information from legal guidelines (Delaware; see Pearson, 1993, 1994). When asked if they believed mediation was better than a hearing with a "special master" or a judge, over half (56%) of these mediation clients said no (Pearson, 1994). As noted by Abel (1982), satisfaction is likely to be a function of how the clients are treated, the amount of time mediators spend with the clients, and the degree of inconvenience required to attend sessions. Thus, the more "efficient" the institution is, the less likely people are excited about using it (Abel, 1982).

Obviously, there are clients who are dissatisfied with mediation. Kelly and Gigy (1989) found that in their sample of a voluntary, private, comprehensive, fee-for-service mediation program, 14% of men and 26% of women were dissatisfied. Kelly and Duryee (1992) found that in a court-mandated custody and visitation mediation program, 43% of the men and 17% of the women were dissatisfied with the outcome of mediation. The rates of dissatisfaction for court-mandated sessions were certainly higher for men. When couples are dissatisfied with mediation, the reasons cited for dissatisfaction were that the sessions were tension-filled and unpleasant (46%–57%), they stimulated feelings of anger and defensiveness (44%–47%), the process was confusing (20%–30%), and the process was rushed and the parents felt they were given assembly-line treatment (25%–33%; Pearson & Thoennes, 1985b, 1988a, 1989). Thus, the researchers concluded that obtaining an agreement is not synonymous with resolving all the emotional or even legal issues involved in a divorce (Pearson & Thoennes, 1985b). Indeed, approximately one third of the parents who reached agreements in mediation still maintained that they made little or no progress in their case (Pearson & Thoennes, 1985b).

It is not clear how comparable these findings of dissatisfaction with mediation are with findings of dissatisfaction with litigation. Some research has shown that those who litigate their divorces are not necessarily dissatisfied with the entire litigation process but are thoroughly dissatisfied with court hearings in particular (Dingwall & Eekelaar, 1988). Bautz (1988) found indirect support for this point in her study. She found that the litigation group's average response was "I have mixed reactions: I am satisfied with some things and dissatisfied with others" (p. 57). As Pearson and Thoennes (1988a, 1989) noted, in their studies 70% of the litigants were satisfied with their attorneys. The litigants, however, strongly disliked exposing private issues in a public forum, the impersonality of the court experience, its negative (i.e., "criminal") overtones, and the degree of control exercised by legal actors. Thus, as Dingwall and Eekelaar (1988) pointed out, it is not the entire litigation experience litigants find dissatisfactory but mainly the court hearing that is strongly dissatisfactory. In addition, another research team (Pearson & Thoennes, 1988a) concluded that dissatisfaction rates are in fact similar for mediation and litigation because custody/visitation disputes are so emotionally taxing that any method used to resolve them will be unnecessarily unpleasant and evokes defensive reactions.

Assuming for the moment that there is a somewhat higher level of dissatisfaction found in litigated cases, one possible explanation for this finding is that, even in the best of circumstances, parents may expect more of the legal system than it can deliver (W. L. F. Felstiner & Sarat, 1992). Studies have found that 50%–60% of those with a dispute over custody or visitation are dissatisfied with the court experience, 40%–50% of those exposed to a custody evaluation are dissatisfied, and even those who did not contest custody or visitation report 40% dissatisfaction (Pearson & Thoennes, 1985a). Parents come to their lawyer requesting several pieces of information: the legal rules that will be applied, the probabilities of achieving various results, a definite estimate of the costs they will incur, the specific time line for different portions of the case, and the roles that different actors will play (Sarat & Felstiner, 1986). Unfortunately, there are no standard answers that lawyers can provide to parents (Sarat & Felstiner, 1986). Lawyers and judges have wide discretion in interpreting the legal possibilities in divorce law. This level of discretion is greater than in areas of law in which rules significantly narrow the scope of latitude in lawyer negotiations and judicial decision making (e.g., criminal law; W. L. F. Felstiner & Sarat, 1992). In addition,

> vindication, the last dollar of support, meticulous estimates of property value, a neat and precise division of property, a visitation scheme that

covers a very wide range of contingencies, and equitable arrangements that govern the future as well as the present may be theoretically possible, but even approximations require extensive services that middle-class clients generally cannot afford. (W. L. F. Felstiner & Sarat, 1992, p. 1461)

Parents face the realities of the high cost of comprehensive legal representation and the inability of the substantive law in this area to give them definite answers to many of their questions (Sarat & Felstiner, 1986). Thus, it may be that the litigants' expectations of mediation and litigation are different. Litigants may expect more certainty from the adversarial process, and sometimes more certainty than the adversarial process can deliver. In addition, as noted earlier, litigants particularly dislike the court hearings (Dingwall & Eekelaar, 1988). It may be that this dislike of the public court hearing overshadows feelings toward the adversarial process in general as opposed to litigants necessarily preferring the mediation process.

METHODOLOGICAL CONCERNS

A complex set of methodological questions need to be considered to put the findings concerning satisfaction and dissatisfaction with dispute resolution methods into perspective. Important issues include the validity of self-reports of satisfaction, issues concerning comparison groups, passage of time, specific questions assessed, and gender differences.

Validity of Self-Reported Satisfaction

At a fundamental level, client satisfaction does not necessarily correlate well with positive outcomes. For example, Kidder, Judd, and Smith (1986) reviewed parental ratings of satisfaction in compensatory educational programs and found that parents are generally satisfied, even though objective measures of outcome are extremely negative (i.e., subsequent criminal records, poor health, lower occupational standing, and earlier deaths of the participants in the treatment group). Kidder et al. concluded that the parents are basically telling researchers that they appreciate the special attention, the investment of resources, and the good intentions. Gutek (1978) also noted striking discrepancies between objective measures and satisfaction ratings in several areas. For example, there were large discrepancies between national surveys of marital satisfaction versus national divorce rates, large discrepancies in objective ratings of absenteeism or job turnover and subjective ratings of satisfaction with working conditions, and large discrepancies in social indicators such as satisfaction with neighborhood and the objective indicators such as crime rate in the area (Gutek, 1978). She concluded that research participants report high satisfaction ratings on nearly everything social scientists ask them about and that those ratings are not strongly related to objective measures, whatever they are (Gutek, 1978). People live in both a subjective world and an objective one, so clients' reaction to their contacts with governmental agencies is important (Gutek, 1978). Gutek argued that measures of satisfaction should not take the place of objective measures, however, nor should objective measures take the place of subjective ratings, such as satisfaction. Both are important but must be considered separately. In the case of mediation, Kressel et al. (1989) also stated that overall satisfaction should not be confused with objective evaluation of the quality of the services provided.

Comparison Groups

One of the problems with understanding satisfaction/dissatisfaction is the glaring lack of appropriate comparison group data (Levy, 1984). For example, mediation has been studied with large numbers of clients and in longitudinal designs that provide perspectives on consequences over a 2- to 9-year period (Emery, 1994; Kelly, 1996; Pearson & Thoennes, 1985b, 1986, 1988a, 1989). Although not always completely successful, attempts at random assignment to comparable treatments have been made (Emery, Matthews, & Kitzmann, 1991; Emery & Wyer, 1987a; Margolin, 1973; Pearson & Thoennes, 1989; Thoennes et al., 1991). Mediation researchers have also investigated a variety of mediation services, both quasi-private and public, using a wide variety of measures (Kressel, 1985; Pearson & Thoennes, 1989). There are no empirical investigations on the work of lawyers or courts in negotiating divorce settlements that come close to this scope or level of detail (Kressel, 1985; Levy, 1984). In addition, there have been no attempts to alter the court hearings to ascertain if there are other procedures that would increase user satisfaction.

It would not be an overstatement to say that the issue of appropriate comparison groups is critical in designing valid research. For example, mediation researchers generally divide the mediation group into those clients who reach an agreement and those who do not. At times, the agreeing group is further divided into those who reach a complete agreement and those who reach a partial agreement. And, for the group of clinets who fail to reach an agreement in mediation, a division is made between those who eventually negotiate an agreement before going to trial and those who go to trial to resolve disputed issues. The rationale for making such divisions is sound and states that those couples who can negotiate and reach an agreement are somehow fundamentally different from those couples who cannot. And those clients who can negotiate partial agreements or who can negotiate an agreement after mediation have somehow benefited from mediation, even though they cannot resolve all of their issues at the time of mediation.

Interestingly, no similar divisions are made for the litigation group (Levy, 1984). In fact, the phrase *litigation group* is a misnomer because it incorporates couples who hire attorneys to resolve disputes through negotiated agreements without ever resorting to litigation. For example, researchers lump together in one litigation group those couples who reach an agreement prior to going to attorneys and use attorneys to merely codify the agreement; those couples who reach agreement through negotiations between attorneys; those couples who need a custody evaluation before reaching an agreement; those couples who have contested hearings over various issues during the course of their trial but resolve some of those issues in the hearings; and those couples who have to resolve all of the issues at a trial (Kressel, 1985; Levy, 1984). A good case can be made that these divisions constitute fundamentally different groups. The litigation category is thus heterogeneous; however, it has nearly always served as a homogeneous comparison group for all mediation groups.

By lumping all litigation clients together in one group and using it as a comparison group for the various mediation groups, mediation researchers inappropriately reduce the overall satisfaction levels of some of the litigation clients (Kressel, 1985; Levy, 1984; but see Emery, 1994; Emery & Wyer, 1987a; Emery, Matthews, & Wyer, 1991). It may be effective in indicating that mediation is more satisfactory than litigation, but this practice is not appropriate if the goal is to truly understand the differences between mediation and litigation and the clients who use each process.

Another problem with comparison groups is that the majority of mediation studies examine only issues of custody and visitation (Depner et al., 1995; Depner, Cannata, & Simon, 1992; Dillon & Emery, 1996; Donohue et al., 1985, 1989, 1994; Donohue & Weider-Hatfield, 1988; Emery & Jackson, 1989; Emery & Wyer, 1987a; Kitzmann & Emery, 1993, 1994; Kressel et al., 1994; Pearson & Thoennes, 1984, 1985a, 1985b, 1986, 1988a, 1988b, 1988c, 1989; Ricci et al., 1991; Slaikeu, Culler, Pearson, & Thoennes, 1985; J. A. Walker, 1989). Most of the participants in these studies, therefore, can only rely on mediation for a portion of the issues in their divorce dispute (Kelly, 1991). Mediation clients who resolve only custody and visitation issues many times also have contested issues relating to property and financial matters that must be resolved through litigation (Kressel et al., 1994; Pearson & Thoennes, 1985b). Thus, the entire issue of satisfaction becomes murky.

A serious question can be raised concerning whether the couples are able to separate their experiences to the point that their feelings toward one system do not color their views toward the other system. For example, Pearson and Thoennes (1985b) found that approximately 33% of the participants in their sample stated that they had reached a permanent agreement on custody/visitation; however, these same people also stated that little or no progress had been made on their case. Pearson and Thoennes reasoned that the disjunction in these views may relate to the fact that many of the participants (50%) also report having contested financial issues they may be trying to resolve in the traditional way without much luck. In addition, when clients use only the litigation system, they do not usually participate in any process that divides the divorce issues as mediation does into financial (e.g., child support, spousal maintenance, property, and future income) and nonfinancial issues (i.e., custody and visitation).

Comparing couples' assessments of mediation, with only a subscribed set of issues, with litigants who use a particular system for all of their issues seems to confound two variables: the disputed issue and the type of resolution method. As an example, no researcher has asked clients of the litigation process about their satisfaction levels with only that portion of the court process dealing with custody and visitation and ignored their feelings toward the process for all other issues. The confounding influence of the simultaneous use of litigation and mediation to resolve contested issues has never been explored empirically (Kelly, 1991) or discussed in terms of mediation theory. Kelly noted that the most that can be drawn from these studies is that the moderately positive findings favorable to custody/visitation mediation cannot be generalized to the more complex divorce process encompassing all disputed issues that need to be resolved.

In addition, comparing court-based programs with private, fee-for-service programs is problematic. The two researchers who have done the most extensive work on private programs (Irving & Benjamin, 1992; Kelly, 1991) used a mediation model that differs from court-mandated custody mediation along at least two dimensions: A larger number of sessions were allowed to reach agreement, and the scope and complexity of issues mediated are much broader. Thus, comparisons are problematic at best. There is now, however, one jurisdiction that has recently passed legislation that mandates clients to attend comprehensive mediation programs (i.e., Minnesota, 1999b). Whether these programs will provide the opportunity for fairer comparisons with private mediation remains to be seen. For instance, although the complexity of the issues addressed should be identical, research will have to determine if the law on the books matches the law in action. In addition, private, voluntary programs typically attract a much different client base than court-mandated programs. Thus, differences in clients served make comparing comprehensive programs (i.e., programs that resolve all issues) with court-based programs theoretically and empirically difficult. Generally, comprehensive programs provided by private, voluntary, fee-for-service programs attract clients who tend to be young (in their 30s), middle-class, well-educated professionals who are mostly cooperative and fair-minded (Irving & Benjamin, 1992; Kelly, 1989; Pearson, 1991). Clients in court-mandated programs tend to be working class, have a poor education, and are either underemployed or unemployed (Irving & Benjamin, 1992). Thus, for an adequate comparison, clients from comprehensive private programs would need to be matched on these important characteristics to couples mandated by the court to attend a court-based program.

As noted above, the issue of an appropriate comparison group for court-mandated clients becomes complex because court-mandated clients use both mediation and litigation to resolve their disputes. In addition, it would be difficult to identify both mediation and litigation clients who use only their respective dispute-resolution system to resolve custody and visitation disputes and do not have any financial matters to resolve that would complicate the analysis. One mediation research team (Pearson & Thoennes, 1988a) concluded that at least when looking at the issue of child adjustment, there is too much variation in the litigation experience to make meaningful comparisons between children of litigation versus mediation couples (e.g., some attorneys push for a full court battle whereas others are much more flexible and attempt to ameliorate hostility). It is very likely that the variation in the litigation experience highlighted here is also found in the mediation experience (e.g., mediators who are demanding and forceful in their recommendations as opposed to more conciliatory mediators who allow clients time to discuss important issues and assist clients to reach their own decisions). These variations make it difficult to compare litigation and mediation couples and their children on a variety of issues (e.g., satisfaction, compliance with court orders, and mediated settlements). Until researchers develop experimental designs to control for these variations, meaningful comparisons between these two groups will remain questionable.

Passage of Time

The passage of time is another important variable in assessing satisfaction levels (Kelly, 1989, 1990b; Pearson & Thoennes, 1988a, 1989). During the first year after mediation, satisfaction with mediation remains high with both those clients who reached agreement and those who did not. For example, between 70% and 90% of those who produced agreements and 50% and 82% of those who did not were glad they tried the process (Cauble et al., 1985; Little et al., 1985; Lyon et al., 1985; Pearson & Thoennes, 1986). Only about 20% of those who did not reach agreements in mediation reported that they regretted they had tried the mediation process (Little et al., 1985). Those litigants interviewed 4 to 5 years after mediation, however, were far less satisfied. Only about 65% who produced agreements and 40% of those who did not produce an agreement said they were satisfied with their mediation experience.

Pearson and Thoennes (1986) argued that there can be several reasons for this drop in satisfaction over time. Over time, there are many issues for which noncompliance can develop (e.g., child support, visitation, decisions concerning education, religious practices, and conflicts over the role of new partners). Noncompliance by an ex-spouse may temper the good feelings a litigant had toward mediation because its positive results start to disappear (Pearson & Thoennes, 1986).

Specific Questions Assessed

There is also the question of what actually is being measured. For example, research that asks if a person would recommend mandatory mediation or recommend mediation to a friend may not necessarily be the same as research that asks individuals whether they are satisfied with the overall outcome or process or with particular aspects of either the outcome or process. As noted earlier, asking slightly different questions is likely to yield slightly different answers (Gutek, 1978). Kelly and Duryee (1992) found that the satisfaction rates differed depending on the question asked. When asking process versus outcome questions of court-mandated clients, these researchers found that there was no significant difference between the men and women on a question measuring satisfaction with the *process* of mediation. There was a significant difference, however, between ratings of men and women on a question measuring satisfaction with the *outcome* of mediation. Men were significantly less satisfied with the outcome of mediation. Some researchers have asked if clients would recommend mediation to their friends or recommend mandatory mediation and have used the answers to these questions, in addition to basic questions concerning overall satisfaction, as the basis of measures of satisfaction (Cauble et al., 1985; Little et al., 1985; Lyon et al., 1985; Pearson & Thoennes, 1985b, 1988a, 1989). There may be an important difference in the construct being measured between studies that compare global assessments of mediation with studies that break satisfaction down into the separate elements of process and outcome. Furthermore, using different terms to assess satisfaction means losing the ability to make comparisons across studies (Gutek, 1978).

One research group conducted a procedural justice versus distributive justice analysis of parent satisfaction in mediation and litigation cases. In other words, the researchers asked whether elements of the legal process or elements of outcome (getting what one wanted) were more important for parent satisfaction. The researchers found that both were important for parent satisfaction. The relative importance of procedural fairness and attaining a favorable outcome differs depending on the disputants' gender and level of conflict in the relationship (Kitzmann, & Emery, 1993). For women, obtaining a desired outcome was important in determining overall satisfaction with the process, whereas for men procedural fairness was more important. The researchers argued that although both parents were petitioning for sole physical custody, in nearly every case the physical custody was given to the mother. Mothers are therefore in a superior position with regard to custody issues. Thus, the fairness of the processes became salient for the men.

Levels of conflict among couples relate to measures of satisfaction. In the low-conflict couples, obtaining a desired outcome was a significant predictor of satisfaction, but procedural fairness was not. The results were reversed for the high-conflict couples; for them, procedural fairness was a significant predictor of satisfaction, whereas obtaining a desired outcome was not. Kitzmann and Emery (1993) concluded that

> the structural characteristics of the dispute resolution process (such as how adversarial the process is designed to be) may be less important than participants' perception of the degree of conflict or hostility and participants' relative vantage points in the negotiation process. (p. 559)

This suggests that satisfaction with the method of dispute resolution is intimately related to internal family dynamics. In any event, using different terms and levels of specificity to assess satisfaction makes it difficult to compare results across studies (Gutek, 1978).

Gender Differences

It is clear from our discussion that there are gender differences in reactions to mediation, yet not all research has revealed them. Researchers at a voluntary, private, fee-for-service mediation program found few differences in the assessments of men versus women to the mediation experience (Kelly & Duryee, 1992), and when they did, the differences tended to favor women (Kelly & Duryee, 1992). For example, as noted earlier, women were more satisfied than were men with the outcome of mediation (Kelly & Duryee, 1992). Women also reported significantly greater confidence in their ability to stand up for themselves, and women were significantly more likely to report that mediation allowed them an opportunity to express their views, put aside their anger, and focus on their children (Kelly & Duryee, 1992).

A second research group found that women who litigated were more satisfied with both the process and the outcome of the dispute resolution, both at the time of the divorce and 1 year later, to perceive the decision as fair and to perceive that they won what they wanted (Emery, Matthews, & Kitzmann, 1991; Emery & Wyer, 1987a). Men were more likely to be satisfied with mediation rather than litigation, with fathers consistently preferring mediation to litigation (Emery, Matthews, & Wyer, 1991).

Yet a third research group found that satisfaction rates are similar for men and women (Pearson & Thoennes, 1988a, 1989). They reported comparable levels of satisfaction with the division of property, child support, and willingness to recommend mediation (Pearson & Thoennes, 1988a, 1989). The assessment of issues relating to the experience of mediation, however, was very different and did not necessarily favor women (Pearson & Thoennes, 1988a, 1989). Although women did report some favorable reactions (i.e., mediation helped them better understand their spouse's point of view, focus on the children, keep discussions on track, identify problems, and understand their own feelings), women are much more apt to also report negative reactions to mediation (i.e., feeling pressured into an agreement by the ex-spouse, never feeling comfortable expressing their feelings, being tense and angry during mediation, and feeling the mediator directed the terms of the agreement; Pearson & Thoennes, 1988a, 1989).

Why is it that Pearson and Thoennes, Emery and his colleagues, and Kelly and Duryee found such different results concerning the experiences of women and men while analyzing data from court-sponsored mediation programs? There are many possible reasons. Mediation programs vary from jurisdiction to jurisdiction and from state to state (Kelly, 1996; Ricci et al., 1991). Although all were court sponsored, it does not mean that the programs were similar. Second, participants in Kelly and Duryee's (1992) study were from a county (Alameda) in California, participants in Emery and Wyer's (1987a, 1987b) study were from one town (Charlottesville) in Virginia, whereas participants in Pearson and Thoennes's (1985b, 1988a, 1989) study were an aggregate of several samples: one from Denver, Colorado; one from Los Angeles, California; one from the Connecticut Superior Court; and one from Hennepin County, Minnesota. It may be that the participants in Alameda, California and Charlottesville, Virginia differ in substantial ways from the participants in the other studies and that those differences were not measured in the study. Ricci et al. (1991) concluded that because of the widespread variability in court services and case processing among jurisdictions within a state, it is not possible to generalize for a region or the state from the experience of one court.

Third, the response rates for two of the three studies were quite low. The response rate for Kelly and Duryee's (1992) study was 20%. Because of incomplete questionnaires, only 7.3% of the original sample questionnaires were used. This sample cannot be considered representative of even the county where the research was conducted. Response rates for Pearson and Thoennes's (1985a, 1985b, 1988a, 1988b, 1988c, 1989) study were somewhat better but inconsistent across the sites studied (i.e., 36% for Los Angeles, 35%–40% for Connecticut, and 90% for Hennepin County, Minnesota), and attrition rates across the sites for the follow-up interviews ranged from 15% to 30% (Cauble et al., 1985; Little et al., 1985; Lyon et al., 1985; Pearson & Thoennes, 1985b). There is little discussion of how these different response and attrition rates may have affected the results in these studies.

Only one research study found that men who mediate were significantly more positive compared with women (Emery & Wyer, 1987b). According to these researchers, however, men's favorable mediation ratings in that setting were due to their extreme dissatisfaction with court processes (Emery & Wyer, 1987a; Pearson, 1994).

There is also an often quoted finding that women are able to terminate mediation sessions and do so for the "right reasons," such as feeling overwhelmed, that a fair agreement could not be reached, that issues are too complex, that they lacked financial knowledge, that they are emotionally drained, and that they are unprotected and unable to have their say (Kelly & Duryee, 1992). This finding is thus used to substantiate claims that because women have the opportunity to and do terminate sessions, there is no undue pressure on them to reach agreements with husbands who may have superior skills in negotiation. This result was found with clients in a private mediation setting, and these women tended to be better educated, have higher income, and have spouses who were more cooperative. In the court-mandated sample that Kelly and Duryee (1992) analyzed, there is no parallel finding. Kelly and Duryee only stated that a quarter of the couples from the court sample also terminated mediation and then suggested that the reasons may be similar to those reported by the women in private mediation. It is unclear whether the court-mandated sample of clients was actually asked if and why mediation was terminated. It is very important to assess if women in these court-based programs are as able to terminate sessions and for what reasons. It would be important to know if there are a group of women who reach agreement, but do so to end the negotiations and still experience the feelings noted above (i.e., they were overwhelmed, they lacked financial knowledge, they were never comfortable expressing their feelings, they were pressured by their ex-spouses, and they felt the mediator directed the terms of the agreement). Most important, future research should always consider the potential for disparate responses by men and women both during the design phase of the study and the analysis of data.

CONCLUSION

Analysis of satisfaction (and dissatisfaction) with legal procedures to obtain a divorce is complex. Specific attention must be paid to the questions asked, when in time from the final divorce the questions are asked, the full spectrum of legal procedures being used by the couple to obtain a divorce and the comparison groups used to make inferences about the data collected. Even with the most carefully collected data, it may well be that satisfaction with the dispute resolution method used to obtain a divorce has more to do with the internal dynamics of the family and level of conflict than it does with the method. Thus, conclusions drawn to date concerning relative client satisfaction with both mediation and litigation still must be considered tentative.

7

INCREASED COMPLIANCE WITH COURT ORDERS

Although it seems logical to suggest that people who are more satisfied with the process and outcome of legal processes are more likely to comply with court orders (Tyler, 1990), the research reviewed in this chapter indicates that this relationship is not significant in this context. Compliance with court orders and settlements, however, is an important goal of mediation in its own right. Compliance with court orders could be seen as both a benefit for the litigant and a benefit for the legal system. Compliance, particularly with orders concerning child support, is a benefit for the litigants in that it reduces significant economic distress for custodial parents after divorce (Dillon & Emery, 1996). It is estimated that postdissolution litigation occurs in approximately one third of all divorces in which children are involved (Emery & Wyer, 1987a; Foster & Freed, 1973). Although there are discrepancies in reporting between noncustodial and custodial parents, evidence from a study of matched pairs of custodial–noncustodial parents' reports indicates that only 47%–66% of noncustodial parents are actually paying all that is owed in child support, and between 4% and 13% are paying nothing at all (Braver, Fitzpatrick, & Bay, 1991). There is, therefore, a great number of children and their custodial parents who are receiving either no child support or less than what has been ordered, resulting in significant economic hardship. Thus, compliance with court orders would reduce the need by either custodial or noncustodial parents to return to court to enforce portions of the divorce agreement (i.e., visitation, division of property assets, and child support), which can be financially draining, emotionally demanding, and extraordinarily time consuming.

Compliance can also be seen as a benefit for the legal system in that if litigants willingly comply with court orders, there is less need for additional court hearings or other state involvement in these cases. One of the major reasons enforcement proceedings occur is over nonpayment of child support (I. Cohen, 1998). In Arizona, for example, if a custodial parent is receiving Aid to Families With Dependent Children and not receiving regular support payments or if a parent is particularly negligent in paying child support, the Expedited Child Support Enforcement Unit of the Attorney General's Office will take over litigation to enforce child support orders.[1] Another enforcement option that is becoming more popular is the "special master" programs. Some California statutes provide for appointment of "special masters" in high-conflict cases (Santa Clara County, California, 1997). The special masters are generally experienced mental health professionals who take over management of the cases and, in addition to other duties, closely monitor compliance with court orders.

Moreover, proponents of mediation argue that one of the substantial benefits of using mediation to resolve divorce disputes is that it is a cooperative process that gives control to the parents in making decisions and thus leads to increased compliance with the resulting agreements (Benjamin & Irving, 1995; Dillon & Emery, 1996; Emery, 1994; Emery, Matthews, & Wyer, 1991; Irving & Benjamin, 1992; Kelly, 1990a, 1990b, 1991; Pearson, 1994; Pearson & Thoennes, 1988a, 1989). There are studies that modestly support the idea that mediation leads to greater compliance (Bautz & Hill, 1989; Emery, Matthews, & Wyer, 1991; Kelly, 1990b; Pearson & Thoennes, 1985a, 1986; Thoennes & Pearson, 1985). As we show in the remainder of this chapter, the research is not uniformly or overwhelmingly supportive. Because mediation is typically only mandated for those parents who are disputing visitation and custody, and it is most often used voluntarily by disputants who are parents, the remainder of the chapter focuses on compliance issues most pertinent for these parents: visitation and child support agreements.

VISITATION

Two studies found mixed support for claims that, at least in the short term, mediation clients complied with visitation orders at a higher rate compared with litigation clients (Pearson & Thoennes, 1985a, 1986). Pearson and Thoennes (1985a) found that, at 3 months postdivorce, their Di-

---

[1] Mediation agreements become orders of the court after they have been ratified by the judge.

vorce Mediation Research Project (DMRP) sample of custodial parents reported that visitation was "rare or unpredictable": 30% for clients who tried mediation (i.e., both successful and unsuccessful), 30% for litigation clients, and 50% for noncontested cases. Noncustodial parents, however, reported that visitation was rare or unpredictable at rates of 0% for successful mediation clients, 30% for unsuccessful mediation clients, and 30% for litigation clients. Thus, there is obvious discrepancy in the reports of custodial versus noncustodial parents, and this discrepancy is expected and has been found in other studies (Braver, Wolchik, Sandler, Fogas, & Zvetina, 1991; Braver et al., 1993). It can be assumed that the parents' reports "bracket" the true number of visits (Braver, Fitzpatrick, & Bay, 1991). Interestingly, even with the discrepancies, both reports modestly favor mediation. Unfortunately, Pearson and Thoennes did not report whether the differences between the groups were statistically significant and did not give rates for noncontested cases reported by noncustodial parents.

Pearson and Thoennes (1985a) then reported compliance rates for visitation agreements for a group of participants whose divorces were final 4–5 years earlier. They found that 60% of the litigation group reported regular visitation as opposed to only 46% of those clients who were successful in reaching agreements in mediation. Unfortunately, Pearson and Thoennes again did not report if the group differences are statistically significant, and they reversed the method of reporting, which makes comparisons between this study and the previous one difficult. Instead of reporting the percentage of clients in each group who report rare or unpredictable visitation, as was done in the first sample, for this latter sample Pearson and Thoennes reported compliance rates for those clients who report regular visitation. Thus, both the question reported and the direction of the answers given do not match the earlier sample. It is unclear how many of the clients in this sample reported rare or unpredictable visits or if this question was even asked. It could be as high as 40% of the litigation group and as high as 54% of the mediation group, which are much higher percentages than reported in the earlier study and support litigation as opposed to mediation. In addition, 60% of the noncustodians who tried mediation reported they were visiting regularly, whereas 80% of the litigation noncustodians reported they were visiting regularly. Again, 40% of the noncustodial mediation clients could be visiting rarely or unpredictably, whereas 20% of the noncustodial litigation clients could be doing so. It appears that in this latter group, litigation clients were more compliant with visitation orders, but it is difficult to determine if they were significantly so and how this relates to the first sample.

A third study (Kelly, 1990b) found that at final divorce, a significant difference was found in noncompliance with visitation or custody agreements between litigation (30%) and mediation (12%) groups. There are, however, no figures given for compliance with visitation or custody agreements 2 years postdivorce.

CHILD SUPPORT

Four longitudinal studies and one cross-sectional study compare compliance rates for mediating and litigating clients. The results of one cross-sectional study are confusing and make the findings unclear (Bautz & Hill, 1989). In Bautz and Hill's article describing the study, Table 2 details the analysis of child support payments and reports the sample size of the litigation group as 56 and the mediation group as 30, whereas in the Method or study section of the article, the number of participants in the study was listed as 52 for the litigation group and 68 for the mediated group. There is no explanation as to why the litigation sample has more participants than were enlisted in the study and why the mediation sample has fewer, or what subset of the original mediated sample this group represents. Thus, unless further clarification is made available, the results of this study are unclear.

In the first longitudinal study, Pearson and Thoennes (1985a, 1986) reported that, for their DMRP sample, at 3 months postdivorce, support payments were "absent or irregular" for 33% of the mediation clients, 33% of the litigation clients whose cases were uncontested, and 50% of the litigation clients whose cases were contested. At 12 months postdivorce, the researchers reported that the percentage in every category increased but was greatest for the group of litigation clients whose cases were contested. Twenty-one percent of those who reached an agreement in mediation returned to court for contempt citations, to take out temporary restraining orders, or to change custody, visitation, or child support. The rate was 31% for those who did not reach an agreement in mediation and 36% for the litigation group (13% had been back twice as opposed to 6% for the successful mediation group; Pearson & Thoennes, 1988c). The authors indicated that the rates were statistically lower for mediation clients but did not indicate if the three figures were statistically significantly different.

Unfortunately, these rates do not hold over time. For the sample of clients interviewed 4–5 years postdivorce, Pearson and Thoennes (1988c) found there were not significant differences between the litigation and successful mediation clients. On the basis of self-report data, approximately 25% of each group (i.e., successful mediation clients, unsuccessful mediation clients, and the litigation groups) reported returning to court on a custody-visitation matter. And, in their study of Delaware mediation clients, Pearson and Thoennes (1989) again found identical rates of relitigation in various categories.

Pearson and Thoennes (1984b) also reported on a combined visitation/child support variable on a separate sample of clients, the Denver Custody Mediation Project. At 3 months postdivorce, 85% of the successful mediation clients reported that their ex-spouse was "generally complying with all terms of the agreement," whereas only 60% of the unsuccessful mediation clients, those clients who rejected an offer of mediation and the contested litigation cases, were doing so. In addition, reports of "serious disagreements" were at 14% for successful mediation clients but between 30% and 40% for all other groups. It is interesting that at 9 months postdivorce, the rates changed. The percentage of successful mediation clients who reported that their ex-spouse was generally complying with all the terms of the agreement was now 79% (vs. 85% earlier), and 67% of litigation clients reported compliance (vs. 60% earlier). It appears that the groups are regressing to a similar mean. Reports of serious disagreements were 6% for successful mediation clients and 33% for litigation clients, but no rates were reported for unsuccessful mediation clients or those who rejected an offer to mediate. Again, the researchers did not report whether these rates were statistically significantly different. The researchers did report an additional analysis and indicated that when they controlled for differences in cooperation between the spouses in the successful mediation versus unsuccessful mediation groups, the differences in rates were smaller but the pattern persisted. However, the researchers did not report the exact rates or differences and did not report the rates for the unsuccessful mediation group for the 9-month follow-up. At 2-year follow-up, only 13% of the mediation clients successful in reaching an agreement had filed for court modifications, as opposed to 35% of the litigation clients. Unfortunately, there are no figures given for mediation clients who did not reach an agreement or those who reached only partial agreement (Pearson & Thoennes, 1988c). And again, there is no indication if this difference is statistically significant.

A second longitudinal study reported that at divorce and at 1 year postdivorce, there were modest differences between mediating and litigating clients in terms of no or partial compliance with spousal support orders (23% litigation vs. 7% mediation), and no or partial compliance with child support reported by custodial women (23% litigation vs. 19% mediation) or by noncustodial men (9% litigation vs. 0% mediation; Kelly, 1990b). Unfortunately, as with the Pearson and Thoennes data presented above, the researcher did not report whether these differences were statistically significant. In any event, by 2 years postdivorce, these differences had disappeared. The litigation group became more compliant over time, whereas the mediation group became less so (Kelly, 1990b). Interestingly, when Kelly analyzed the contributions of other measured variables to noncompliance from before the divorce to 2 years postdivorce, satisfaction with the divorce process/outcome was not significant. What Kelly did find was that there was a gender difference in variables associated with noncompliance. For men, there was a significant correlation between noncompliance at 2 years postdivorce and two variables: the degree of conflict in the marriage and the amount of anger reported at their ex-spouse 2 years post-divorce. For women, a report of noncompliance at 2 years postdivorce was significantly negatively related to one variable: their ex-spouses' income before the divorce. In other words, women whose spouses made less before the divorce were more likely to report noncompliance 2 years after the divorce than women whose ex-spouses had higher incomes before the divorce (Kelly, 1990a, 1990b). This result is also consistent with a study by Braver, Fitzpatrick, and Bay (1991; see below). Thus, satisfaction with the divorce process and outcome hypothesized by many mediation advocates to be a significant contributing factor to why mediation clients have higher compliance rates was not found to be so. According to one group of researchers (Pearson & Thoennes, 1985a), nonpayment of child support seems to be a phenomenon rooted outside the initial custody dispute and dispute resolution method used to resolve custody. Instead, three other variables appear to be much more significant in predicting noncompliance: level of conflict, level of anger, and the payee's income.

In a third longitudinal study, Emery, Matthews, and Wyer (1991) reported that at 2 years postdivorce, a review of court records indicates that overdue child support notices were sent to 71% of the litigation fathers but only 51% of the mediation fathers. This difference, however, did not reach statistical significance and is probably not reflective of overall compliance rates in that it only assessed those cases for which legal action was taken. Previous studies reviewed earlier (Kelly, 1990b; Pearson & Thoennes, 1985a, 1985b, 1986; Thoennes & Pearson, 1985) used a method of self-report that may have yielded different rates of compliance.

CONCLUSION

Probably the safest conclusion is that mediation may produce modest improvements in compliance with visitation and child support agreements in the short term but that these modest improvements do not hold up for the long term (Pearson, 1994). To reach more secure and concrete conclusions, however, researchers need to address many of the methodological issues addressed in the previous section on increased satisfaction.

For example, specific questions asked would need to be standardized so that results could be compared across studies. The questions asked (i.e., "rare and unpredictable" visitation vs. "regular" visitation; "absent or irregular" child support vs. "generally complying with all terms of the agreement") and the method of data collection (i.e., self-report or court records) need to be consistent across studies. Asking slightly different questions is likely to yield slightly different answers (Gutek, 1978). Court records could underestimate both the amount of visitation and payments of child support.

In terms of child support, judges often fail to require that decrees contain the provision that support be paid through the court, and payers might choose to pay payees directly, bypassing the court processes altogether (Braver, Fitzpatrick, & Bay, 1991). In addition, interviews with custodial parents only can be problematic. Custodial parents' report of support payments as a percentage of what is owed is approximately 27% lower than their matched noncustodial parents' report (Braver, Fitzpatrick, & Bay, 1991). Thus, relying on only court records or only the custodial parent's report of payments provides an incomplete picture. Comparison groups also need to be equivalent. Suitable divisions need to be completed within the litigating group reflecting level of conflict, and the intervention needed to resolve these cases. Once divided, these subgroups can then be compared with the clients successful in reaching a full agreement, clients successful in reaching a partial agreement, and unsuccessful mediation groups. Passage of time also needs to be assessed. Because results show that within 2 to 5 years all differences between mediation and litigation groups disappear (Kelly, 1990b; Pearson & Thoennes, 1984b), researchers need to carefully select participants so that those with wide differences in lengths of time since divorce are not included in the same sample. Finally, statistical significance tests need to be computed for the results of comparisons to indicate if the differences were meaningful.

A study of matched pairs of custodial and noncustodial parents' reports of compliance with child support indicated that the most powerful predictor of compliance is the payer's ability to pay (Braver, Fitzpatrick, & Bay, 1991). Variables making up the index of ability to pay included noncustodial parent's income, how much child support was owed, how much child support was owed per child, and the percentage of noncustodial parent's income that was owed. The strongest predictor of compliance yet identified, however, was the payer's employment. When the researcher looked only at families in which the noncustodial parent was employed for the full 12 months prior to data collection, reports of compliance with support orders were much greater than those given when the noncustodial parent was unemployed during the same period.

8

DECREASED DIVORCE
PROCESSING COSTS

Increasing the efficiency of the legal system is one of the driving forces behind the evolution and proliferation of mediation (Fix & Harter, 1992). Therefore, a critical goal of mediation is to decrease costs for the litigants and the legal system, including costs associated with legal fees and time spent in the legal process reaching a resolution, costs associated with additional litigation hearings and relitigation of issues, and costs incurred by courts processing divorce cases. This chapter considers each of these divorce processing costs.

DECREASING LITIGANTS' COSTS AND TIME EXPENDED

Legal fees in contested divorces can be extremely high, consuming a substantial part of the assets and reducing the standard of living for each partner for a period of time after the divorce (Sales et al., 1993a, 1993b; Schlissel, 1992). It has also been argued that mediation decreases the cost of securing a divorce. Some research appears to support this assertion. In comparing a comprehensive, private, voluntary, fee-for-service mediation program with a litigation approach in California, Kelly (1990a, 1990b) found that the greatest cost savings were experienced by the mediation parents. The average divorce costs for couples in the mediation sample

99

were $5,243, whereas the average divorce cost for couples in the litigation sample was $12,234—a 100% difference. Although the clientele in this study were upper-middle-class professionals, Pearson (1994) also found a difference in her studies of public mediation. The average legal fee for an individual who successfully mediated was $1,650, whereas purely litigation respondents spent an average of $2,360 per person. Pearson also found that when mediation was unsuccessful, the cost per individual was $2,010. In an earlier article, Pearson and Thoennes (1982) conducted analyses of attorney fees and looked at these in relation to when the case was referred to mediation. They found that in order for mediation to produce these savings, parties must be diverted to it early in the dispute and mediation must succeed in resolving the dispute (Pearson & Thoennes, 1988a). Mediation conducted before the clients have been to court to establish temporary orders yielded attorneys fees of $874, whereas mediation after obtaining temporary orders yielded attorneys fees of $1,940 (Pearson & Thoennes, 1982). As a comparison, the control group attorney fees were $1,076 prior to temporary orders and $1,500 overall (Pearson & Thoennes, 1982). Thus, it would appear that attorney fees for mediation clients are actually more than attorney fees for litigation clients when the mediation clients are unsuccessful in reaching an agreement. The 1982 article noted that not all of the data from the sample were analyzed at the point the article was published; therefore, comparison between the 1982 article and data contained in Pearson (1994) is unclear.

Despite the compelling logic for predicting decreased costs associated with mediation, two researchers (Ellis, 1990; Keilitz et al., 1992) found no cost savings in a comparison of litigated and mediated cases. In a large study covering four jurisdictions in different states, Keilitz et al. (1992) compared mediated and nonmediated sites and asked attorneys to estimate the amount of time they spent on cases that went to mediation and those that did not. The attorneys estimated they spent less time on mediation cases, but their fees did not reflect this result. Keilitz et al. reasoned that attorneys may be using a fixed-fee billing procedure. Thus, total costs remain the same regardless of whether the couple use mediation. Another study (Bahr, 1981) found a savings of $535 per case when private mediation was compared with litigation, rather than the $5,000 difference noted by Kelly (1990a, 1990b). Thus, mediation produces some cost savings in attorney fees, although these savings are neither great nor consistently found across studies (J. Folberg & Milne, 1988; Pearson & Thoennes, 1988a).

As already noted, one factor affecting cost is the time spent in the legal process. The research findings regarding this variable appear to mirror cost findings. Two groups of researchers (Emery & Wyer, 1987a; Trost, Braver, & Schoeneman, 1988) found that settlements are reached more quickly in mediated cases as compared with litigated cases. In viewing the Superior Court of Arizona in Maricopa County both prior to and subsequent to the implementation of mandatory mediation, Trost et al. (1988) found that the mandatory mediation sample took significantly less time to obtain divorces than did two comparison groups—a group measured before mandatory mediation was instituted and two groups in another county taken before and after the mediation rule was instituted in Maricopa County. Pearson (1994), however, found that only successful mediation translated into time savings. Cases moved the slowest (14.2 months) if they were mediated unsuccessfully and needed both mediation and litigation. Successfully mediated cases needed only 8.5 months, and litigation cases needed 10.8 months.

Once again, the logic supporting the above findings is compelling. Successfully mediated cases move the fastest because both of the parties needed to make decisions are in the same room at the same time, and the parties are generally inclined toward agreement or become inclined fairly quickly or mediation is terminated. Litigated cases can take longer for any number of reasons. If both parties are represented by attorneys, they have the added complexity of coordinating communications between two parties and two lawyers. Lawyers tend to have many cases active at any one time and thus may not necessarily be available to consult when the clients and the opposing counsel are ready to negotiate. It may also be the case that clients choosing to hire attorneys are less inclined toward agreement and thus take more time to negotiate agreements. Cases needing mediation and litigation have both the problem of negotiating with two lawyers and the additional time it takes to attend mediation, have it fail, and then be referred back to the litigation system. Referrals to mediation and back to court take added time.

Mirroring the findings on cost, not all research on case-processing time has reached the same conclusions. Keilitz et al. (1992) found inconsistency in the time needed to process cases between the four sites in their study. In three of the four sites, mediation proceeded at a faster pace than litigation (Keilitz et al., 1992). Results also indicated that for those clients who reached agreement, case-processing times were the fastest in two jurisdictions (i.e., Brevard County, Florida and Las Vegas, Nevada) and were also the slowest in two other jurisdictions (Mecklenburg County, North Carolina and Santa Fe, New Mexico). Keilitz et al. concluded that there is no pattern, either faster or slower, for cases referred to mediation, but they pointed out that they were unable to control for other potentially confounding variables (i.e., legal, economic, and social factors) that could account for differences in case-processing times. For example, local court rules governing procedural issues (e.g., whether a hearing must be held prior to cases being referred to mediation) can have a significant impact on case-processing times (Keilitz et al., 1992). These rules vary from jurisdiction to jurisdiction and have nothing at all to do with the quality of the mediation or litigation offered.

Moreover, there are no strong conclusions that can be drawn from current research concerning litigant cost and time from initial filing to final dissolution. If there are any cost savings attached to mediation, they are likely to be enjoyed by the higher socioeconomic clients who choose to attend private mediation services and have all divorce issues resolved there. In addition, jurisdictional differences in local court rules and procedural issues are likely to have more of an impact on case-processing times than the dispute resolution method. It is important to sort out how these differences in rules and procedures affect case-processing times so that the differences in dispute resolution method can be fully understood.

DECREASING THE NUMBER OF LITIGATION HEARINGS AND RELITIGATION

Divorce litigation comprises the major portion of civil caseloads in many large court systems (Gerber, 1990; Schlissel, 1992; Shepard, 1990). Reducing the number of initial hearings and the amount of relitigation in divorce cases was an early goal of mediation (Keilitz et al., 1992). Mediation proponents argue that it has achieved this goal (Clement & Schwebel, 1993; Depner et al., 1992; Emery, 1994; Emery et al., 1987; Irving & Benjamin, 1995; Kelly, 1990a, 1990b, 1996; Kelly & Duryee, 1992; Margolin, 1973; Pearson & Thoennes, 1989; Smoron, 1998). It is argued that mediation clients are much more likely to reach agreement out of court as opposed to litigation clients (Emery et al., 1987; Kelly, 1996). For example, across studies, settlement rates for divorce mediation are between 50% and 85% whether in court-sponsored volunteer or mandatory programs (Depner et al., 1992; Emery, 1994; Kelly, 1996; Kelly & Duryee, 1992; Pearson, 1994; Pearson & Thoennes, 1984b, 1989) or in private, voluntary, comprehensive programs (Irving & Benjamin, 1995; Kelly, 1990a, 1990b). Furthermore, both in the short term and over the course of 1 to 2 years postdivorce, mediation is argued to reduce relitigation by up to 30% (Clement & Schwebel, 1993; Pearson & Thoennes, 1982). Although those clients who reach agreement are the least likely to return to court (Pearson & Thoennes, 1989), even those clients who did not reach agreement in mediation are less likely to return to court compared with their litigation counterparts (Pearson & Thoennes, 1989). At least in the short term, these patterns do not differ for users of mandatory (Pearson & Thoennes, 1989) or voluntary (Kelly, 1990a, 1990b, 1996) mediation programs. Thus, at first glance, mediation appears to be much more successful in discouraging relitigation. At a closer look, however, the picture does not remain so optimistic. Both Kelly (1990b) and Pearson and Thoennes (1989), in addition to others, found that in the long term, initial differences in relitigation rates between mediating and litigating groups disappear.

Assessing a voluntary, fee-for-service, comprehensive mediation program, Kelly (1990b) found that at between 1 and 2 years postmediation, 15% of both mediation and litigation couples had returned to court or had seen an attorney about a change in their agreements. In a sample of couples who mediated and litigated their cases in a court-sponsored program 5 years prior to interview, there were no differences in relitigation rates; approximately 25% of each group had returned to court (Pearson & Thoennes, 1989). And in a sample of couples from Delaware who mediated child support matters only, equal numbers of couples from mediated and litigation groups returned to court (Pearson & Thoennes, 1989). Emery, Matthews, and Kitzmann (1991) assessed mediating and litigating groups in a court-sponsored program and found there were no significant differences between the groups for returns to court. Emery et al. found that returns to court were frequent (approximately 66% of all families had further disputes within a 2-year period). In a 9-year follow-up to their original study sample, these researchers found that their original results were confirmed (Dillon & Emery, 1996). There were no differences between mediated and litigated groups on the number of changes attempted and made on custody, visitation, and support arrangements and on the forum used to make changes (Dillon & Emery, 1996). There were also no differences comparing groups on total contacts with the legal profession in the 9 years since the initial settlement. Dillon and Emery concluded that there were no effects on subsequent relitigation attributable to the dispute resolution method in the short or long term.

Methodological Concerns

A complex set of methodological questions need to be considered to put these findings into perspective. Important issues include specific question assessed, specific advice given by mediators and attorneys, the comparability of control groups, passage of time, and the level of conflict between the spouses.

Specific Question Assessed

In many studies, it is unclear if the relitigation category refers to returns to court for any reason or returns to court for only contested matters (Fix & Harter, 1992; Johnston et al., 1985; Kressel et al., 1994; Milne, 1978; Pearson & Thoennes, 1989). This information is important to know for two reasons.

First, the underlying level of conflict between ex-spouses can be quite different and the term *relitigation* can be a misnomer. Relitigation, on one hand, can refer to mutually agreeable changes in custody of a child, wherein parents file papers with the court merely detailing the change, or a payee's salary can change so that a new wage assignment will need to be filed with the court. Although both of these instances can be counted as a postdecree action or relitigation, in neither of these instances does the entry of new documents into the file signify a contest between the parents or actual relitigation of an issue. These instances would be better classified as postdecree actions rather than as relitigation. The parents have merely agreed to a change and filed papers with the court codifying the change. On the other hand, relitigation can refer to parents who argue bitterly over a change in custody of a child, or over a change in levels of support because of changes in levels of salary. The parents can participate in protracted and hostile hearings over the matters. These instances clearly indicate a breakdown of the original agreement and a severe conflict and contest between the parents. The term *relitigation* seems appropriate for these instances. Postdecree actions and relitigated issues should be counted as such and not be confused.

Second, in addition to understanding the level of conflict between couples, one must also understand the precise definition used to assess relitigation rates to compare studies. It is critical to ascertain whether the researchers are asking the same question; otherwise the comparisons across studies are meaningless. Unfortunately, of all the studies that publish rates of relitigation, only three studies defined the term *relitigation* (Irving & Benjamin, 1983; Keilitz et al., 1992; Meierding, 1993). Irving and Benjamin (1983) broke down their relitigation rate figures into an overall relitigation rate for successful mediation clients who participated in their follow-up interviews (71%); however, the authors also noted that 80% of this figure was for "automatic" changes to the record. They went on to state that only 10% of the clients successful in reaching an agreement returned to court 3 to 6 months postagreement, although it is not clear in the article how this 10% figure is derived from the 71% relitigation figure stated earlier; presumably the 10% figure represents contested matters (Irving & Benjamin, 1983).

Meierding (1993) was the clearest in her description of relitigation rates. She broke down her relitigation categories for mediation clients into overall (10.6%), agreed-upon changes (3.2%), and contested changes (7.4%). Unfortunately, both of these studies only published relitigation rates for clients who successfully reached agreement. There are no data available for clients who did not reach agreement in mediation, and both studies have no control group of clients who used litigation to resolve their dispute. Without a control group with which to compare these results, it is difficult to draw any substantive conclusions regarding the value of this program in reducing overall relitigation rates.

In the one empirical study that attempted to classify returns to court as contested (relitigation) versus noncontested (postdecree actions), no actual data were provided. Keilitz et al. (1992) reported finding that a higher proportion of mediation cases (as compared with litigation cases) file a modification of residential custody or visitation, but they also indicated that nearly half of the parties report that they have made these modifications on their own without contest. Statistics were not provided on exact numbers of mediating and litigating clients relitigating, nor were any data provided for the numbers of clients for whom the relitigated issue was uncontested.

It is difficult to draw any definitive conclusions regarding relitigation rates from studies that report rates of relitigation for only one subgroup of mediation clients (i.e., clients successful in reaching agreements), that have no control group for comparison, or that give review statements as opposed to statistical data. To understand the full effect of mediation, researchers must report rates for all those clients who received mediation (i.e., successful, not successful, and partially successful in reaching an agreement) and have adequate comparison group data.

Specific Advice by Mediators and Lawyers

There may be a difference in how clients are instructed by their mediators and lawyers to proceed with uncontested postdecree changes to their divorce agreement that produce differences in relitigation rates, regardless of method used to resolve the initial divorce dispute. Although there is no systematic research on how many mediation programs encourage clients to codify mutually agreed-to changes with the court to reduce the chances of any misunderstandings at a later time that may result from these changes, researchers have found that some programs do encourage this practice (Keilitz et al., 1992; Trost & Braver, 1987). This practice may inflate relitigation rates for mediation clients, particularly if rates are not broken down into uncontested postdecree actions versus contested relitigated issues. It may also be the practice of some divorce attorneys to encourage clients to codify agreed-to changes with the court. Unfortunately, there is no research concerning divorce attorneys' practices on this issue, so it is unclear whether litigation clients' relitigation rates are also inflated in this way or whether there is a difference between the number of mediators versus lawyers who encourage this practice.

Comparability of Control Groups

As noted earlier, one of the problems with understanding mediation research generally and relitigation rates specifically is the lack of appropriate comparison group data (see previous section on rates of satisfaction and lack of comparison group data; Levy, 1984; Roehl & Cook, 1985). Mediation research has been conducted using large samples, longitudinal designs, random assignment, different methods, and a variety of public and private services (Emery, Matthews, & Kitzmann, 1991; Emery & Wyer,

1987a; Irving & Benjamin, 1995; Keilitz et al., 1992; Kelly, 1996; Kressel, 1985; Margolin, 1973; Pearson, 1981; Pearson & Thoennes, 1982, 1985a, 1985b, 1989; Thoennes et al., 1991). There are no empirical investigations on the work of lawyers or courts in negotiating divorce agreements that come close to this scope or level of detail (Kressel, 1985), and no studies have been conducted that alter aspects of the court experience that could possibly alter relitigation rates. Adequate comparison group data are critical for valid research (Levy, 1984), and it is sorely lacking in mediation research generally.

A second major issue concerning comparison groups, also noted earlier, is the lack of breakdowns in the litigation samples that would reflect similar breakdowns in the mediation samples. For example, it is common in mediation studies to separate groups into mediating clients (a) who reach agreement during mediation, (b) who do not reach agreement during mediation, (c) who reach partial agreement during mediation, and (d) who reach agreement after mediation has ended but prior to any court hearings (Kressel, 1985; Levy, 1984). The rationale for making these divisions is that those couples who can negotiate and reach an agreement are somehow fundamentally different from those couples who cannot. In addition, those clients who reach agreement after mediation but before going to trial have somehow benefited from mediation, even though they could not resolve any or all of their issues in mediation. Unfortunately, similar breakdowns are not done for the litigation group. For example, litigation clients could be grouped into those clients (a) who reach agreement through negotiations between attorneys, (b) who do not reach agreement and must litigate, (c) who have contested hearings over various issues during the course of their divorce but resolve many issues prior to trial, and (d) who resolve all issues at trial. For example, those clients who reach agreement prior to going to an attorney and use the services of an attorney merely to codify the agreement should arguably remain in a class by themselves. They are not true litigation clients because there is nothing to litigate, nor are they mediation clients. These clients could represent the least conflictual group of all divorcing clients.

One notable exception to this methodological oversight exists. Emery and his colleagues (Emery, 1994; Emery, Matthews, & Wyer, 1991; Emery & Wyer, 1987a) specifically stated that subdividing one group (mediation), without doing so with the other (litigation), creates inappropriate comparison groups (Emery & Wyer, 1987a).

Even where the researchers have attempted to provide appropriate comparison groups, there is a danger of a different confound in the design. For example, in one of the largest multisite samples of mediation, the comparison sample of litigation cases was not collected at the same locations as the mediation samples (Pearson & Thoennes, 1985a, 1986). The control group sample was selected from filings in Colorado, whereas the mediation samples came from Los Angeles, California; Hennepin County, Minnesota; and jurisdictions across Connecticut. The study thus has some multijurisdictional comparisons that can be done for the mediation sample, but how these mediation samples compare with the Colorado-based litigation sample is unclear. There is no empirical method to assess if the differences found between the litigation and mediation groups are due to differences in procedural rules between the jurisdictions or to true differences in participants. It is important to have comparable groups, both in terms of breakdowns of participants within categories and in terms of collection of data from the groups at the same geographical locations at the same point in time.

A large part of the problem in obtaining appropriate comparison groups is that, traditionally, judges, court administrators, and lawyers have blocked any efforts at true randomization, which would require that either all divorcing clients within a jurisdiction or a specific percentage of clients be randomized to mediation versus litigation groups (see Thoennes et al., 1991). Furthermore, clients often refuse to be randomized to a certain group. There is only one very early study that accomplished true randomization of participants to experimental and control groups (Margolin, 1973). In this study, 150 consecutive, divorced couples who were unable to reach agreement on visitation were referred to the Conciliation Court for randomization to either a counseling group or a litigation group. Although one third of the control group failed to report to the Conciliation Court, Margolin was able to track all of these cases so that, at least in terms of relitigation rates, data could be obtained in all cases. Follow-up data, which occurred at 4 months postdecision, showed that 12% of the mediation clients had relitigated, whereas 79% of the litigation group had returned to court. Margolin did not, however, define the term *relitigation of issues*, so it is unclear if these figures reflect uncontested postdecree actions or actual relitigation and how many of each occurred for the mediation and litigation groups. The postdecree period was also very short, so it is unclear if the rates would regress to a similar mean overtime as occurred in several other studies (Kelly, 1990b; Pearson, 1994).

Two recent attempts at an experimental assessment of a mandatory mediation program addressing visitation/custody issues (Oregon) and child support issues (Indiana) were also dismal failures in randomization and point out another important problem in obtaining adequate matched samples: self-selection (Newmark et al., 1995; Thoennes et al., 1991). In Oregon, the original purpose of the study was to compare the use of mediation and custody evaluations in custody and visitation disputes involving domestic abuse. The research had to be modified, however, because mediation had become such a popular method of dispute resolution that most clients who were assigned to the custody evaluation group refused to do so and self-selected into the mediation group.

The program in Indiana was based on a temporary, local court rule where no sanctions were imposed by the court for failure to appear at mediation, and the attorneys representing mediation clients admitted to encouraging clients not to attend mediation sessions (Thoennes et al., 1991). Nearly 66% of the eligible clients referred to the two courts designated to use mediation ignored orders to appear for the orientation or mediation sessions. Only approximately 33% complied with the orders to appear. Of those 33% who complied with the orders, 56% were excluded from the research because their dispute was not relevant to the research (e.g., dispute over property) and another substantial percentage were excluded because they could not be given mediation appointments prior to their scheduled preliminary court hearing (the authors do not specify this last figure). In the final analysis, Thoennes et al. (1991) indicated that only 11% of the total cases referred to the mediation courts actually received mediation services. From this limited sample, the researchers found that the mediation and litigation groups were significantly different on several variables. The mediation group had significantly more postdivorce couples, as opposed to couples negotiating the initial divorce, than did the litigation group. Thoennes et al. speculated that the postdivorce couples who obtained mediation were viewed as "troublesome" by both attorneys and judges, who then welcomed additional assistance in settling the dispute (i.e., 40% of these postdivorce cases had made previous attempts to modify child support). The litigation group, on the other hand, were primarily initial divorce cases. The differences between the mediation and litigation groups made meaningful comparisons regarding relitigation rates for these two groups impossible.

With the exception of Margolin (1973), the result of this lack of institutional support for sound research is that generally only participants who volunteer for a study (Emery & Jackson, 1989; Pearson & Thoennes, 1984b; Pearson et al., 1982) are involved in this research. Researchers have approached clients and asked them either to be in one of the two groups (mediation or litigation) or to agree to be randomly assigned to one of the two groups (Emery & Jackson, 1989; Newmark et al., 1995; Pearson et al., 1982; Pearson & Thoennes, 1984a). Social psychological research on volunteers has shown that people who volunteer can be qualitatively different from people who do not volunteer for research projects (Bell, 1962; Lasagna & von Felsinger, 1954; Maslow & Sakoda, 1952).

Even mediation researchers have found differences in those who accept and reject any offer of free mediation (Pearson et al., 1982). Pearson et al. (1982) and Pearson (1991) found that clients willing to mediate have more education, have higher incomes both before and after separation or divorce, and communicate better; men have higher occupational status. Interestingly, men who are ambivalent about the divorce are more willing to try mediation. Emery, Matthews, and Wyer (1991) also found similar results. Mothers who reject mediation tend to be of significantly lower income than those mothers who accept, and fathers who refused mediation were more likely to work in blue-collar jobs. Differences in relitigation rates could then just as easily be caused by differences between the groups and not by the quality of the dispute resolution process (Levy, 1984).

In the mediation studies that report relitigation rates, only four recent studies have attempted even a quasiexperimental design (Emery & Jackson, 1989; Emery & Wyer, 1987a, 1987b; Pearson & Thoennes, 1984b, 1985a, 1985b; Thoennes et al., 1991), and in two of these studies the quality of the randomization has been called into question either by the authors themselves (Thoennes et al., 1991) or by others (Levy, 1984). The remaining studies that report relitigation rates either have no control group (Davis & Roberts, 1988; Irving & Benjamin, 1983; Johnston & Campbell, 1987; Kressel et al., 1994; Meierding, 1993; Milne, 1978, Saposnek et al., 1984) or have a noncomparable control group (Fix & Harter, 1992; Thoennes et al., 1991).

Thus, there is no way to clearly indicate if rates of relitigation for either mediating or litigating clients are due to (a) initial differences or self-selection into the mediation and litigation groups, (b) mediators or lawyers encouraging their clients to codify uncontested postdecree changes with the court, (c) differences in the number of uncontested postdecree actions versus contested relitigation, or (d) failure of the dispute resolution method to fully resolve the issues. Until researchers have a better understanding of the practices of most mediation programs and divorce attorneys, or at the very least can categorize returns to court into contested (relitigation) and uncontested (postdecree actions), it is unlikely that we will have a clear understanding of how the dispute resolution method affects relitigation rates. As a result of these problems, published findings regarding relitigation rates are difficult to interpret.

Passage of Time

Probably the most consistent finding concerning relitigation rates is that there are no significant differences between mediating and litigating groups in the long term. Kelly (1990b) found that the differences in her groups had vanished by the 2-year follow-up. Pearson and Thoennes (1989) found that in their sample interviewed 4 to 5 years postdivorce, there were no differences in the frequency of reported disagreements over visitation and child support. In a 9-year follow-up study, Dillon and Emery (1996) found that there were no differences in number of changes attempted and made on custody, visitation, or support arrangements or in the forum used to make these arrangements.

Thus, it is important to understand at what point in time studies to assess relitigation or postdecree actions. Studies that assess differences in the short term (i.e., less than 1 year; see Margolin, 1973) are more likely to find different rates of relitigation than those that assess it in the long term. Whatever positive effect mediation may have, if any, will likely be found only for the short term (Kelly, 1990b).

Level of Conflict Between the Spouses

Finally, the level of conflict between the ex-spouses is also important in assessing relitigation rates. Several studies that report relitigation rates focus on mediation programs designed for very high-conflict cases. The clients of these programs are predominantly postdecree couples with long histories of litigation. The programs studied are generally offered only after mandatory or brief settlement-focused mediation has failed and as an alternative to a court-ordered custody evaluation (Johnston & Campbell, 1987; Kressel et al., 1994; Milne, 1978). Because past behavior is often the best predictor of future behavior (Mischel, 1968), it seems reasonable to assume that these clients will be more litigious after mediation than those clients without the long history of contentiousness and relitigation. And, not surprisingly, these studies often report higher rates of relitigation (i.e., Johnston & Campbell, 1987, 36%; Kressel et al., 1994, 44%) than do studies with either a mixed pre- and postdivorce participant pool or those studies with mostly predivorce participants (Margolin, 1973, 12%; Meierding, 1993, 10.6%; Pearson & Thoennes, 1989, 13%; Pearson & Thoennes, 1985a, 21%). Unfortunately, these studies of high-conflict cases do not report relitigation rates for a high-conflict control group of litigation clients, so it is impossible to assess whether these specialized mediation programs have a differential impact on these clients in terms of their continued rate of relitigation over that of a litigation sample.

There are myriad events and circumstances that influence people's lives that make it unlikely that a time-limited intervention, which is focused on producing agreements, can have significant long-term effects on the ability of the parents to follow through on child support, child custody, and visitation obligations and cooperatively settle future disputes without returning to court (Keilitz et al., 1992). Although mediation may deter relitigation in the short term, over a longer period of time a substantial number of parents will return to court regardless of which forum they used to resolve their initial divorce case (Thoennes et al., 1991). The relationship between divorcing parents (e.g., their ability to communicate and work together) and the employment status of the payee (Braver, Fitzpatrick, & Bay, 1991) have much more to do with postdecree litigation than does the forum used for the initial divorce (Pearson & Thoennes, 1988b). In addition, in some counties and states, parties were encouraged by their mediators to return to mediation or court to modify agreements as circumstances changed (Trost & Braver, 1987; Keilitz et al., 1992). In a study of a mandatory mediation program, Thoennes et al. (1991) found that there were no significant differences in the compliance rates between mediated and nonmediated child support and visitation agreements, even in the short run and even with the mediating group composed of more postdivorce, litigious couples. Thoennes et al. found that relitigation of child support issues was common and occurred in approximately 33% of both mediated and litigated cases. In Thoennes et al.'s study, over half of the mediated cases returned to deal with enforcement of child support and arrearage issues; in the litigated cases nearly half were seeking to increase support levels. I. Cohen (1998) also agreed that child support was the overwhelming issue that caused families to return to court. Of the cases that returned to court, 60% were to enforce child support orders.

What can be concluded from this research? Pearson (1994) argued that the safest statement that can be made is that while mediation is not more effective than litigation in preventing relitigation, these agreements are probably no more unstable than those agreements originating from lawyer negotiations or judicial decisions.

DECREASING THE COSTS FOR THE COURTS OF PROCESSING DIVORCE CASES

A companion goal to that of reducing the number of initial hearings and the amount of relitigation in divorce cases is the goal of decreasing costs for the courts in processing domestic relations cases by reducing caseloads (Pearson, 1981; Pearson & Thoennes, 1982). Some early research estimating court costs claimed that mediation programs saved the court system substantial amounts in that having litigants attend mediation to resolve their disputes was much less expensive than resolving these same disputes through the litigation system (i.e., trials or formal custody evaluations; see Bahr, 1981; Doyle & Caron, 1979; McIsaac, 1981; Milne, 1978; Pearson, 1981; Pearson & Thoennes, 1982; W. W. Weiss & Collada, 1977). For example, one researcher (Bahr, 1981) stated that if mediation services were available for all custody disputes in the United States, the court system in 1978 would have saved at least $9.6 million in court costs. Another researcher evaluated the mediation program in Los Angeles and found that it saved the court $280,362 in 1979 (McIsaac, 1981) and between $990,000 and $1,140,000 in 1982 (McIsaac, 1983). Yet another group of researchers (Cauble et al., 1985) evaluating the mediation program in Hennepin County, Minnesota, found that it saved the court $139,000 in 1982.

Not all researchers have been as optimistic in their cost estimates. S. Cohen (1982, cited in Pearson & Thoennes, 1988a), evaluating the mediation program in Clackamas County, Oregon, estimated that mediation actually cost more to conduct than trials (i.e., $307–$338 per case vs. trial costs of $96–$247). Fix and Harter (1992) concluded that if mediators' time and the staff required to implement mediation programs are taken into account, mediation programs would increase the total resources expended by the court on a per-case basis. And after nearly 20 years of investigating and publishing on all aspects of mediation, Pearson (1994) stated that mediation programs appear to have little impact on the courts' overall caseload. This finding is not unique to divorce mediation. Other researchers have also found that mediation programs do not produce aggregate cost savings for the courts (MacCoun, Lind, Hensler, Bryant, & Ebener, 1988). In an analysis of the New Jersey Automobile Arbitration Program, MacCoun et al. (1988) found that because people liked the mediation program, they were likely to use it and less likely to settle their disputes outside the courts. Thus, the increases in the use of mediation offset the economic gains from less use of the litigation system (Tyler, 1997). In other words, people who would have allowed their cases to be dismissed or would have reached an agreement through private settlement were now seeking court-sponsored mediation (Tyler, 1997). In addition, in MacCoun et al.'s study, the court-sponsored mediation program did not reduce the length of time for cases to be resolved or the legal fees (Tyler, 1997).

Methodological Concerns

To understand these disparate findings, we must investigate how the cost estimates were derived. Some of the issues include representativeness of cost estimates, individual cost items, overhead costs, and fees.

Representativeness of Cost Estimates

The more detailed and specific the cost estimates, the less likely it is that the results will indicate a large cost savings. For example, Bahr (1981) was creative in deriving his cost estimate for nationwide savings, and in doing so combined pieces of data from several different jurisdictions and extrapolated the results to a national estimate. He took per-hour cost estimates of trials versus mediation services for a sample in Los Angeles, California (H. McIsaac, personal communication, 1979, cited in Bahr, 1981). He then combined these figures with the percentage of divorce cases with children involving a custody contest and the percentage of nonmediated cases that settle prior to trial found in a sample from Hennepin County, Minnesota (Cauble et al., 1985). He then computed a mean number of cases that reach agreement in mediation based on studies using samples from several jurisdictions (see Bahr, 1981) and constructed his cost estimates. Although creative, these estimates may not be fully accurate for a variety of reasons.

Data taken from one jurisdiction in one state at one point in time cannot be assumed to be representative of the entire United States population (Ricci et al., 1991). Per-hour costs of trials versus mediation taken from one county in one state (i.e., Los Angeles, California) very likely do not equal court and mediation costs in other counties in California, much less other counties across the nation (Ricci et al., 1991). At the time the estimates were derived, Los Angeles had the highest caseload of any mediation program. It has been found that as the caseload numbers increase, the cost of service per case declines (Fix & Harter, 1992). Indeed, S. Cohen (1982) found that mediation costs are higher than trial costs in another jurisdiction, Clackamas County, Oregon, where caseloads were much smaller. If Bahr (1981) had used the cost figures from S. Cohen (1982) and made the necessary recalculations, a much different nationwide cost figure would result. Problems are only compounded when data are combined across nonrandomly selected participants and jurisdictions.

Individual Cost Items

There is little detail given in McIsaac (1981, 1983), S. Cohen (1982), or any of the articles concerning the individual cost items that are included in the mediation and trial cost figures. For example, Cauble et al. (1985) included mediator and clerk time in assessing mediation costs but excluded overhead costs for the mediation program. In addition, they did not state what cost items they used to calculate hearing/trial costs. McIsaac (1981) computed trial costs by including employee costs of all the participants in a trial (i.e., commissioner, court reporter, court clerk, and sheriff), then added fringe benefits and overhead percentages to the per-day total of employee costs. When calculating the conciliation costs, McIsaac (1981) only quoted a number but did not indicate how many mediators' salaries were used or if it included clerk or secretary time (as he included for trial costs). In his cost estimates of the Los Angeles Court in 1982, McIssac (1983) only cited the total cost savings of $990,000–$1,140,000 but did not give any indication of how these figures were calculated. Without detailed information concerning all costs included in overall estimates of cost savings for a jurisdiction or for the nation, it is unclear what is actually being measured and what to conclude from the results.

Overhead Costs

A good example of this is provided by one of the most important but overlooked costs: overhead costs. Only one of the researchers' estimates (McIsaac, 1981) included overhead costs of either the trial court or mediation program. Employee costs are not the only expenses in operating a court or mediation program. And depending on whether the program is court-connected or the services are contracted out to private mediators, the overhead costs may be quite different. In fact, in discussing the Denver Custody Mediation Project (CMP), Pearson (1981) indicated that "even if we assume an overhead of 100 percent for project administration, the cost of mediating falls far below the cost of litigating" (p. 10). The following year Pearson and Thoennes (1982) calculated the cost savings of processing 100 cases in mediation versus 100 cases in litigation using these same CMP figures. Yet, it appears that the researchers included the overhead costs for the courts in conducting uncontested and contested hearings[1] but did not include any mediation program overhead costs in their calculations (Pearson & Thoennes, 1982).[2] Without overhead costs included, Pearson and Thoennes concluded that mediation saves between $5,610 and $27,510 per 100 cases (depending on whether the litigated cases are calculated to require 4 hours or 9.8 hours in operation costs for a court to resolve the case). If the figures presented in this article were recalculated to include a 100% "project administration" figure (as was suggested in the 1981 article), mediation actually costs the public $13,890 *more* than processing 100 litigated cases under the 4-hour court time figure ($59,540 vs. $45,650). If the 9.8-hour court time figure is used, the savings of processing mediated cases versus litigated cases is $8,010. These figures are quite different than those presented by Pearson and Thoennes (1982) when omitting program administration or overhead costs for mediation but including it for calculating costs of court hearings ($5,650 savings vs. $13,890 additional costs and $27,510 savings vs. $8,010 savings, respectively).

In some states, it was also found that courts required at least two hearings and maybe more on mediated cases before they were resolved (Fix & Harter, 1992; Trost & Braver, 1987). If the cost of only the second hearing is added to the 100-case figures presented by Pearson and Thoennes (1982), the cost savings plummets even more.

This example highlights an important aspect of cost calculations. Including all the costs of operating a mediation program is essential to understanding the true cost savings of mediation versus litigation.

---

[1] "Since the hourly cost of operating a Colorado trial court in 1981 was approximately $125, the cost for the half hour of bench time would be about $63" (Pearson & Thoennes, 1982, p. 28).

[2] "Based on average direct costs of offering mediation services in Denver Custody Mediation Project, excluding program overhead" (Pearson & Thoennes, 1982, p. 29). In figuring the savings, Pearson and Thoennes calculated that the direct average cost per case of providing mediation services is $195. They found that 80% of the mediation cases then stipulated and thus needed only a noncontested hearing to resolve their case (20% needed a contested hearing). In the litigation sample, Pearson and Thoennes found that only 50% of the litigated cases needed a noncontested hearing, whereas 50% needed a contested hearing. Only 11% of the mediation sample needed a public-sector custody evaluation, whereas 35% of the litigation sample did so. In addition, they found that in Los Angeles, California, and in Portland, Oregon, court administrators estimated it takes 4 hours of bench time to complete a contested hearing, whereas the lawyers in Denver estimated it takes 9.8 hours of bench time to complete a contested hearing.

Fees

Several jurisdictions either charge for mediation on a sliding-fee scale or levy additional charges to divorce petition filing fees, marriage licenses, or motion filings to garner money to support the conciliation courts or court-connected mediation programs. None of these income sources are included in the cost estimates. For example, McIsaac (1981) indicated that in 1981 California instituted a $15 increase in divorce filing fees, a $5 charge for marriage licenses, and a $15 charge for filing motions to modify or enforce custody and visitation orders to support the conciliation courts. He did not, however, indicate the total amounts these fees garner in support of the conciliation courts and how this amount figured into his overall estimates of cost savings for the court.

Assumptions About Cost Benefits

The importance placed on these cost estimates cannot be overstated. Estimates produced by McIsaac (1981) was a central reason the California legislature passed a law in 1980 making mediation mandatory in child custody and visitation disputes (Pearson, 1994). Cost efficiency is also the driving force behind proliferation of mediation programs in other jurisdictions (Fix & Harter, 1992). Minimizing precious judicial time devoted to divorce cases by diverting these cases to a separate and cheaper alternative dispute resolution program is extremely attractive for court administrators who make decisions concerning the allocation of scarce resources. As noted earlier, high rates of agreement are found in the group of parents who mediate their agreements (i.e., 50%–85%; Kelly, 1996). Thus, it should be expected that this finding would translate into significant cost savings for the courts.

Unfortunately, this is not necessarily the case. Fix and Harter (1992) pointed out that early proponents of mediation assumed favorable answers to the following series of important questions without having any data to support their assumptions. In addition, Fix and Harter (1992, p. 20) indicated that subsequent studies have been unable to provide sufficient answers to these questions because of difficulties in determining values for many of the relevant variables:

1. At what stage are cases diverted to the mediation (Alternative Dispute Resolution, or ADR) track—how many court resources have already been expended in filing cases, pretrial conferences, motions, and discovery?
2. What is the cost to the court of the ADR program compared with its savings in litigation-related expenses? Have other resources been investigated, such as increasing case manage-

ment, hiring more judges and magistrates, and procuring more courtrooms?

3. What is the success rate of the ADR program? How many of its cases are not fully resolved and require subsequent judicial resources?

4. Of those cases successfully resolved in the ADR program, how many—had they not been in the program—would have gone to trial? How many would have settled or have been dismissed prior to trial?

As noted, there is little information available to answer these questions, but what is available is not necessarily encouraging.

Time Line for Diversion

In relation to the stage at which cases are diverted to mediation and how many court resources have already been expended at the point they are referred, researchers found that mediation clients in one jurisdiction attended a court hearing both before and after mediation (Trost & Braver, 1987). In a second study, researchers found that 40% of the clients indicated that they had not been before a judge or commissioner prior to being referred to mediation, 30% of the clients indicated that they had been before a judge or commissioner prior to referral to mediation, and another 30% indicated that they had been before a judge or commissioner two or more times (Fix & Harter, 1992). Therefore, 60% of all mediation clients in this study had been before a judge or commissioner one or more times before they began mediation. The structural problem of requiring hearings, or merely allowing hearings prior to referral to mediation, for certain clients in certain jurisdictions is that it reduces the possible cost savings of having a mediation program. As noted above in the section on overhead costs and using calculations made by Pearson and Thoennes (1982) and Pearson (1981), the savings are minimal to nonexistent if two hearings are required in mediation cases and overhead costs are included in cost calculations.

In the unmediated cases in Fix and Harter's (1992) study, it is noted that more than 68% of the attorneys in these cases indicated that they had not been before a judge or commissioner before starting serious settlement negotiations, 16% had appeared once, and only 10% had appeared two or more times. Although unmediated cases in which all negotiations are conducted through attorneys may be costly for the litigants in attorney fees, they appear to be less expensive for the courts by reducing the number of pretrial hearings.

In addition, referral processes for cases to mediation vary widely from jurisdiction to jurisdiction, even within states. In many states, judges have the discretion to assign cases to mediation at whatever point they decide is appropriate (e.g., Colorado Revised Statutes, 1998). Under this scenario, the case could have extensive court action prior to being referred to mediation. And since many mediation programs handle only child custody and visitation issues, no matter how many court resources are expended prior to referral to mediation, these clients must then return to court to resolve property and financial matters after mediation (S. Cohen, 1982). Requiring that clients use both litigation for resolving some issues and mediation for resolving others is arguably much more expensive for the courts than just using one system to resolve all matters. It is essential that this hypothesis be addressed empirically. Such studies should use equivalent comparison groups for both mediation and litigation clients, so that accurate cost-effectiveness estimates can be calculated and appropriate modifications of referral processes can be made to increase the cost-effectiveness of mediation programs.

Cost of Using Additional Resources

To ensure accuracy in determining the cost of mediation programs, researchers need to investigate and include alternative resources. At least in one jurisdiction, researchers found that "affirmative case management" or better management of caseloads had a greater influence on settlement rates than did the introduction of a mediation program (Trost & Braver, 1987). Although Trost and Braver concluded that mediation would be most beneficial in jurisdictions that were well managed, they also stated that similar improvements in settlement rates could be achieved through better case management itself or through the use of quasijudicial processes (Trost & Braver, 1987). Other than this one study, however, there has been little published research on alternative court-based processes (i.e., other than mediation) that could assist parties in settling cases.

The recent changes in the law concerning "special masters" and "family court advisors" are important programs to evaluate with empirically sound research methods. It was recently argued at a national conference of the Association of Family and Conciliation Courts that these special masters, who are assigned to monitor and control particularly high-conflict cases, can have a significant effect in reducing court hearings (Mitchell, 1998). The American Academy of Matrimonial Lawyers has passed a resolution to support arbitration as a means of resolving contested divorce cases and has trained many of its members as arbitrators (Schlissel, 1992). To date, there have been no empirical studies evaluating divorce arbitration programs. It is critical that these and other dispute-resolution or monitoring programs be identified and evaluated so that the best, most cost-effective set of processes can be developed to help litigants resolve the initial divorce or ongoing family disputes.

Success of Mediation Programs in Resolving All Disputed Issues

The success of the mediation services in resolving all disputed issues also affects costs. For example, many mediation programs handle only child custody and visitation issues, leaving clients to resolve property and financial matters in court (S. Cohen, 1982). Even for those litigants who are able to successfully mediate child custody and visitation issues, and who do not relitigate these mediated issues, the vast majority still need to return to the court system to resolve disputes over financial matters. One study in Britain (Ogus, McCarthy, & Wray, 1987) found that parents generally preferred to settle all issues together as opposed to only being allowed to settle a few. In a second study (Cauble et al., 1985), over 50% of the clients involved in custody/visitation mediation anticipated that there would be major problems surrounding the division of property; about 33% anticipated problems determining child support levels, and 40% of these same clients stated that the ability to mediate financial issues would have been helpful. In another study (Pearson, 1993), 76% of the fathers and 64% of the mothers favored considering both visitation and child support at the same time. Moreover, it is not just parents who admit that it is often difficult to separate child-related issues from financial issues. As early as 1985, the Domestic Relations Division in Hennepin County, Minnnesota, attempted to obtain permission to hire attorneys to help mental health professionals handle mediation of financial issues for the clients (Cauble et al., 1985). Unfortunately, the judges in the county were unwilling to approve this proposal (Cauble et al., 1985). Thus, most successfully mediated cases are not fully resolved by the mediation program and require subsequent judicial resources. Hiring attorneys to assist in conducting court-connected mediation sessions to resolve financial issues was recognized as a need and was suggested as early as 1985; however, the judges were unwilling to approve this proposal (Cauble et al., 1985). Empirical studies of this issue would be helpful in determining if lawmakers need to consider having mediation cover all issues (including financial issues) so that these programs can become more cost-effective.

Types of Cases Referred to Mediation

At least in the case of Neighborhood Justice Centers that conduct mediation for other types of civil cases, Roehl and Cook (1985) concluded that cases referred to mediation often were those that would have been dismissed or dropped very early in the court process. The researchers concluded that mediation offered relief to the citizens but had little impact on court caseloads. It is unclear whether this same conclusion would hold for initial divorce or postdecree domestic relations cases. This is a critical question that needs to be addressed empirically.

Another important issue is that only a very small portion of all divorce cases ever end in a hearing (Dingwall & Eekelaar, 1988; Kressel et al., 1989; MacCoun, Lind, & Tyler, 1992; Pearson, 1994; Thoennes et al., 1991; Tyler, 1989). Approximately 10% of all divorce cases are settled in court, while the remaining 90% are settled out of court by attorneys or the parties themselves (Dingwall & Eekelaar, 1988; Emery & Wyer, 1987b). And custody disputes only occur in 10%–20% of the divorce cases *with minor aged children* (Keilitz et al., 1992; Thoennes et al., 1991). Thus, the number of contested custody disputes in initial divorce cases is extremely small. There are, however, a number of cases that return to court for re-litigation postdivorce (Emery, 1994).

In addition, only a very small proportion of cases are referred to and then attend mediation. In Arizona in 1984–1985, only 6.6% of the randomly selected sample were ordered to mediation (Trost et al., 1988). In another study of four jurisdictions in four states (Keilitz et al. (1992), a likewise small number of cases were referred to mediation (Brevard County, Florida, 2%; Las Vegas, Nevada, 2%; Mecklenburg County, North Carolina, 5%; and Santa Fe, New Mexico, 9.5%). A significant portion of those mandated to mediation do not comply (e.g., 22% in the Arizona study; Trost & Braver, 1987). In a study of a pilot mandatory mediation program in Marion County, Indiana, 41% of those ordered to mediation failed to appear for the mediation intake appointment and 38% with an appointment failed to appear for the mediation session (Thoennes et al., 1991). Thus, both in voluntary and mandatory mediation jurisdictions, a significant number of couples who are either eligible or ordered by the court to attend do not do so.

Even if 60% to 90% of the contested custody divorce cases that would be settled at trial (as opposed to through attorney negotiations or between the parties themselves) can be settled as a result of mediation, it will probably not have a large impact on the court system (Pearson, 1994). These cases still only represent a fraction of the 10% of all divorce cases that would go to trial.

Several authors have argued that although there are only relatively few couples who actually attend mediation and settle their cases, they are part of an elite group that would burden the court system with hearings and litigation were it not for mediation (Fix & Harter, 1992; Keilitz et al., 1992; Pearson, 1994; Trost & Braver, 1987). These participants are determined to fight over custody and visitation matters. Their cases tend to be the most time consuming, are generally emotionally bitter, and are extremely complex (Pearson, 1994). Thus, if mediation can settle a substantial number of these cases, the total impact may not be great but it is still likely to be felt and appreciated by the judges and court workers (Pearson, 1994). It may also be helpful for the parents themselves. Protracted disputes and uncertainty over the residential and financial status of children can have potentially disastrous effects on families. If the argument in support of mediation programs is that many litigious couples are removed from the court, then mediation can be considered a success. Unfortunately, for the most angry couples interventions by mediators do not appear to be able to overcome the couple's hostilities so that they can produce agreements acceptable to both (Bickerdike, 1998; Bickerdike & Littlefield, in press). Thus, if cost-effectiveness is the goal, it appears that mediation is unlikely to save money and achieve that goal, or at least it is still an open question.

Although the above studies have found either that the number of hearings both pre- and postdecree are similar for mediated and litigated cases or that in some mediated cases the clients file more postdecree actions, other authors have argued that mediation is still cost-effective for courts. Pearson and Thoennes (1982) factored into their estimates of cost the amount of time it takes to conduct uncontested versus contested hearings. They reasoned that with mediation cases, approximately 80% (i.e., 60% in mediation and 20% after mediation but prior to trial) settle and require only one uncontested hearing, with these hearings estimated to take approximately 30 minutes. Contested hearings are estimated to take anywhere from 4 to 9.8 hours. Pearson and Thoennes also argued that mediation saves an estimated $5,610 to $27,510 per 100 cases. Unfortunately, these figures may be optimistic in two ways.

First, it has been found in several courts that mediated cases require at least two hearings, not one (Keilitz et al., 1992; Pearson, 1994; Trost & Braver, 1987). Thus, using Pearson and Thoennes's (1982) figures, the resulting savings would be from $570 to $22,470 per 100 cases. The savings would be even less in the jurisdiction where 30% of the mediating clients had been before the court two or more times (Fix & Harter, 1992). Second, Pearson and Thoennes also stated that their cost estimates do not include the overhead costs of maintaining a mediation service but only include the "average direct costs" of offering mediation services. Including both two hearings and overhead costs, cost savings for processing 100 cases is much less clear. Costs of processing 100 cases could actually cost $18,930 *more* than litigation if contested hearings are estimated to be 4 hours and would be a modest savings of $2,970 if contested hearings are estimated to take 9.8 hours. Cost-effectiveness of mediation relative to litigation is extremely difficult to calculate, and reliable comparative data on costs are not currently available (Roehl & Cook, 1985).

CONCLUSION

There are no strong conclusions that can be drawn from current research concerning litigant or system costs. If there are any cost savings for clients who attend meditation, the savings are likely to be realized by those clients who resolve all their issues in mediation. Mediation system cost-effectiveness relative to litigation is extremely difficult to calculate, and reliable comparative data on costs are not currently available (Roehl & Cook, 1985). In regard to time costs, case processing times are more likely to be affected by differences between jurisdictions in local court rules regarding procedural issues than they are to be affected by dispute resolution method used.

When computing costs, it is important to focus on the costs associated with relitigation. Mediation may deter relitigation in the short-term. Over a longer period of time, however, a substantial number of parents will return to court regardless of the forum they used to resolve their initial divorce case (Dillon & Emery, 1996; Thoennes et al., 1991). What does predict relitigation is the quality of the relationship between the ex-spouses (e.g., level of anger and ability to cooperate) and the employment status of the noncustodial parent who is required to pay child support (Braver, Fitzpatrick, et al., 1991). Moreover, mediation is probably no more or less effective than litigation in preventing relitigation (Pearson, 1994), and these agreements are probably no more or less stable than those agreements originating from lawyer negotiations or judicial decisions (Pearson, 1994).

III

NEW DIRECTIONS FOR MEDIATION RESEARCH AND THEORY TO INFORM POLICY AND PRACTICE

9

FUTURE MEDIATION RESEARCH

Part of the lesson we have learned from our critical review of mediation research is that there are serious methodological problems, and these problems impede our developing a clear understanding of mediation's strengths and weaknesses. This in turn makes it very difficult to improve mediation policy and practice. Thus, any discussion of future directions for mediation scholarship must start by identifying the methodologies that will be most likely to generate reliable and valid knowledge about mediation. This chapter considers research designs used in another area of study, psychotherapy research, to better understand how psychotherapy researchers have dealt with many of the problems that we find in mediation research, and it explores how these methodologies could be applied to study mediation more effectively.

PSYCHOTHERAPY RESEARCH METHODS

Looking to psychotherapy research designs is particularly helpful in that psychotherapy researchers have a long history of debating the relative merits of different designs to answer important research questions (Bergin & Garfield, 1994; Chambless et al., 1996; Kazdin, 1998; Kendall & Chambless, 1998; Roth & Fonagy, 1996; Seligman, 1995; VandenBos, 1996). Furthermore, psychotherapy research has already informed other aspects of

125

mediation research. For example, research has shown that improvement in both marital relations and long-term compliance with divorce court orders is found only if the therapists-mediators can work on fundamental elements of the relationship by teaching problem-solving skills and teaching the couple about their particular maladaptive communication patterns as opposed to merely producing a behavioral or mediated agreement without this level of understanding (Pruitt, 1995).

In psychotherapy research, there are reasonably well-defined research design rules that researchers agree to follow so that they (or anyone else) who knows these rules can agree on the knowledge obtained or replicate the research design (American Psychological Association Division 12, 1995; American Psychological Association Task Force on Psychological Intervention Guidelines, 1995; Borkovec & Castonguay, 1998; Chambless & Hollon, 1998; Chambless et al., 1996; Seligman, 1995). Psychotherapy researchers agree in general terms on issues of measurement, design, methodology, statistics, and the ways in which these different things affect what can and cannot be concluded (Borkovec & Castonguay, 1998; see the discussion of efficacy and effectiveness studies below). There is, however, more lively discussion and controversy concerning the potential interpretation of study results, how the results may offer clues to revision of theories, and how well the results generalize to settings and clients beyond those specific to the study in question (Beutler, 1998; Borkovec & Castonguay, 1998; Garfield, 1998; Goldfried & Wolfe, 1998; Jacobson & Christensen, 1996; Persons & Silberschatz, 1998; Sechrest, McKnight, & McKnight, 1996; Seligman, 1995).

In using these agreed-upon research methods, psychotherapy researchers want to demonstrate cause-and-effect relationships and build a knowledge base. For example, by randomly assigning clients to therapy and no-treatment conditions, researchers want to make the two groups equal on all factors except for the presence or absence of therapy (Borkovec & Castonguay, 1998). If the two groups have different outcomes, the researchers can reject several competing explanations for the differences, for example, history, maturation, repeated testing, instrument drift, statistical regression, attrition, selection bias, and interactions between selection bias and other factors (Borkovec & Castonguay, 1998). In other words, there was something contained in the therapy condition that was not in the no-treatment condition that caused additional change. Although several competing factors can be ruled out by the no-treatment group design, there may be several other ways the groups differed and any combination of these ways can account for the therapy group's superior outcome (Borkovec & Castonguay, 1998). Thus, the cause-and-effect conclusions that can be drawn from this design are limited in their ability to specify additional causal factors involved (Borkovec & Castonguay, 1998).

The use of placebo groups or comparisons to alternative therapies allows researchers to rule out additional causes associated with factors common to all therapeutic relationships and to state that something specific in the therapy condition, beyond effects of common factors, caused the change (Borkovec & Castonguay, 1998). By building on previous research and increasing the specificity of the questions asked, psychotherapy researchers have developed a solid knowledge base of empirically supported therapies (Kendall & Chambless, 1998).

Two task forces from the American Psychological Association (American Psychological Association Division 12, Clinical Psychology, Task Force on Promotion and Dissemination of Psychological Procedures, 1995; American Psychological Association Task Force on Psychological Intervention Guidelines, 1995) were convened to develop specific guidelines for assessing the strength of research designs in drawing conclusions from psychotherapy research. These guidelines were recently clarified by Chambless and Hollon (1998) and Kendall (1998), who argued that efficacy is best established through randomized clinical trials (also referred to as *randomized controlled trials*, hereinafter RCTs) or group designs in which clients are randomly assigned to treatment conditions or a carefully controlled single case design. They further specified the terms *efficacious and specific*, *efficacious*, and *possibly efficacious* as labels to designate the different levels of research support available for specific therapeutic interventions (Chambless & Hollon, 1998). Along with other specific design and statistical design considerations for all categories, the term *efficacious and specific* refers to a treatment that has been found to be superior to other treatments or a placebo treatment, the research has been replicated by one or more independent research teams, the results have not been contradicted by others, diagnosis was done with a structured diagnostic interview, outcome assessments tap significant dimensions of the problem under question and have demonstrated reliability and validity, and multiple methods of outcome assessment were used (Chambless & Hollon, 1998). The term *efficacious* refers to a treatment that has been found to be efficacious in at least two studies by independent research teams and the findings are not contradicted by others (Chambless & Hollon, 1998). The term *possibly efficacious* refers to a treatment that is supported by only one study or to research that has been conducted by one team of researchers.

Following the pronouncement of these designations, experienced researchers were asked to analyze the research base and determine which therapies meet the specifications noted above, and an entire issue of a prestigious journal was devoted to publishing the findings (Kendall & Chambless, 1998). It was noted that much of the urgency for defining empirically supported therapies at this level of specificity was created by the real possibility that the courts and legislative bodies would define, nonempirically, the types of psychotherapy that could and could not be practiced and reimbursed in a burgeoning system of managed health care

(Beutler, 1998). Nevertheless, the discipline rose to the challenge and now has a set of guidelines, an active and ongoing discussion of the meaning of these guidelines, and an initial determination of which therapies meet the requirements of these guidelines (Kendall & Chambless, 1998; Pilkonis, 1999).

Mediation researchers likewise wish to acquire knowledge and establish cause-and-effect relationships; however, at this point there is little discussion, much less agreement, on the rules of research evidence needed to make claims concerning such cause-and-effect relationships. For example, researchers claim effectiveness of mediation programs in the following cases: There is no control group on which to compare results of the mediation group or in some cases an experimentally nonequivalent control group; no random assignment of clients to groups, thus no initial equivalence of groups; no clear, step-by-step manual detailing mediation interventions, thus no clear definition of the intervention performed, no manipulation checks on the intervention actually delivered to the clients, or no ability to replicate the study; and no agreed-upon measures of outcome, thereby making comparisons across studies impossible. In terms of the guidelines specified for psychotherapy research, all mediation research to date would fall under the lowest level of support or validation, that is, "possibly efficacious."

Matching the Research Question to the Research Design

One of the basic issues that needs to be addressed in conducting any study is to consider whether the study design was adequate to answer the question being asked in the study. The match between question asked and study design is critical for drawing conclusions from any study. If a mediation researcher wants to ask whether his or her particular model of mediation is effective, or more effective than other models, or whether his or her model is best for a certain population, there are certain research design conditions that would need to be used. The most cogent statement of this question–design match found in psychotherapy literature is presented by Kazdin (1994) in Table 9.1.

Notice first that the basic requirement of each of these different research designs is at least two groups of participants. To make any meaningful conclusions regarding whether one treatment is effective or what particular parts of a treatment are effective, researchers need to contrast the results produced by one group of experimental participants with something meaningful—generally the results of another group of participants who differed in a systematic way from the first group. Thus, studies of a particular therapy model that only has one participant group have no basis of comparison, and thus conclusions drawn from these studies are extremely limited. With notable exceptions (Emery & Jackson, 1989; Emery, Mat-

TABLE 9.1
Research Question/Research Design Match

Question asked	Study design	Basic requirements
Does treatment produce therapeutic change?	Treatment package study	Two groups: a treatment and either a no-treatment group or a wait-list control group
Which treatment is the more or most effective for a particular population?	Comparative outcome study	Two or more different treatments for a given problem, applied to at least two groups from this population
What client, family, or therapist characteristic(s) is critical for treatment to be effective?	Client and therapist variation study	Treatment as applied separately to different types of cases, therapists, and so on
What processes occur in treatment that affect within-session interactions between therapist and client and may contribute to treatment outcome?	Process study	Treatment groups in which client and therapist interactions in sessions are tape-recorded, coded, and analyzed
What components are necessary and sufficient to facilitate therapeutic change?	Dismantling treatment study	Two or more treatment groups that vary in the components of treatment provided
What components or other treatments can be added to enhance therapeutic change?	Constructive treatment study	Two or more treatment groups that vary in components that are provided
What changes can be made in a specific treatment to increase its effectiveness?	Parametric study	Two or more treatment groups that differ in one or more aspects of a particular treatment

Note. From "Methodology, Design, and Evaluation in Psychotherapy Research," by A. E. Kazdin, 1994, in A. E. Bergin and S. L. Garfield (Eds.), *Handbook of Psychotherapy and Behavior Change* (4th ed.), p. 21. New York: Wiley. Adapted with permission.

thews, & Kitzmann, 1991; Emery, Matthews, & Wyer, 1991; Emery & Wyer, 1987a), much of the research in mediation is conducted with only one mediation group (Davis & Roberts, 1988; Irving & Benjamin, 1983, 1992, 1995; Johnston & Campbell, 1987; Kressel et al., 1994; Meierding, 1993; Milne, 1978; Saposnek et al., 1984) or a nonequivalent control group (Fix & Harter, 1992; Kelly, 1990a, 1990b; Kelly & Duryee, 1992; Pearson & Thoennes, 1982, 1984b, 1985b, 1986, 1989; Thoennes et al., 1991). Although the research is interesting, the conclusions that can be drawn from these studies are extremely limited. None of the experimental-group-only studies can answer the question of whether the results could also have occurred by any number of alternative explanations: chance, spontaneous remission, maturation, history, repeated testing, instrument drift, statistical regression to the mean, attrition, selection bias, and interactions between selection bias and other factors (Borkovec & Castonguay, 1998).

A reasonable strategy to develop a knowledge base is to use a series of studies with different methods to assess the effectiveness of a treatment. For example, an initial study of a treatment may be the treatment package study design or comparative outcome study design (see Table 9.1). The results from these study designs, if positive, can tell us that (a) the therapy contained an active ingredient that caused some degree of change beyond that caused by factors common to all therapy or placebo conditions or chance, and (b) this was true for particular clinical problems, clients, settings, methods, therapists, and ways of measuring improvement used in this particular study (Borkovec & Castonguay, 1998). This information is very important and indicates that additional basic knowledge can be gained by continuing research to

> evaluate the causative contributions of separate and combined elements of a therapy (dismantling or component control designs), of the addition of a new therapy element to an already established therapy (constructive or additive designs), and the levels of dimensions of therapeutic process thought theoretically to mediate a technique's causative effects (parametric designs). These designs allow increasingly specific cause-and-effect conclusions and thus markedly enhance our basic knowledge ("this" causes "that") about therapeutic change. (Borkovec & Castonguay, 1998, p. 137)

In mediation research, specific elements of different models could be assessed in this manner and would add significantly to the current knowledge in the field. For example, one of the long-standing models of mediation is Coogler's (1978) structured mediation model (as modified by Grebe, 1987). This model could first be assessed using a treatment package or comparative outcome design. If shown to have more positive outcomes than a no-treatment, placebo, or litigation condition, it could then be assessed by using dismantling or constructive treatment designs to ascertain the elements that are most likely to cause the positive change. For example, Coogler drew on Deutsch's (1973) theory of conflict resolution in establishing the requirement that each of the parties provide a financial deposit before mediation begins. Coogler believed that this financial commitment ensured equal commitment of both parties to the process. This theoretical assumption could be tested in a dismantling design in which one group of participants is not required to provide financial deposits whereas a second group of participants is required to do so. Outcomes could then be compared for the two groups of participants to assess the effect of this requirement. Another requirement of Coogler's structured mediation model is that private caucuses between the mediator and one spouse are prohibited. Again, this element could be added to the basic requirements of the model to assess if it has an additive effect on measured outcomes.

There are other assumptions contained in various models of mediation, state statutes, and local rules that are believed to facilitate change in the couple's ability to negotiate and to allow them to develop an agreement. For example, in some models of mediation there is an assumed correct order for issues to be settled (Coogler, 1978; Mosten, 1997). Some mediators argue that male–female mediator teams should be used (Emery et al., 1987), and still others argue for lawyer–therapist teams (Black & Joffee, 1978). It is generally assumed by court-sponsored mediation programs that screening questionnaires will correctly identify spousal abuse cases (Thoennes et al., 1995). It is also generally assumed by court-sponsored programs that separating the negotiations concerning custody/visitation from the negotiations concerning property and financial issues will protect the custody/visitation decisions from becoming excessively tied to financial issues (e.g., contesting custody to negotiate lower child support payments or contest the divorce generally; Emery, 1994; Emery & Wyer, 1987a; Weitzman, 1985). Some argue that attorney participation in mediation sessions is destructive and thus attorneys are excluded (Marlow & Sauber, 1990), whereas others argue that attorneys are needed in mediation sessions to balance the power of the mediator (McEwen et al., 1995). It is also argued that one attorney participating only as an advisor for both clients reduces acrimony between the couple created by having separate representation (Coogler, 1978). These assumptions are often conflicting and have never been subjected to the level of scrutiny found in psychotherapeutic research to determine which ones have any overall merit or add to the effectiveness of any mediation intervention or model.

A way to address this problem is to use an RCT design (also known as a "horserace") by having skilled mediators become proficient in several models of mediation, and then by studying these models with representative samples of parties facing representative sets of problems (A. I. Schwebel et al., 1994). It is important to take a closer look at RCT designs to understand all the requirements of such a design, to discuss how the requirements of an RCT design compare with designs used in mediation research, and to consider if RCTs could offer additional guidance for mediation researchers conducting research in the future.

RCT–Efficacy Studies

Within the different types of psychotherapy designs listed in Table 9.1 (e.g., treatment package, comparative outcome, and client and therapist variation), there are two agreed-upon research methods that researchers have developed to standardize their research (Borkovec & Castonguay, 1998; Kendall & Chambless, 1998; VandenBos, 1996): efficacy designs (RCT) and effectiveness designs (Chambless & Hollon, 1998; Seligman, 1995). Efficacy studies are experimental studies that are tightly controlled and generally contrast one kind of therapy to a comparison group or groups (treatment package or comparative outcome studies). These studies attempt to answer the question whether, under the most controlled circumstances, a particular psychological treatment works and for whom (Chambless & Hollon, 1998; Seligman, 1995). The criteria for RCT–efficacy studies (Chambless & Hollon; Seligman) include the following:

1. The clients are randomly assigned to treatment and control conditions with appropriate sample sizes.
2. Controls are rigorous and generally include one group of clients who receive no treatment at all and a second group of clients who receive a nonspecific treatment (a placebo treatment that controls for such influences as rapport, expectation of gain, and sympathetic attention).
3. Treatment manuals are developed with either highly detailed scripting of the therapy protocol or particular points where a therapist has flexibility built into a highly organized therapy. Therapist adherence to these protocols is assessed by reviewing videotapes of sessions and therapists are given additional instruction where appropriate to ensure strict compliance.
4. Clients are seen for a specific number of sessions.
5. The outcomes are well defined, for example, clinician-diagnosed disorder in accordance with the *Diagnostic and Statistical Manual of Mental Disorders* (4th ed., hereinafter *DSM–IV*; American Psychiatric Association, 1994) or number of panic attacks within a specified period, using multiple methods of assessment.
6. The clients meet criteria for a single diagnosed disorder or meet criteria for a specific dual diagnosis.
7. Raters and diagnosticians are "blind" to which group the client comes from.
8. The clients are followed for a specific period after termination of treatment with a thorough assessment battery.
9. Results are replicated.

Efficacy studies are favored by academic clinicians and researchers because they are able to control for many extraneous variables that could potentially confound the research results (Seligman, 1995). In addition, extensive reviews of the conclusions that can be drawn from these studies have been published and have yielded important information for practicing psychotherapists concerning "what works for whom" (Roth & Fonagy, 1996; Seligman, 1994, 1995). For example, these studies indicate that cognitive therapy, interpersonal therapy, and psychotropic medications are all moderately effective in reducing symptoms of unipolar depression; exposure therapy and the medication clomipramine both relieve symptoms of obsessive–compulsive disorder, but exposure therapy has a longer lasting effect; cognitive therapy works very well for panic disorder and bulimia and is better at relieving the symptoms of bulimia than the psychotropic medications alone; a flooding therapy plus a psychotropic mediation does better at treating symptoms of agoraphobia than either alone; systematic desensitization therapy is very effective in reducing the symptoms related to specific phobias; aversion therapy is only marginally effective with sexual offenders; and the drug disulfram (Antabuse) does not have a lasting effect on reducing the symptoms associated with alcoholism (Seligman, 1995). In fact, most researchers agree that the efficacy study is the "gold standard" for determining whether a treatment works and for whom and whether it is empirically supported (Chambless & Hollon, 1998; Jacobson & Christensen, 1996; Persons & Silberschatz, 1998; Seligman, 1995; Shaddish & Ragsdale, 1996).

It is safe to say that only one set of studies with even remotely similar levels of controls found in efficacy studies conducted in psychotherapy research has been conducted in mediation research (Dillon & Emery, 1996; Emery, 1994; Emery & Jackson, 1989; Emery, Matthews, & Kitzmann, 1991; Emery, Matthews, & Wyer, 1991; Emery et al., 1987; Emery & Wyer, 1987a, 1987b; Kitzmann & Emery, 1993, 1994). Although many proponents would like to, in mediation research one cannot realistically draw the types of very specific cause-and-effect conclusions psychotherapy researchers are able to with any degree of certainty. We next examine the controls for efficacy studies in greater depth and assess them in terms of the research designs used in mediation, and thus the conclusions that can be drawn.

Random Assignment

In psychotherapy studies, clients generally volunteer for the study and are then randomly assigned to a specific treatment or one of the control groups.

> There are several characteristics [that are important to consider] (e.g., age, sex, motivation for participation), circumstances of participation (e.g., how referred, order of appearance or entry into the study), and other factors that might if uncontrolled, interfere with the interpretation of group differences. (Kazdin, 1994, p. 35)

By randomly assigning participants to conditions, one assumes that these variables are distributed evenly among groups (Kazdin, 1994).

Another issue to consider is that merely randomly assigning clients to conditions may not produce equivalent groups. The production of equivalent groups varies as a function of the size of the sample within the group (Kazdin, 1994). When the total sample of a study is small or the groups have only 10–20 participants, the chances that the groups will *not* be equivalent are very high (Kazdin, 1994). The result is that at the end of the study, the researcher will not be able to conclusively say that the difference between groups is due to the intervention and not to the nonequivalence of groups (Kazdin, 1994). As an example, for a statistical significance test to be able to detect a medium amount of difference between two groups at 80% power (I. Cohen, 1988), a researcher needs approximately 50 clients per group (Chambless & Hollon, 1998). In other words, to have some reasonable assurance of the strength of findings and thus claims made in relation to those findings, both random assignment of participants to groups and relatively large sample sizes are needed.

In nearly 20 years of research, there have only been three studies in which mediation clients who volunteered to participate in a research protocol were then randomly assigned to conditions (Emery & Wyer, 1987a; Margolin, 1973; Pearson & Thoennes, 1984b). Unfortunately, in Pearson and Thoennes's study, 50% of the participants randomly offered mediation refused, and evidence indicates that they were the more acrimonious couples (Emery & Wyer, 1987a; Pearson & Thoennes, 1984b; Pearson et al., 1982). Thus, the true randomness of the client assignment in this study is called into question. Random assignment to conditions is important as a means of ensuring that the groups are equivalent at the beginning of the study so that any differences measured at the end of the study can be attributed to the treatment and not to initial differences between the groups.

There are several ways to achieve this randomization. As noted earlier, researchers have already used the procedure in which clients are asked to volunteer to participate in a research protocol and are then randomly assigned to conditions (Emery & Wyer, 1987a; Margolin, 1973; Pearson & Thoennes, 1984b). Although an argument can be made that volunteers are substantially different from nonvolunteers, research studies conducted in this manner use analyses to determine if those volunteering are substantially different from those not volunteering on a variety of variables. If no significant differences are found between the groups, the results from the volunteers can be generalized to the larger population of participants. A procedure to substantially increase the number of divorce disputants willing to serve as participants in this research is for the research project to pay the costs of mediation and litigation (A. J. Rush, personal communication, January 10, 2000). For example, in psychotherapy research, the therapeutic services are traditionally paid for out of grant funds.

A second method to increase participation in random assignment is to analyze client willingness to be randomized to research conditions. Researchers could consider a two-step process (A. J. Rush, personal communication, January 10, 2000). First, ask potential volunteers whether the conditions to which they would be randomized are acceptable, and randomize those for whom the conditions are acceptable. Second, for those who do not agree to be randomized, place them in the condition for which they prefer. Then, track the results for all participants. By detailing this extra step and monitoring the progress of all participants, the researchers would not lose the data of potential participants who are unwilling to be randomized.

Interestingly, in the case of mediation, it is theoretically possible to conduct even more sound research than can be found in psychotherapy research. Since divorce files are public information, mediation researchers can obtain access to at least the court files of *all* divorcing clients in a jurisdiction or a sample of jurisdictions, not merely those who volunteer for a service. Obtaining information concerning all participants is important because there is a long history of research concerning the differences between those clients who volunteer for a service and those people who do not volunteer (Bell, 1962; Jung, 1971; Lasagna & von Felsinger, 1954; Maslow & Sakoda, 1952; Pearson et al., 1982; Reber, 1985). By comparing the participants who volunteer for the intervention with those who do not on several variables, one can determine if there are significant differences between the two groups. Psychotherapy researchers will never have the ability to obtain this type of detailed information on all participants obtaining psychotherapy in a jurisdiction because no records kept on psychotherapy clients are open to the public.

State statutes or local rules in nearly every jurisdiction in the United States mandate certain clients with certain problems to attend mediation (i.e., those with custody or visitation disputes and, in some states, any disputed issue in a divorce). Although judges and court administrators are willing to follow this mandate, they have thus far been hesitant to go the additional step and order that, for a short time, all these court-mandated clients participate in a research study that randomly assigns them to specific conditions (i.e., litigation, placebo, or mediation). If judges do so, adequate samples of clients could be assigned to these conditions and more empirically valid conclusions drawn concerning the effectiveness of mediation. Without this level of control in research design, the basis for these laws (e.g., the assumptions concerning the superiority of mediation to reduce conflict between parents and increase compliance to divorce agreements) is speculative at best.[1]

The two studies that have attempted to achieve this randomization, without a court mandate, found that many clients circumvented the randomization procedure by simply failing to appear at the designated courts, intake appointments, or mediation sessions (Thoennes et al., 1991), or they refused to consent to the assignment to one of the two groups (Newmark et al., 1995). In the first case, the protocol allowing this randomization and the statute related to it in the particular jurisdiction being studied, and in many jurisdictions across the nation, lacked penalties for those clients who failed to appear. This was then exacerbated by the fact that local lawyers were hostile to the research protocols and encouraged their clients not to attend the specified appointments, essentially because there would be no legal recourse for failing to attend. Therefore, the mediation studies to date are extremely different from the efficacy studies in terms of randomization of clients to treatment and control groups. Thus, the conclusions that can be drawn from many of these mediation studies are questionable because important confounds and alternative explanations cannot be ruled out (e.g., chance, spontaneous remission, maturation, history, repeated testing, instrument drift, statistical regression, attrition, selection bias, and interactions between selection bias and other factors; Borkovec & Castonguay, 1998). It is theoretically possible, however, to randomly assign court-mandated mediation clients to a treatment or control group and obtain this level of control.

Concerning sample sizes in mediation research, much of the research in mediation is conducted with very small sample sizes or with large sample

---

[1] Some may be concerned that mandating clients to mediation might violate researcher ethics or the U.S. Constitution's 14th Amendment's Due Process Clause. As to the former issue, is it unethical to deny someone court-sponsored mediation or avoidance of mediation? The answer is identical to that commonly agreed upon in medical ethics. Until a treatment's effectiveness has been proven, it is not an ethical violation to randomly assign participants to the treatment or control group to determine the impact of a proposed intervention. As this book demonstrates, we cannot say with scientific certainty that all types of mediation are effective for all types of couples. Thus, treatment outcome research on mediation is not ethically comprised.

As to the latter issue, violation of the U.S. Constitution's 14th Amendment's Due Process Clause, if the disputants had no control over their assignment to one condition or the other (mediation or no mediation), they could argue that the procedure violated due process. A problem with this argument is that some states already impose conditions on litigation, such as mandatory mediation for cases with contested child custody/visitation. If couples were assigned to mediation, did not want it, and were unhappy with the outcome, they would not have to enter into a mediation agreement and could then go directly to litigation. The more difficult legal problem is for those who wanted mediation but were denied it for experimental reasons (i.e., random assignment). If mediation is a legal right in their jurisdiction, they are being denied a right conferred on others. But is there a legal right to mediation, either constitutionally created or because a state legislature mandates it? We believe there is no such constitutional right. A state that mandates mediation legislatively could just as easily remove that right until its effectiveness is proven. If there is no such right, courts could then randomly assign clients, in the same way courts try out other dispute resolution innovations. Unfortunately, it is beyond the scope of this book to further explore these important issues.

sizes, but with no corresponding equivalent comparison groups (see Irving & Benjamin, 1995, Table 10.1, pp. 409–411, for a complete breakdown of sample sizes for all research studies in mediation). Because there is only one truly randomized study in mediation research (Emery & Wyer, 1987a), and the sample size of that study is 32 mediation participants versus 26 litigation participants, the above-noted caution clearly holds. When the total sample of a study is small or the groups have only 10–20 participants, the chances that the groups are *not* equivalent at the outset are very high (Kazdin, 1994). In other words, to have some assurance of the strength of findings, both random assignment of participants to groups and relatively large sample sizes (e.g., 50 participants) are needed. Mediation research could benefit greatly from a true RCT design with at least 50 participants per group.

Control Groups

For a psychotherapy treatment to be found to be effective and empirically supported, receiving treatment needs to be shown to be more effective than receiving no treatment at all and more effective than receiving a nonspecific or placebo treatment. These comparisons are important to show that the effect of treatment goes beyond the consequences of mere passage of time or receiving attention from a professional and the expectation of change (Chambless & Hollon, 1998). This finding is also important for theory in that it increases confidence in the model on which the treatment was based; it is important for practice because it suggests that certain types of training and experience may be required to produce the therapeutic effect (Chambless & Hollon, 1998).

There has never been a study of mediation that has used this level and specificity of control groups. For example, there has never been a placebo group of clients who were given a nonspecific treatment to control for such influences as rapport, expectation of gain, and sympathetic attention (Seligman, 1995). This issue is particularly important because the effect of participating in a "special project" that is enthusiastically promoted and thus being treated with special attention, regardless of the quality of the program, has consistently been found to have strong positive effects on reports of satisfaction (Gutek, 1978; Kidder et al., 1986; Kressel et al., 1989), which are the measures mediation researchers rely on most heavily for evidence of success (Benjamin & Irving, 1995; Emery, 1994; Emery & Wyer, 1987a; Kelly, 1996; Kelly & Duryee, 1992; Kressel et al., 1989; Pearson, 1994; Pearson & Thoennes, 1989). The confounding effects associated with special attention, dubbed the "Hawthorne effect," are well documented in the social psychology literature (Mayo, 1933; Riggio & Porter, 1990).

One strategy to control for placebo effects would be to design a special program, structured such that clients were given time and attention, as well as discussion of pertinent issues, without necessarily duplicating the mediation or litigation treatment condition. An example of this would be a "bibliodivorce" group similar to the bibliotherapy groups conducted in psychotherapy research (A. J. Rush, personal communication, January 10, 2000). This could consist of a didactic course with a set of readings, detailing the nuances of court procedures and divorce law (e.g., child support guidelines, custody and property law), but presented in laymen's terms. This course is arguably an active treatment, in that it provides a great deal of information about legal decision making that is presented in writing and by an instructor, and might lead clients to understand that what they are considering arguing about is not worth the cost of legal or mediation fees. A pure bibliodivorce group could be mandated, much like mediation is currently mandated in some jurisdictions.[2] It would control for what mediation researchers and practitioners argue is the "change agent" (i.e., what actually causes the change) in their programs. For example, within the legal model of mediation (Coogler, 1978; A. I. Schwebel et al., 1994), the structure of the procedure followed and the order of issues presented are argued to be the change agents. Under the therapeutic model of mediation, the mediator's sophistication at assisting the couple resolve their emotional blockages is argued to be the change agent that allows couples to resolve their issues. Neither of these models argues that providing information alone concerning the legal parameters of how divorce decisions will be made is the change agent, although both do provide this information. The biblidivorce group would control for this factor. The bibliodivorce group could also be part of a Dismantling or Constructive Treatment Design (see Table 9.1) in that it could be added to or deleted from traditional mediation or litigation services to ascertain if it has any additional benefit, above and beyond traditional treatments.

In addition to placebo group problems, there has also been no attempt to create a straight control group of clients who are put on a waiting list to ascertain how many cases spontaneously settle as a result of the passage of time alone. One early study found that 21% of nonmediated custody disputes in which a custody study is ordered are resolved without a trial (Doyle & Caron, 1979). It would be important to replicate these results paying particular attention to who the clients are who settle without mediation and the level of intervention required to do so.

Thus, the results of most mediation studies cannot be said to adequately distinguish between effects associated with special attention or effects associated simply with the passage of time. Conducting a mediation study with a placebo and wait-list control group would be possible and

---

[2] If one uses an analysis similar to that presented in Footnote 1, such a group would be ethical and legal.

essential to making claims that mediation is more effective than doing nothing, more effective than giving clients empathetic attention, or more effective than giving clients information in an organized fashion.

Treatment Manuals

In efficacy studies, the value of the research is questionable if the actual treatment that was provided is not clearly specified so that it can be replicated in other studies (Chambless & Hollon, 1998). Thus, many treatment manuals have been created to address these issues. These manuals provide information about how a treatment is to be delivered and often offer a session-by-session script (Chambless & Hollon, 1998; Kazdin, 1994). They contain explicit descriptions of the kinds of techniques and strategies that are involved in the treatment (Chambless & Hollon, 1998). The manuals are generally not sufficient in themselves; additional training and supervision of the practitioner is generally required (Chambless & Hollon, 1998). They are, however, a giant step forward in standardizing treatment for research. These manuals minimize variability in the delivery of a specific treatment, increase the sensitivity of a test that compares different treatment conditions, and allow replication of the treatment in other studies (Kazdin, 1994). In addition, the use of manuals reduces the variability between therapists who offer the treatment (Crits-Christoph & Mintz, 1991). All of these issues are extremely important to ensure that the treatment being tested is what is actually being delivered to the clients (Yeaton & Sechrest, 1981). These manuals provide benefits to both practitioners and researchers in that they can then be given to practitioners who can use them and provide feedback to researchers concerning their experiences with the treatments in actual practice (Kazdin, 1994). In addition, revision of the manuals can be made on the basis of practitioners' comments. Although there is debate in the psychotherapy literature concerning the benefit of treatment manuals (Davison & Lazarus, 1995; Henry, Strupp, Butler, Schacht, & Binder, 1993; Persons, 1991), it has been argued that on balance the benefits of manuals far outweigh the burdens (Shoham & Rohrbaugh, 1996).

Although, as noted in chapter 5, there are several descriptions of mediation models used in research and practice (Coogler, 1978; Emery et al., 1987; J. Folberg & Taylor, 1984; J. M. Haynes, 1981; Irving & Benjamin, 1995; Kelly, 1983; Mosten, 1997) and at least one provides a session-by-session analysis of what is required in each session (i.e., Emery et al., 1987), no models of mediation have been specified in step-by-step treatment manuals so that adherence to the proscribed intervention by the mediator could be assessed by an independent research team (Kelly, 1996). If the adherence issue is assessed at all, the only types of studies available are retrospective studies asking mediators what they did or asking clients what occurred in mediation and studies of nonrandomly selected mediators who have agreed to tape-record a nonrandomly selected set of their sessions. The researchers who have developed detailed descriptions of the models of mediation used did not then subsequently videotape or audiotape mediation client sessions to ensure that the proscribed treatment was the one that was actually delivered. Thus, it is unclear what is actually being practiced and unclear if there is a differential result for the different models of mediation. Although these different models are argued to exist (A. I. Schwebel et al., 1994), it is unclear whether anyone practices them in the form intended and if it makes a difference in terms of outcomes for particular clients (Yeaton & Sechrest, 1981).

It is interesting, as noted above, that some mediation researchers and practitioners have developed fairly definitive outlines for the content of mediation sessions (Coogler, 1978; Emery et al., 1987; J. Folberg & Taylor, 1984; J. M. Haynes, 1981; Irving & Benjamin, 1995; Kelly, 1983; Mosten, 1997). It would be possible and advantageous to translate these outlines into specific, step-by-step *scripted* manuals so that future researchers could conduct studies using the manuals and assess both the strength of the mediation intervention and adherence by the mediator to the proscribed treatment.

Limited Number of Sessions

In efficacy studies, clients are generally seen for a specified number of sessions so that all clients obtain the same treatment for the same length of time. In mediation, policies and rules differ jurisdiction by jurisdiction regarding the number of mediation sessions or hours allotted to complete a case. Overall, mediation clients are seen for a variable number of sessions ranging from 1 to 10 or even more (Dillon & Emery, 1996; Kelly, 1990b; Pearson, 1994; Ricci et al, 1991). In a statewide study of the 56 court-sponsored mediation programs in California, 27 programs do not impose any limits on the number of sessions or hours for mediation, 14 programs impose a limit but allow additional time if the mediator believes it would result in a better outcome or agreement for the clients, and only 4 programs set a firm limit on maximum number of hours or sessions to complete a case (Ricci et al., 1991). In addition, the majority of the programs allowed clients to return to mediation free of charge to revise their agreement as needed, 9 programs required a "significant change" to return, and 4 programs set a fixed window of time that the clients were allowed to return (Ricci et al., 1991). It is unclear, however, whether these policies affect the actual number of sessions offered clients. The average number of sessions actually provided the clients for each of these groups of programs was not reported (Ricci et al., 1991). It has been found that the most dissatisfied mediation clients are the ones participating in programs limited to only one session (Pearson & Thoennes, 1989). What is much less clear, however, is the number of sessions that would be adequate to produce satisfied customers or the effect of the number of sessions (if any) on long-term compliance.

There is some evidence in the community mediation literature that mediation with clients that addresses relational issues between the parties have greater long-term compliance rates than those mediation models that focus merely on obtaining an agreement (Pruitt, 1995). Those programs that address relational issues also tend to offer a greater number of sessions (Irving & Benjamin, 1995; Kelly, 1996). With detailed treatment manuals, mediation researchers could conduct studies varying the number of sessions to ascertain the most effective number of sessions per type of treatment. The information provided by such a study would be extremely helpful in that court-mandated programs would have solid evidence on which to provide service in a cost-effective manner. Psychotherapy researchers, for example, found that there is a specific "dose–response curve" concerning the number of sessions offered and benefits to the clients (Howard, Kopta, Krause, & Orlinsky, 1986). In other words, at a certain number of total sessions, adding sessions had a positive effect; however, the positive effects of continuing to add sessions tended to decrease after a total of 10 sessions. It would be extremely helpful to ascertain if there is a similar dose–response curve for the number of mediation sessions.

Well-Defined Outcomes Using Multiple Methods of Assessment

In efficacy studies, the specific outcomes measured need to be an adequate test of the particular dimension of the presenting problem addressed by the therapy. In addition, it is recommended that the measurement of the outcomes be conducted using instruments with demonstrated reliability and validity (Chambless & Hollon, 1998) and that these outcomes be measured using different methods (e.g., self-report, report of a significant other, or physiological measures). It is also suggested that researchers go beyond assessment of the particular presenting symptoms to examine the effects of the treatment on general measures of functioning and quality of life and consider whether there are also negative effects for clients receiving the treatment (Chambless & Hollon, 1998).

Outcomes measured in mediation are rarely defined with precision so that a true comparison can be made between studies. For example, as noted earlier, one outcome measure included in many studies is the rate of relitigation. Yet, most studies are unclear concerning whether their operationalization of relitigation refers to any further court action on a case, including mutually agreed-upon changes (e.g., agreed-upon changes in residence) or only those issues that are contested and relitigated (e.g., contested custody changes).

An additional complication is the method used to assess outcomes.

Some mediation studies ask the divorced parents, or in many cases only the custodial parent, about compliance with court-ordered visitation or support (Braver, Fitzpatrick, & Bay, 1991; Braver, Wolchik, et al., 1991, 1993). Other studies obtain this information from the court files. It is unclear whether data from these two sources yield similar results; therefore it is unclear whether studies using these different methods of assessment can be compared. Only rarely have mediation researchers collected both data from the court files and data from direct interviews with the clients (Emery, Matthews, & Wyer, 1991; Emery & Wyer, 1987a). Without precision in definition of outcomes and method used to assess them, it remains unclear what is actually being measured and makes comparisons across studies impossible. This is not to say that it is impossible to define outcome variables and methods of assessment with precision. It would be very helpful if future mediation researchers precisely defined the outcome variables of choice and method of assessment so that others can replicate the studies and comparisons can be made across studies.

Diagnostic Criteria

In efficacy studies, the treatments being tested are generally designed to target a specific disorder (e.g., major depression, obsessive–compulsive disorder, or panic disorder) or dual diagnosis (e.g., borderline personality disorder with other diagnoses). Thus, potential clients are carefully screened by diagnosticians to determine if they meet criteria for the disorders. The specific diagnoses are operationalized either in accordance with the *DSM–IV*, cut scores on other reliable and valid questionnaires, or standardized interviews identifying the clinical problem. Although the *DSM–IV* is arguably not the definitive system of classification, at least within psychotherapeutic research there exists a set of criteria and a standardized instrument for diagnosing specific conditions. From a methodological standpoint, specific criteria are critical to permit replication of the findings by other investigators and to allow for the possibility of analyzing client characteristics across studies (Kazdin, 1994).

Mediation is an interesting example of a treatment that is also directed at a specific client-related problem (e.g., inability to negotiate a divorce agreement), but the screening of clients occurs at a much different level. Research in mediation often includes all clients who would agree to participate in the study without any or very little prescreening. Traditionally, the researchers who have been interested in psychological variables have given their clients standardized questionnaires that assess for various psychological disorders after including the clients in the mediation research, as opposed to screening the clients for the presence of these disorders before accepting them into the study (Emery & Wyer, 1987a; Kelly et al., 1988). Methodologically, this practice is acceptable given that psychological processes in mediation research have been looked at as a continuous variable, and thus it is much less important to assess if a client meets some arbitrary cut point or set of criteria of a psychological disorder than it is to indicate whether symptoms associated with psychological distress actually worsen or improve after mediation. Therefore, formal psychological assessment in terms of DSM–IV diagnoses is never carried out prior to mediation and does not need to be.

There are, however, other issues that have been identified as important for premediation assessment or diagnosis. These are cases of spousal abuse or power imbalances between the parties (see chapter 3). Unfortunately, the state of the art in diagnosing these two problems is nowhere near the state of the art in diagnosing many psychological disorders. For example, there is no generally agreed-upon set of criteria relating to a relationship that includes spousal abuse (i.e., the level or types of abuse or violence and the characteristics of the victim, perpetrator, or the relationship) or relating to a power-imbalanced relationship that would guide diagnosticians in determining the couple's dispute inappropriate for mediation. In addition, because there is not a set of criteria, there is also no standardized instrument that can make these designations. There is also a great deal of controversy in the literature concerning whether relationships with spousal abuse should be allowed in mediation at all (Bryan, 1994; Fischer et al., 1993; Grillo, 1991). There is some research in the psychotherapy literature, however, that has begun to define at least two levels of abuse or violence between couples (Holtzworth-Munroe et al., 1998; O'Leary, 1993), relationship patterns that are consistent with higher levels of violence, and possibly when therapy is less likely to provide an avenue for change in these relationships (Holtzworth-Munroe et al., 1998). Mediation could benefit a great deal from research designs directed toward the goal of using this literature to further define both concepts of spousal abuse and power imbalances and then specify criteria related to both types of relationships that would make them inappropriate for mediation.

Beyond the issue of spousal violence and power imbalances, there is a second level of diagnosis in mediation research in terms of the legally relevant client case characteristics that have never been adequately assessed or addressed. Clients involved in mediation are involved because they have a specific set of contested issues (i.e., custody, visitation, and financial matters) and also have a set of family-relevant legal issues (e.g., number of children, ages of both children and parents, employment history, and employment prospects of parents). Most of the research has investigated clients who are contesting custody/visitation; however, there has been little attempt to determine if these clients are also contesting other issues involved in a divorce (i.e., financial issues). There has been no adequate empirical attempt to ascertain if mediation with these limited sets of issues is somehow different from mediation with all issues, or the ways in which it may be different (e.g., short- or long-term satisfaction and compliance, number of sessions), or the ways in which mediation with custody and visitation issues only may affect resolution of the other disputed issues. As noted above, court-sponsored programs make the assumption that resolving custody/visitation issues through mediation is somehow preferable to resolving no issues through mediation or all issues through mediation. Because the clients of comprehensive, volunteer, fee-for-service programs are so different from the clients of court-sponsored programs, it would be important to conduct a study of court-sponsored programs in which clients were randomly assigned to resolving all their issues versus resolving only custody/visitation issues, as is currently done.

Blinded Raters and Diagnosticians

Efficacy studies in psychotherapy generally use trained diagnosticians to determine whether a client is eligible for the study; to assess whether there is therapist adherence to treatment manuals and therapist competence in treatment provision; and to reinterview the clients at the end of the study to determine the level of symptoms the client is still experiencing. Precision in diagnosis, treatment provision, and therapist competency, as noted above, allow a corresponding precision in measures of outcome.

Once in the study, the sessions with the clients and therapists are either videotaped or audiotaped. Trained raters then code these tapes so that statistical analyses can be conducted on the client–therapist interactions. Both the diagnosticians and raters are unaware or "blind" to the treatments that the clients will receive or have received. This control is extremely important for ensuring several important goals. The diagnosticians are able to make a diagnosis based on the symptoms the client presents and are not consciously or unconsciously swayed to portray the symptoms as less or more severe on the basis of the treatment the client received. In terms of the raters, the fact that they are blind to the treatment condition can provide a check on treatment adherence (i.e., whether the therapists carried out the treatment as detailed in the manual) and treatment-provision competency (i.e., whether the therapist delivered the treatment as intended and with special skill; Kazdin, 1994).

In terms of mediation research, development of specific criteria for relevant diagnoses, development of specific step-by-step *scripted* treatment manuals that move beyond session-by-session analyses (Emery et al., 1987), and the determination of whether the treatments provided were those specified and whether the treatments are provided competently have not been done. In addition, definitions of, and criteria for, diagnosis of the issues identified as important in client assessment at the beginning of mediation (e.g., spousal abuse and power imbalances) have not been developed. Theorizing and research are needed to help identify such relevant diagnoses. For example, there have been preliminary theorizing and research in the area of spousal abuse that could form the basis for such a diagnosis that would be useful in mediation work. This research has identified risk factors that indicate a higher likelihood of future acts of severe violence in marital relationships (L. E. Walker, 1984) and define different levels of spousal abuse (Fischer et al., 1993; Holtzworth-Munroe et al., 1998; O'Leary, 1993). There has also been preliminary research conducted on developing a protocol to process spousal abuse cases in mediation (Magana & Taylor, 1993) and a survey of policies and procedures used in courts across the United States in responding to domestic violence (Thoennes et al., 1995). Such work could form the basis for diagnosing spousal abuse and be used to modify mediation to fit these clients' special needs or eliminate these couples from mediation because of the negative effects it could have for the abused spouse.

In addition, blind rating is important to ensure lack of bias in the analysis. For this to occur, criteria are needed for rating the precision and competence with which mediators are to follow the treatment manuals. Once these criteria are established, mediation sessions with clients could be audiotaped or videotaped, and the raters blind to the specific treatment provided could be trained to code these tapes on these variables. This process will allow precision in the measurement of the variables noted above and in the ensuing results.

Follow-Up

Follow-up measures in efficacy studies are very important; researchers can assess whether a treatment effect lasts over time and whether different treatments have different stability over time (Chambless & Hollon, 1998). For example, it is generally believed that cognitive–behavioral or cognitive therapy alone may have more stable effects than other therapies because it teaches clients coping skills (Hollon & Beck, 1994). In addition, some new evidence indicates that social functioning and related symptoms may be helped by interpersonal psychotherapy but that it may not emerge until well after the therapy has ended (Chambless & Hollon, 1998; Fairburn, Jones, Peveler, Hope, & O'Connor, 1993; Weissman & Markowitz, 1994).

Psychotherapy researchers know, however, the many difficulties in analyzing follow-up data. For example, follow-up periods vary greatly study to study, ranging from a few months to several years. In addition, there is often significant attrition during the follow-up period. Furthermore, clients typically seek additional treatment during the follow-up period. All of these issues make it difficult to evaluate the long-term effects of the experimental treatment (Baucom, Shoham, Mueser, Daiuto, & Stickle, 1998). These issues are extremely important, and documenting each one (i.e., the exact period for follow-up, whether and what kind of additional treatments clients obtained, and which clients drop out of the study) allows decisions to be made concerning the analysis of any follow-up data generated.

Although there have been follow-up mediation studies, these studies have never included the other controls noted above. It is unclear, for example, if one model of mediation produces differential effects for a specific group of clients at treatment or at follow-up. Thus, the results of follow-up studies can be confounded by a number of variables that were never measured (e.g., number of sessions, model of mediation used, severity of problems, and number of contested issues). Like psychotherapy clients, mediation clients are free to obtain additional mediation sessions. Without repeated measures, assessment of clients' status at any one point can be misleading and may be susceptible to bias resulting from differential attrition from the study (Chambless & Hollon, 1998).

Despite these problems, the value of follow-up data is clear. Again, mediation research could conduct follow-up studies in which meaningful results could be obtained and added significantly to the base of knowledge in this area. The one study (Dillon & Emery, 1996) that used the most sound experimental methodology and conducted a 9-year follow-up with clients had many of the same problems noted above. Attrition was high; only 36% of the original mediation sample and 27% of the original litigation sample could be located for follow-up. The follow-up occurred at one point in time and used only a retrospective, self-report measure for data collection.

Replication of Results

In efficacy studies, replication of results, particularly by an independent team of investigators, is critical to drawing conclusions about whether the treatment works (Chambless & Hollon, 1998). This replication helps protect scholars from drawing conclusions based on one aberrant finding and provides protection against researcher bias or results tied to a particular setting or group of therapists (Chambless & Hollon, 1998; Dobson, 1989; Robinson, Berman, & Neimeyer, 1990; see also Gaffan, Tsaousis, & Kemp-Wheeler, 1995).

Replication of research studies has rarely occurred in mediation research, and when done, it has not involved independent research teams. Only one research team (Emery, Matthews, & Wyer, 1991; Emery & Wyer, 1987a) replicated their work. Although this work is the most empirically sound in all of the mediation literature, the first study published had only 20 participants per group, and the second study had 15 and 16 participants in each group. Technically, the second study is a replication, but the sample sizes are extremely low, leaving questions about its statistical power to find significant differences between the groups or, equally importantly, to prove no initial differences between the groups.

A significant stumbling block to replicating mediation research, particularly by independent teams of researchers, is the lack of specific step-by-step scripted treatment manuals, clearly defined outcome measures, and screening criteria or screening instruments. With the notable exception of Bickerdike (1998) and Bickerdike and Littlefield (in press), it would be extremely difficult for an independent team of researchers to replicate the work of others without these methodological advances. This is not to say, however, that it cannot be done. The state of the art in mediation is such that manuals could be developed and assessment criteria defined so that in the future independent research teams could replicate studies. Results found from these replication studies would provide much stronger evidence concerning the effectiveness of mediation than currently exists today. Bickerdike (1998) and Bickerdike and Littlefield (in press) had in fact carried out new and exciting research that meets many of these suggestions. Although there is no detailed treatment manual with adherence checks for the mediators, he developed detailed process and outcome measures and published reliability and validity data for these measures that would make replication of his work possible.

In summary, an RCT is the gold standard for determining empirically supported therapies. Because of the continued attention and debate by scholars in developing these designs, the designs have developed over time to be the strongest available design to rule out potential confounds or alternative explanations. Because the structure and process of mediation are very similar to psychotherapy in several significant ways, an RCT should be applied to mediation. Mediation is an intervention often used with clients experiencing a great deal of emotional distress. It is also designed to facilitate change and is directed toward a specific psycholegal problem (e.g., inability to negotiate a divorce agreement). The process includes meeting with a third party to discuss the issues and negotiate a resolution. Clients are often mandated to attend therapy (e.g., people arrested for drug/alcohol abuse or domestic violence), and these clients often are not allowed to choose the particular therapist or intervention program. In some cases, therapy clients are also mandated by the court to attend a specific number of sessions (e.g., domestic violence or drug/alcohol cases). And theories about the mechanisms of change have been used in specific mediation models. Although very similar in these various ways, research in mediation has not risen to the level of specificity found in the RCTs of psychotherapy research. There is only one research group in the mediation area that comes close to using such a design (Emery, 1994; Emery, Matthews, & Wyer, 1991; Emery & Wyer, 1987a). Conclusions that could be drawn from mediation research studies would be much stronger if researchers would use several aspects of the RCT design in the future (i.e., random assignment, larger sample sizes, nonspecific or placebo groups, step-by-step scripted treatment manuals, well-defined outcome measures, multiple methods of assessment, and clearer diagnostic criteria).

Effectiveness Studies

The second class of studies in psychotherapy research, effectiveness studies, attempts to answer the question of whether psychotherapy works as it is actually carried out in practice with typical clients, as opposed to psychotherapy provided in a research laboratory with carefully screened clients. In other words, effectiveness studies attempt to establish the generalizability, feasibility, and cost-effectiveness of a treatment (Jacobson & Christensen, 1996). Effectiveness studies are typically less controlled, often use different assessment and outcome measures than efficacy studies, and attempt to answer the question of whether a particular psychological treatment works with more diagnostically complex client problems in actual clinical settings (Chambless & Hollon, 1998; Seligman, 1995). It is useful to consider to what extent evidence from efficacy studies outlined above can be applied to clients actually seen in clinical practice (Chambless & Hollon, 1998). In essence, it is important to establish that the effect can be adequately transferred from laboratory research to the clinical setting (Jacobson & Christensen, 1996).

In the case of mediation, the question is whether mediation works as it is actually practiced in private or court-sponsored programs. Because there are no true efficacy studies, clear conclusions concerning the efficacy of mediation (or any model of mediation) still need to be established. Psychotherapy researchers recognize, however, that randomized clinical (or controlled) trials may not represent true clinical practice because these studies omit or control for many elements present in clinical practice, and thus additional research designs are needed (Chambless & Hollon, 1998; Seligman, 1995). These elements include the following (Seligman, 1995):

1. Psychotherapy is generally not of a fixed duration.
2. Psychotherapy is self-correcting.
3. Clients come to therapy after actively shopping for the type of therapy and therapist.
4. Therapists have less access to specific training and supervision.
5. Clients tend to have multiple problems.
6. Psychotherapy is most always concerned with the improvement in the general functioning of clients as well as amelioration of particular symptoms associated with a disorder.
7. Research is generally not carried out by unbiased evaluators.

Let us consider these elements in relation to mediation research and determine what information could be gained, beyond that in RCT designs, in conducting effectiveness studies in mediation.

Fixed Duration

Psychotherapy is not generally of a fixed duration, but instead ends when the client, therapist, or both believe the client is experiencing a significant reduction in symptoms (Seligman, 1995). The argument is that allowing only an arbitrary number of sessions limits the effectiveness of treatments as they actually occur in practice. This may be true for those clients who pay for services themselves; however, this argument becomes less true for those clients who rely on health maintenance organizations (HMOs) for their mental health care benefits. HMOs generally limit mental health care benefits either by designating a cap on the amount of money they will provide to subsidize mental health care benefits or by specifying a certain number of sessions that the client is allowed with a mental health provider.

Mediation is not generally limited to a certain number of sessions; however, for the vast majority of clients who attend court-sponsored programs, there is a limited *range* of sessions allowed. Generally, these programs allow for up to six sessions. Voluntary, fee-for-service programs, however, generally allow many more sessions (e.g., 10 or more; Kelly & Duryee, 1992). There is, therefore, a discontinuity between the two providers—court-sponsored and private programs—in the number of sessions provided. There is also an inherent confound between these two providers. The number of sessions is confounded with the number of issues settled. In court-sponsored programs, custody and visitation are generally the only issues negotiated, whereas in private programs, all issues including financial issues are generally negotiated.

Some argue that randomized clinical trials can compare therapy of a fixed duration with one that varies according to the therapist's and client's judgment (Jacobson & Christensen, 1996). The benefit of such a study would be that it combines the methodological rigor of RCTs with simultaneously allowing for specific conditions found in clinical practice (Jacobson & Christensen, 1996). For example, one group of participants would be given a set number of sessions, whereas for a second group the number of sessions would be determined by the therapist and client. Results for the two groups could then be compared.

An important issue for mediation research would be to designate the issues to be settled for each program so that the number of sessions could be assessed in terms of what is actually settled in those sessions. It may take more sessions when all issues are negotiated in mediation. In court-sponsored programs, it would also be important to assess whether the clients have financial issues to settle, which are not addressed in the mediation sessions offered. These additional areas of contest that are not addressed may have an impact on the issues to be addressed in mediation. Simultaneously, it would be critical to ensure that the model of mediation used in each group was consistent.

As noted earlier, psychotherapy researchers found that there is a specific "dose–response curve" concerning the number of sessions offered and benefits to the clients (Howard et al., 1986). In other words, up to a certain point, adding sessions had a positive effect; however, the positive effects of additional sessions tended to decrease after 10 sessions. It would be extremely helpful to ascertain if there is a similar dose–response curve for the number of mediation sessions.

Self-Correcting

It is argued that, on the one hand, psychotherapy is self-correcting in that if a particular technique is not working, the therapist has the freedom to choose another or a blend of techniques and fit them to the idiosyncratic needs of their clients (Persons, 1991; Seligman, 1995). Efficacy studies, on the other hand, are not self-correcting. If the particular model being tested fails to assist the parties, no other treatment is substituted within the confines of the research study. (Often, however, clients who do not respond to the treatment given in the study are referred to other programs or offered another type of treatment outside the confines of the research.) In a study comparing treatments with detailed manuals to therapist-driven individualized client treatment, it was found that therapists using the set protocol produced better results (Schulte, Kunzel, Pepping, & Schulte-Bahrenberg, 1992). This finding needs to be replicated with other therapists and client populations, but it does provide intriguing information.

Mediation is also self-correcting in that mediators can choose techniques that fit the needs of each couple. Unfortunately, there have never been scripted manualized, randomized clinical trials of mediation, so there is no basis for comparison in this domain. It is, however, an important comparison to make in future studies.

It is also argued that the self-correcting nature of therapy is actually an empirical question (Jacobson & Christensen, 1996). That is, little is actually known about the extent to which therapists modify their treatment techniques in response to client reactions (Jacobson & Christensen, 1996). For example, there may be limits to a therapist's training that could accommodate changes in techniques (Jacobson & Christensen, 1996). A suggested study would be to conduct an RCT where in one condition therapists had to rigidly follow a manual, in another condition therapists could use their clinical skills as they wished, and in a third condition a flexible treatment manual could be developed (Jacobson & Christensen, 1996). These concerns are equally valid for mediation research. It is unclear whether mediators are flexible in the techniques they use. And although no manuals have been developed to date, the above design would certainly be a beginning point toward understanding the benefit of pursuing development of manuals in mediation in the future and the type of manual (i.e., step-by-step or flexible) that would be most beneficial for the therapists and clients.

To look at self-correction in a more microscopic way, some have also suggested that process research be conducted using techniques such as task analysis (Rice & Greenberg, 1984). This strategy would yield a much better measure of a therapist's ability to modify techniques than an RCT or an effectiveness study (Jacobson & Christensen, 1996). Within this paradigm, strains in the therapeutic alliance and attempts to repair them could be assessed by way of raters coding videotapes of actual sessions. Likewise, task analysis of exchanges in mediation sessions would also yield critically important information regarding strains in the mediator–client relationships and attempts to repair them. The information gained by such analysis would be extremely helpful in theorizing about the specific mechanisms of change in mediation.

Therapy/Therapist Shopping

There are no studies that can provide direct evidence regarding if or how many therapists clients are likely to interview before settling on a therapist (Jacobson & Christensen, 1996). In addition, the number of therapists available to screen may be severely limited by policies imposed by HMOs. Most HMOs develop a truncated list of therapists from which the client must choose for mental health treatment, or the HMO contracts with one practice group for mental health services for their insured customers. There are also at least three groups of therapy clients who are mandated to attend therapy and often have little choice in the therapist or the therapy. People arrested for domestic violence and alcohol- and illicit drug-related problems are often mandated to attend treatment in lieu of imposition of jail time, fines, or both. Generally, only those who can afford to pay for services or have insurance that will reimburse providers are allowed any choice in who they see for services. In any event, to understand if this assumption is indeed true, we need detailed, structured interviews in practice settings of clients seeking therapy and matching reports with corroborating evidence when possible (Jacobson & Christensen, 1996).

It is also an empirical question that applies to mediation clients, particularly those who choose to attend voluntary, fee-for-service programs. Interestingly, the vast majority of mediation clients are much like the mandated therapy clients in that they are mandated to attend a court-sponsored program, and thus they do not have the opportunity to actively shop for either the type of mediation or the mediator who will provide it. Thus, the efficacy study that uses specific therapists would not be exceptionally different from mediation as it is practiced for the majority of clients. It would, however, be important to assess whether outcomes would be more positive if clients were given a choice of mediators. Again, an RCT could be designed wherein the amount of active selection clients are allowed can be varied in a systematic way (Jacobson & Christensen, 1996). Outcomes of the various groups could then be compared.

Training and Supervision

The therapists in efficacy studies are required to participate in extensive training, have their interactions with clients tape-recorded, and be monitored for adherence to the treatment protocol and the competence with which they are providing the therapy. Rarely is this level of training and supervision found in clinical practice (Chambless & Hollon, 1998). Although some mediators involved in research studies or specific mediation programs have had the benefit of extensive, focused training, most studies or practices do not videotape or audiotape sessions, provide adherence checks for mediators providing the intervention, or provide ongoing supervision to ensure competence in providing the intervention. In addition, models of mediation have not been developed with the level of specificity found in psychotherapeutic practice (i.e., step-by-step scripted treatment manuals). Thus, providing a high level of training, supervision, or checks on adherence to the treatment models available in RCTs is not possible. Mediation research, however, could benefit greatly from these research design innovations.

Multiple Problems

It is argued that clients in efficacy studies are often limited to those with only one diagnosable disorder and that single-diagnosis clients are rare and do not adequately represent the population of clients most practitioners are likely to see in their clinics (Seligman, 1995). Although it may have been true in the 1970s, more recently researchers are beginning to expand the diagnosable client population for these studies, allowing for comorbidity of disorders (i.e., one participant to have two or more disorders) as long as the primary diagnosis is there (Jacobson & Christensen, 1996).

Mediation clients also tend to have multiple problems (e.g., diagnosable mental disorders, subclinical levels of psychological distress, or complex legal issues). In any divorce, there are myriad issues to be settled, as well as the possibility of serious psychological and emotional distress either being exacerbated by the disruption of the divorce or appearing for the first time due to the stress of a divorce. In mediation, the precision of diagnosis of either psychological problems or legally related divorce issues is much less strict. Again, it would be helpful to use an RCT to address questions about the feasibility of using mediation with clients who are experiencing multiple problems. Researchers could stratify clients on the basis of psychologically related, relationship-related problems and/or legally relevant case characteristics. These categories could then be varied systematically.

General Functioning

Efficacy studies are often criticized for only measuring outcomes related to the specific symptoms under study and ignoring more general areas of client functioning. In psychotherapy practice, on the other hand, therapists are more concerned with overall functioning than merely the specific symptoms that brought the client to therapy.

Similar criticisms could be leveled at mediation research. The vast majority of mediation studies assess two outcome variables: rates of satisfaction with the process/outcome and rates of relitigation. A few mediation studies have, however, assessed such global areas of functioning as psychological functioning of both the parent (depression, hostility, and acceptance of marital termination) and the child, short- and long-term specific behaviors of children, relationships between children and parents, and levels of conflict between parents. Unfortunately, to date, the results of these effort have been at best equivocal (Emery, 1994; Kelly et al., 1988). It may be that the research designs used in mediation research to date (e.g., no randomization, small sample sizes, no clear screening criteria, and no standardized assessment measures of distressed normal population) are not sensitive enough to accurately measure global functioning.

Unbiased Evaluators

As noted above, the importance of replicating studies is critical. Yet, because mediation has not developed research protocols similar to efficacy studies, no studies in mediation have been replicated except for those by Emery and his colleagues. In addition, replication by researchers other than those who developed the theory or model is needed to add credibility to the findings.

Conclusion

In summary, there is no limit to what RCTs can systematically assess in terms of effectiveness. For example, designs can combine efficacy and effectiveness questions and thus can examine interactions between treatments and any number of variables (Jacobson & Christensen, 1996). Interactions such as the level of mediator training and experience, level of supervision of mediators, number of sessions, and degree of flexibility in modifying techniques can be addressed in combined efficacy and effectiveness designs in a methodologically rigorous manner such that many of the extraneous variables and alternative explanations can be ruled out. Knowing how these interactions play out would help greatly in developing models of mediation for court-sponsored mediation programs. States are also currently developing criteria for certification of mediators (Arizona Dispute Resolution Association, 1996). This research could inform the process of designing these criteria and specifying the level of continuing supervision necessary to assure quality in the delivery of services.

Criticisms of RCTs

RCTs, however, are not a panacea. Not all psychotherapy researchers are enthusiastic about RCTs (Jacobson & Addis, 1993; Jacobson & Christensen, 1996). Some argue that the results of the horserace studies have been disappointing, particularly given the expense and time that go into conducting them (Jacobson & Addis, 1993). Problems include the following: researcher allegiance to a therapy, significant overlap in models or treatments, research being set up to identify main effects and not Aptitude × Treatment interactions, randomization obscuring potentially important findings, little attention being paid to therapist competence, and an RCT evaluating existing treatments only rather than being used to develop new ones. Let us consider these issues in greater detail, applying them to our consideration of the possible designs for future research in mediation.

Researcher Allegiance

It is argued that in RCTs generally no differences are found between the treatments, or if differences are found, they have been in the direction of the allegiance and expertise of the investigators (Dobson, 1989; Jacobson & Addis, 1993; Robinson et al., 1990). In other words, in those studies that find differences between the therapies tested, the superior therapy is always the one that is preferred by the researcher conducting the study. A researcher's allegiance to a particular treatment is likely to result in differential expertise across various models of treatment and biases toward their favored treatment (Jacobson & Addis, 1993). These researcher biases are communicated to therapists and can affect treatment process and outcome in many ways (Jacobson & Addis, 1993). Some researchers have tried to control for the bias by conducting a multisite study allowing for different sites to have different biases, yet having one neutral objective evaluation team. This strategy acknowledges that each site will have biases favoring the particular therapy practiced there, but valuable information is obtained by comparing therapies across sites. These studies are, however, extremely expensive to conduct (Jacobson & Addis, 1993). Interestingly, in a recent meta-analysis looking at researcher allegiance over time, Gaffan et al. (1995) found a significant historical effect, wherein both effect sizes and allegiance were large in early years and declined over time, particularly for those studies done after 1987. Thus, it is unclear to what extent researcher allegiance remains a factor in psychotherapy research. One proposed solution is to have professionals of each allegiance represent their preferred approach in one study, thereby allowing each potential treatment the benefit of a proponent (Jacobson & Addis, 1993).

Mediation research will also need to address the researcher bias issue. The suggestion noted earlier in which professionals from each allegiance represent their preferred approach in one study could apply equally to mediators with specific preferences for particular models. An additional complicating factor for this type of large-scale study in mediation research is to tease out the particular results attributable to the constraints of local court rules and state regulations within the jurisdictions studied from those attributable to the model of mediation used.

Overlap Among Models

Altering protocols so that the treatments are distinguishable will preserve the internal validity of a study but severely compromise the scientific value of the conclusions that can be drawn (Jacobson & Addis, 1993). The portions of overlap may be the critical factors that encourage change in clients' behaviors as opposed to the artificially derived separate portions that the testable models reflect. There is likewise considerable overlap in the models of mediation. A. I. Schwebel et al. (1994) noted that all mediation models include the following:

> (1) use structure in the form of rules to promote cooperation, (2) foster self-interested bargaining between equals, (3) help parties manage emotional issues blocking effective problem solving, and (4) improve communication between the spouses and provide information and guidance during sessions. . . . Although practitioners using the four mediation models share the goal of helping divorcing parties reach satisfactory, equitable settlements, the details of what happens in their sessions differ on structural, substantive and process dimensions. (pp. 213–214)

If the "structural, substantive and process dimensions" were exploited such that protocols were developed that distinguish the models, the internal validity of the treatment outcome research would be preserved, but the research would not reveal if nonspecific factors, which are equally applicable to all models, are the mechanisms of change.

Aptitude × Treatment Interactions

RCTs are set up to identify various main effects of treatment but would not reflect the complex reality of practice. For example, there may not be differences in the efficacy of treatments that cut across all therapist and client variables (Jacobson & Addis, 1993). There may be Aptitude × Treatment interactions (Jacobson & Addis, 1993). As suggested by

Shoham-Salomon & Hannah (1991), there might also be more complex interactions (i.e., Client × Therapist × Treatment × Problem × Setting) that cannot be adequately addressed by horserace studies pitting one model against another (Shoham-Salomon, 1991; Smith & Sechrest, 1991; Stiles, Shapiro, & Elliott, 1986).

Similarly, these complex interactions may also occur in the mediation arena. There may well be complicated interactions between the dynamics of the couple's relationship (i.e., cooperative, enmeshed, autistic, or hostile), the personal style of the agent (i.e., argumentative, contentious, congenial, or sympathetic), the type of representation in the case (i.e., both parties self-representing, both parties hiring attorneys, one side self-representing and the other side hiring an attorney), the type of dispute process (i.e., litigation or mediation), and the setting in which the process occurs (i.e., private vs. court-connected), which produce satisfied or dissatisfied customers (Couple Relationship × Agent × Representation × Setting × Dispute Resolution Process). Teasing apart these complex interactions is critical for understanding for whom mediation or litigation is appropriate and under what conditions.

Randomization Obscures Findings

It is difficult to assess the efficacy of a treatment and the role of specific techniques within the treatment when a random sample of couples are treated (Jacobson & Addis, 1993; Shoham-Salomon, 1991). Although they are being explored in some detail in psychotherapy research, matching studies have not been tried either in couple therapy (Jacobson & Addis, 1993) or in mediation. The basis of matching studies is that there is a theoretical reason to hypothesize that one intervention is preferred over another by a segment of the client population (Jacobson & Addis, 1993). Matching studies can be correlational in which matching variables are used to predict a response to treatment (Jacobson & Addis, 1993). Matching studies can also be experimental wherein participants are randomly assigned to either matched or mismatched conditions, and the benefit of the matching is directly tested (Jacobson & Addis, 1993). Such an experimental design is capable of testing whether assigning couples to a particular intervention is successful in obtaining the predicted results (Jacobson & Addis, 1993). It is difficult to assess the efficacy of a treatment and the role of specific techniques within the treatment, when a random sample of couples are treated (Jacobson & Addis, 1993; Shoham-Salomon, 1991).

There is also clinically relevant literature regarding matching the therapy interventions with relevant client characteristics. Three treatment dimensions have been proposed as matching variables:

> (a) personal compatibility, (b) treatment technique, and (c) patient stage of change (Beutler, 1983; Prochaska & DiClemente, 1992 cited

in Goldfried & Wolfe, 1998). Investigators are now attempting to match different interventions and different interpersonal stances, or relational styles, with different types of clients. This has led in practice to the development of several systems of prescriptive psychotherapy, such as Norcross's (1994) prescriptive eclectic therapy, Beutler's (1983) systematic eclectic psychotherapy, and the systematic treatment selection of Beutler and Clarkin (1990). Norcross and Beutler (1997) have suggested four client markers that serve as criteria for matching different styles with different clients: (a) patient expectancies, (b) stage of change, (c) patient's resistance potential, and (d) patient's personality and coping style. This research direction gives promise of increasing the usefulness of findings of group research design for clinical practice. (Goldfried & Wolfe, 1998, pp. 148–149)

To begin to understand which specific matching variables would be important in assigning couples to different models of mediation or to litigation, researchers could begin by assessing the current theories and models of conflict resolution and negotiation and communication (Bickerdike, 1998; Bickerdike & Littlefield, in press; Kressel, 1985). With these theories in mind, researchers could then look to types of couple relationships proposed by Gottman (1993) and Fitzpatrick (1988), the postdivorce types of parenting relationships proposed by Maccoby et al. (1993), and the types of relationships of divorcing couples proposed by Kressel et al. (1980) and Ahrons and Rodgers (1987; Ahrons, 1994), all noted earlier, and theorize about which couples might use the different conflict, negotiation, and communication strategies. A critical review of the models of mediation developed thus far should follow such analyses. A researcher could then theorize about which individual client and couple variables, conflict, and negotiation behaviors might best match (or mismatch) a specific model of mediation.

An example of this type of integrated research was conducted in Australia by Bickerdike (1998) and Bickerdike and Littlefield (in press). Looking beyond the macrolevel couple types, Bickerdike assessed specific divorce process-related emotional issues, such as initiator of the divorce (or disparity between the couple on desire to divorce), attachment level to spouse (and the disparity between attachment levels of both spouses to each other), affective climate during mediation sessions, and affective state disputants bring into mediation. Bickerdike then assessed these process variables in terms of how they then relate to or predict specific negotiation behaviors or strategies found in theories of conflict resolution and negotiation, and then how these behaviors might assist or impede effective mediation (Bickerdike, 1998; Bickerdike & Littlefield, in press). With this level of detail and thoughtfulness, Bickerdike has already added substantially to the knowledge base in the mediation literature.

Therapist Competence

Therapist competence is generally inferred on the basis of the level of experience (Jacobson & Addis, 1993), but rarely is competence actually measured (Smith & Sechrest, 1991). A higher academic degree or greater number of years of experience does not necessarily ensure competence in applying an intervention (Simon, Sales, & Sechrest, 1992). Several criteria could be combined to help increase the likelihood of competence: "doctoral trained therapist; therapist with at least 10 years experience, therapist specialized in type of problem involved; therapist well-versed in empirical and theoretical literature; therapist highly regarded by peers for professional expertise" (Smith & Sechrest, 1991, p. 240). Also, adherence to treatment protocols is not synonymous with competence (Jacobson & Addis, 1993). Therapists must be competent using all treatments in between-models comparisons so that differences found are not confounded with differential competence of the therapists (Jacobson & Addis, 1993). Adherence can be controlled for by adequate, ongoing supervision, which is often lacking. In discussing the need for ongoing supervision to ensure competence standards, Smith and Sechrest (1991) found that researchers are beginning to pay more attention to this important factor. One study noted that weaker treatment effects found in their study (Elkin et al., 1989) as compared with another study (Rush, Beck, Kovacs, & Hollon, 1977) may be due to the fact that therapists in the second study were more closely supervised. Furthermore, a competent therapist may not provide adequate treatment all the time. Similar problems need to be addressed in mediation research. The Arizona Dispute Resolution Association (1996) has developed Rules for Certification of Mediators, which includes a performance portion to the exam. Although not specifically tied to any particular model, this set of rules could serve as a basis for development of specific evaluations of mediators' competence using different models of mediation in mediation research.

Evaluating Existing Models Versus Developing New Ones

An RCT can only evaluate existing treatments; it cannot develop new and better ones (Jacobson & Christensen, 1996). This criticism is equally true if an RCT was to be used in mediation research. There is, however, a need to know if the existing mediation interventions are efficacious, so this criticism of RCTs is only partially fair.

Conclusion

In summary, RCTs are not a panacea, and critics have leveled some important concerns toward those who might advocate for the exclusive use of RCT designs. Process research (e.g., task analysis, Aptitude × Treatment interaction designs) and matching studies are also important to understanding the dimensions of psychotherapeutic interventions. Likewise, these designs will be important in assessing the dimensions of mediation interventions. Again, what is most critical in conducting sound research is that there is a match between the question being addressed and the research design that is adequate for addressing the question.

PRACTICE NETWORKS

Any discussion of methodological issues in mediation needs to consider practice networks. These entities are developing as a means to address the generalizability of treatments across clients, practicing therapists, and settings, as well as the feasibility of providing the service and the cost-effectiveness of doing so (Barlow, 1996; Borkovec & Castonguay, 1998). The American Psychiatric Association has developed a network of over 1,000 practicing clinicians, the Association's Clinical Outcomes Research Network. Clinicians in this network have agreed to have their practices monitored for clients seen, interventions used, and outcomes obtained so that the use of new drugs and/or psychosocial treatments can be evaluated in the settings they are offered as well as by the therapists offering them (American Psychiatric Association, 1993, as cited in Barlow, 1996; McIntyre, 1994). The results found for these 1,000 clinicians can then be disseminated more broadly to other practicing clinicians and can also be evaluated more empirically in clinical research centers (Barlow, 1996).

In the psychologist community, an innovative statewide research program was begun by the Pennsylvania Psychological Association to conduct clinical research in a practice setting (Borkovec & Castonguay, 1998). To date, over 200 clinicians are participating, and the network has developed a core assessment battery that will be given to all clients seen by the practicing clinicians at four points in time: pretherapy, midtherapy, posttherapy, and at 6-month follow-up (Borkovec & Castonguay, 1998). This structure will provide an enormous amount of information. The additional benefit is that once this structure is in place, other emerging theory-driven or practitioner-driven questions can be assessed. The core assessment battery will provide data. In addition,

> correlations between these variables and immediate and long-term outcomes will provide initial guidance in the pursuit of cause-and-effect relationships, by ruling out some relationships and encouraging the experimental evaluation of others. Process research in conjunction with the assessment battery has a potentially enormous contribution to make in isolating likely mechanisms of change associated with client experiences and behaviors, therapist moment-to-moment interventions, and the therapeutic relationships itself. . . . The rigorous integration of qualitative and quantitative methods (e.g., task analysis) can provide theoretically driven, contextual, and sequential analyses of the process of change taking place (or failing to take place) in success and failure cases identified by means of the core assessment battery. Al-

though labor-intensive and time-consuming, process research can provide support for mechanisms of change assumed to be operating in different approaches and can generate further hypotheses about causal factors of change. (Borkovec & Castonguay, 1998, pp. 140–141)

Practice networks in mediation could potentially be an enormous asset for the field. Because there are few recent nationwide studies, and none that have ever used standardized assessment measures, this information could benefit the field in providing a much needed base from which additional studies can be designed and implemented.

SUMMARY AND CONCLUSION

For mediation research to effectively inform policy and practice, several important steps must be taken. First, a clear definition of divorce mediation must be developed. Currently, the term *mediation* describes many different interventions, making scholarly discussion and comparisons across studies extremely difficult (Dingwall & Eekelaar, 1988; A. I. Schwebel et al., 1994). For example, in some jurisdictions, if parties do not reach agreement, the mediator makes a recommendation to the court, whereas in other jurisdictions the process is confidential (Newmark et al., 1995; Ricci et al., 1991). In some jurisdictions, attorneys are required to attend mediation sessions with their clients, whereas in others attorneys are purposefully excluded. Mediators in some jurisdictions are trained professionals with advanced degrees, whereas in others mediators are community volunteers with no required skills. The models of mediation used, the number of sessions offered, and the issues to be settled also vary considerably from jurisdiction to jurisdiction (Ricci et al., 1991). At a more fundamental level, even the goals of the program and desired outcomes from the mediation process are widely different depending on the jurisdiction.

Second, more appropriate comparison group data need to be collected to make reasonable judgments about the effectiveness of mediation versus litigation. Comparisons of mediation with full-scale trials and comparisons of subgroups of mediation clients with a heterogeneous litigation group are inadequate for drawing conclusions about either mediation or litigation. Empirically sound studies of lawyer negotiations; lawyer and client negotiations; and lawyer, client, and mediator negotiations need to be conducted to have an adequate understanding of what should constitute comparison groups in mediation research. Research designs also require control groups to screen out placebo effects. Clients often feel they have benefited from a novel, enthusiastically administered program when the program itself has no inherent value or merit (Gutek, 1978; Kidder et al., 1986;

Kressel et al., 1989). Placebo effects are especially likely to contaminate attitudinal measures (e.g., general satisfaction), which provides the strongest evidence to date in favor of mediation (Kressel et al., 1989).

Third, very few studies have explored the effectiveness of mediation for ethnic minorities. The research does not address whether or how mediators need to adapt the mediation models or mediation process to respond to different racial, cultural, ethnic, and socioeconomic groups of clients (Barsky, Este, & Collins, 1996; Kelly, 1996) as well as differences in the way they resolve disputes. A comprehensive study of the California Family Court Services indicates that in 1991 approximately one third of all the mediation clients are from an ethnic minority (Depner et al., 1995). Given that many ethnic minority families experience divorce and are mandated to attend mediation in many jurisdictions, there is a pressing need for research concerning the provision of mediation to these families.

Fourth, there is an urgent need to closely examine mediation for couples whose relationships include domestic violence/abuse (Newmark et al., 1995; Pearson, 1994). Much of the research to date has been anecdotal. While informative, it does not necessarily assist in developing criteria for determining the level of violence or relationship variables that would necessitate using alternative dispute resolution procedures. Anecdotal evidence also does not assist in developing alternative procedures to deal with these critically important cases. The rates of abuse/violence reported in mandatory mediation clients is as high as 68% (Alaska Judicial Council, 1992); this makes it imperative that clear criteria and alternative procedures to handle these cases are developed. In addition, because the term *mediation* refers to a variety of practices, and because mediators vary widely in their education and training, it is important to focus on the nature of the process recommended for these couples as opposed to the label assigned to the dispute resolution process under investigation (Newmark et al., 1995).

Fifth, just as psychotherapy researchers are long past the stage of referring to psychotherapy as if it were uniform without specifically addressing the particular problem being treated or the treatment used (Jacobson & Christensen, 1996), it is time that mediation researchers also move beyond designing research that assumes mediation is a uniform treatment without specifying the specific model of intervention used or the range of problems being addressed. Various models of divorce mediation must be described and detailed manuals developed so that the models can be well understood and replicated in future studies (A. I. Schwebel et al., 1994). Several models have already been identified in terms of their assumptions about what techniques facilitate change. A. I. Schwebel et al. (1994) discussed four models: the legal model (Coogler, 1978), the labor management model (J. M. Haynes, 1981), the therapeutic model (Emery et al., 1987; Irving & Benjamin, 1989, 1995; A. I. Schwebel et al., 1993; R. Schwebel &

Schwebel, 1985), and the communication and information model (Black & Joffee, 1978). Emery (Emery et al., 1987), Kelly (1983), J. M. Haynes (1981), Coogler (1978), and Irving and Benjamin (1995) have described in some detail the models of mediation used in their studies; however, step-by-step manuals are needed so that replication of their work is possible. Without a clear understanding of the model of intervention being offered and the methods used to assess the reliability of the implementation of the model, it is impossible to state with conviction that what was assumed to be offered was in fact what the client received.

Sixth, research relying on videotaped and audiotaped sessions is needed so that the content of mediation can be analyzed within and across different mediation models. To date, few studies have used actual audio-taped or videotaped data. Instead, researchers have relied on self-reports of both clients and mediators to understand what occurs in the process of mediation. It is unclear how the current self-report data from clients and mediators would correlate with more objective ratings of actual taped data (Thoennes & Pearson, 1985). Even such basic research methodology issues such as coding systems must be developed to analyze the data produced in the sessions. Such systems will need to be sensitive enough to record data that are relevant to litigant issues, couple issues, legal representation issues, and legal system issues. For example, well-validated and replicated results have been found using several different coding systems produced for mo-ment-to-moment data in couple interaction research studies (Gottman & Krokoff, 1989; Krokoff, Gottman, & Haas, 1989; R. L. Weiss & Summers, 1983). These coding systems could serve as a basis for development of coding systems appropriate for moment-to-moment data produced in me-diation sessions. A group of mediation researchers developed a coding sys-tem for analyzing mediation sessions (Slaikeu, Pearson, Luckett, & Myers, 1985). Unfortunately, this coding system was never widely used or repli-cated in additional studies (but see Bickerdike, 1998; Bickerdike & Little-field, in press). It could, however, serve as a bridge between the couple interaction coding systems and the development of a new coding system for mediation research.

Seventh, it has been suggested that the different mediation models need to be tested with different client groups (A. I. Schwebel et al., 1994). By having skilled mediators develop competence in one or more of the models, comparisons can then be made of several of the models with a representative sample of parties facing representative sets of problems (A. I. Schwebel et al., 1994). The research design suggested above by Schwebel et al., comparative trials or RCTs, has been used extensively in psycho-therapy research (Shoham-Salomon & Hannah, 1991). While an RCT provides valuable information, particularly if designed to include questions of effectiveness (Jacobson & Christensen, 1996), so too do process studies using task analysis, Aptitude × Treatment intervention, and matching de-signs. More important, however, there needs to be a match between the question the researcher is asking and the design chosen to answer the question.

Eighth, there is also a need to develop and evaluate "hybrid" alternative dispute resolution processes in family courts (Mitchell, 1998), including arbitration, mediation/arbitration (Kelly, 1996; Schlissel, 1992; Spencer & Zammit, 1976), special mastering, brief evaluation, collaborative law, and unbundled legal service models for divorce disputes (Mitchell, 1998; Mosten, 1997). The arbitration model has been promoted by the American Academy of Matrimonial Lawyers (Schlissel, 1992). This organization has developed a training program and has trained a number of arbitrators to handle divorce cases. There are, however, no empirical studies of the arbitrators using this program. This is unfortunate because the mediator/arbitrator model has been used in community mediation and has been shown to produce more effective mediator and client behaviors during the process (McGillicuddy, Welton, & Pruitt, 1987; Pruitt, 1995). These researchers tested three conditions: straight mediation in which the mediator would not issue any decisions following unsuccessful resolution by the clients (med only); mediation/arbitration in which the mediator would issue a legally binding decision if the clients did not reach agreement (med/ arb[same]); and mediation/arbitration in which another mediator would review the case and issue a legally binding decision if the clients were unable to reach an agreement (med/arb[differ]). In the med/arb(same) condition, disputants engaged in more problem-solving and were less hostile and less competitive. Somewhat surprisingly, in this condition, the mediators/arbitrators were also viewed by the clients as less forceful, and the clients saw themselves as more involved in the decisions. Furthermore, mediators in both med only and med/arb(differ) conditions were less involved than those in med/arb(same) group. In another study, it was also found that satisfaction rates do not differ between those jurisdictions in California where mediators make recommendations to the court in unsuccessful mediation, and thus resemble the med/arb(same) condition, and those jurisdictions where the mediation process is confidential, which resembles the more traditional mediation process (Depner et al., 1995; Kelly, 1996).

Hybrid mediation programs may be particularly suited to settling the multiple issues presented by disputants in divorce mediation (e.g., both custody/visitation and financial issues). For example, one study in Britain found that parents generally preferred to settle all issues together as opposed to only being allowed to settle a few (Ogus et al., 1987), and 40%–57% of custody/visitation clients in a second multijurisdictional study stated that mediating financial issues would have been helpful (Cauble et al., 1985; Little et al., 1985; Pearson & Thoennes, 1988a). Whether comprehensive settlement will benefit from hybrid programs (e.g., combining mediation and arbitration) or some other combination of programs or resources (e.g., using lawyers more fully and effectively in mediation) is an important research direction and question.

Ninth, the only mediation programs that are likely to create changes in conflictual relationships are those that (a) use a therapeutic model of mediation that focuses on such changes in relationship quality between the spouses, (b) allow a greater number of sessions to work through a conflict-ridden history and change ingrained behavior patterns (Irving & Benjamin, 1995), and (c) require follow-up telephone calls to the clients by the mediator and/or follow-up or "booster" sessions with the mediator so that any problems that arise in the first several months can be dealt with quickly (Felstiner & Williams, 1980; Kitzmann & Emery, 1994). One study found that, for parents who reported problems that developed postmediation, these problems began within the first 3 months following completion of mediation (Saposnek et al., 1984). For cases in which the mediators believe the clients may have trouble complying with the terms of the agreement, in which additional social services are needed, or in which dispute resolution skills were not learned well, active and persistent follow-up on the part of the mediator should be the rule (Felstiner & Williams, 1980). Follow-up should be completed by the mediators and not the staff, because the mediators have developed a sense of the case and developed rapport with the clients (Felstiner & Williams, 1980). If the goal is to ensure that clients successfully comply with the terms of their agreements and amicably negotiate further disputes rather than to merely produce agreements to justify program funding, then sustained support to the clients is important (Felstiner & Williams, 1980) and research to assess these models is needed.

Tenth, the benefits of mediation should not be overstated (Pearson & Thoennes, 1988a). Keeping in mind the benefits and drawbacks of efficacy, effectiveness, process, and matching studies, as well as the conclusions that can be appropriately drawn from each design, one must consider the claims currently being made by mediation researchers against the research designs from which the claims are based. "Even the advocates for an approach need to be careful about what standards of evidence that they are willing to accept" (Hollon, 1996, p. 1026). Nearly all the research base for mediation consists of quasieffectiveness studies with few controls for alternative explanations. To date, mediation research cannot indicate whether mediation as it is practiced is more effective than a nonspecific placebo treatment that includes the attention of a professional, active listening, and expectations of gain.

At present, there is no legislative pressure to designate empirically supported mediation interventions; however, as courts experience further budget cuts, there may come such a time in the future. Discussions of the appropriateness of specific designs for drawing conclusions about models of mediation, and designating those empirically supported models before being required to do so by legislative pressure, would greatly enhance the knowledge base in this discipline and its legitimacy.

For example, although many studies find that mediation clients tend to be quite satisfied with the mediation process in the short term, satisfaction appears to decline over time. There also appears to be little consistency in the research findings regarding more basic behavioral changes, such as the power of mediation to increase long-term compliance with court orders, reduce relitigation, and alter or improve ex-spousal relationships (Pearson & Thoennes, 1988a). In addition, the cost savings to clients attending mediation tend to accrue to the more affluent clients who choose to attend voluntary, fee-for-service, private, comprehensive mediation programs that address all divorce issues (Kelly, 1996), as opposed to those clients who are from lower socioeconomic groups and attend mandatory public or court-sponsored, custody/visitation mediation. Public-sector cost savings associated with mediation programs remain an open question, since to date the cost figures used to compute these savings have been incomplete. Cost savings are likely to be found, however, only in mandatory programs in jurisdictions with large caseloads that possibly put restrictions on the number of sessions offered and where the litigants are ordered into the mediation process very early in the divorce process (Pearson & Thoennes, 1988a).

The good news, however, is that although mediation may not always prove to be superior to litigation in altering basic relationship patterns by transforming hostile couples into cooperative ones, or producing long-term compliance with court orders and less relitigation, it also does not generally appear to produce more hostile, less cooperative couples or excessive relitigation when compared with those agreements produced in lawyer negotiations or court orders (Kelly, 1996; Pearson & Thoennes, 1988a, 1988b). And mediation is probably as effective as litigation for a number of people (Pearson & Thoennes, 1988b).

Eleventh, and finally, it may be that the methods and practices that determine constructive negotiations and effective agreements are the same whether used by lawyers or nonlawyer mediators (Kressel, 1985). Several researchers caution that there is little evidence that mediation and litigation are absolutely distinct approaches (Pearson & Thoennes, 1989), nor is there evidence that couples use only one forum to resolve their divorce issues (Pearson, 1991). Couples often use a variety of methods to resolve their issues (Pearson, 1991). There is research that supports the belief that those couples who self-select into a mediation-only option differ in substantial ways from couples who self-select into litigation-only option, which makes obtaining matched samples of mediation and litigation samples nearly impossible (Pearson, 1991).

Rather than focusing on how to obtain better samples of clients in each forum, research must be designed that assesses the qualities that produce sound agreements in each forum, as opposed to pitting mediation against litigation without regard for the similarities between the dispute resolution methods, the variations within each of the methods, self-selection of people to either method, and the widely varying personalities, marital relationships, and circumstances of the litigants (e.g., need for an interpreter; Kressel, 1985; Pearson, 1991). So far, for example, important factors that have been found to explain variations in terms of divorce agreements and the perceived fairness of them, other than the dispute resolution method used to obtain the divorce, are the quality of the relationship between the spouses at the time of separation and employment status of the payee (Braver, Fitzpatrick, & Bay, 1991; Pearson, 1991). A "friendly" relationship between parents predicts financial contributions to the care of a child above and beyond child support and also predicts satisfaction with alimony orders among those who are ordered to pay (Pearson, 1991). The strongest predictor of compliance with child support orders yet identified, however, was the payer's employment history (Braver, Fitzpatrick, & Bay, 1991). In looking only at families in which the noncustodial parent was employed for the full 12 months prior to data collection, reports of compliance with support orders were much greater than those given when the noncustodial parent was unemployed during the same period (Braver, Fitzpatrick, & Bay, 1991).

An important point that has been made is that mediation research needs to "indicate what sorts of behaviors on the part of mediators have what sorts of effects with what sorts of client couples in what sorts of contexts" (Irving & Benjamin, 1995, p. 412). Broadening this admonition would be even more helpful. The question could become not whether mediation is better than litigation with attorney advocacy, but which mode of intervention is most suitable for which types of disputes, for which clients, and for which kinds of desired outcomes (Emery, 1994; Kressel, 1985). In addition, as Levy (1984) noted, evaluations of mediation programs will not yield very useful information until researchers decipher and control for the complexities of lawyer behavior, mediator behavior, lawyer–mediator and client interactions, and preexisting client characteristics.

10

CURRENT MEDIATION THEORY

Correcting past methodological concerns and oversights in mediation research is critical, but it is not sufficient. If we are to improve mediation policy and practice, future mediation scholarship must build a coherent theory or combination of theories of mediation. An obvious place to start this effort is by reviewing existing theoretical scholarship as well as other relevant writings that have potential theoretical significance. That is the purpose of this chapter.

THE EFFECT OF THE TYPES OF MEDIATION SCHOLARSHIP ON CURRENT MEDIATION THEORY

Understanding the theories used in divorce mediation literature is challenging because mediation scholarship is spread across many different disciplines (e.g., law, sociology, economics, communications, social work, anthropology, counseling, and clinical and social psychology). Theories relevant to one discipline are often irrelevant to another discipline, as are variables of interest, empirical research designs, and levels of analysis. In addition, researchers, or researchers and practitioners, from all the different disciplines rarely have collaborated (Rifkin, 1994). The result is that the available theoretical or conceptual scholarship and empirical research do not incorporate the breadth of factors or relevant contexts needed for a complete understanding of the field. For example, mediation scholars from mental health disciplines are soundly criticized for failing to incorporate theories of negotiation and conflict into their work (Bickerdike, 1998; J. Haynes & Haynes, 1989; Jones, 1994; Kressel et al., 1989). And mediation scholars from communications are criticized for failing to integrate interpersonal, social, and cultural contexts into their theorizing (Jones, 1994).

In addition to the distinctions among disciplinary interests and orientations, there are different kinds of scholarship within and across these disciplines. Divorce mediation has been the subject of four types of scholarship: theory-building, process and intervention research, outcome-based evaluations, and conceptual critiques (Lowry, 1993).

Theory-Building Efforts

Several scholars, dissatisfied with the current focus on negotiation and game theory in mediation, have written works discussing new theoretical bases for mediation. These efforts are not necessarily connected with a specific mediation intervention in that the actual interventions are not yet developed, but certainly the theorizing has begun. Examples of this type of approach are Folger and Bush's (1994; see also Bush & Folger, 1994) transformative approach, Cobb's (1994a) narrative approach, and Tjosvold and van de Vliert's (1994) cooperative and competitive conflict theory as applied to mediation.

For example, Bush and Folger's (1994; Bush, 1989; Folger & Bush's, 1994) transformative orientation is argued to originate in an ideology or organizing framework (relational) that is separate from the ideology (individualist) from which traditional forms of divorce mediation arise. Folger and Bush argued that in the individualist ideology, conflict is seen as a problem in which some individual's need is not being fulfilled. The proper response to this problem is then defined as integrative and collaborative problem-solving (Folger & Bush, 1994; Menkel-Meadow, 1984, 1995). In the relational ideology, however, conflict is not seen as a problem to be solved but as a potential for growth in two dimensions.

> Growth in *empowerment* involves realizing and strengthening one's capacity as an individual for encountering and grappling with adverse circumstances and problems of all kinds. Growth in *recognition* involves realizing and strengthening one's capacity as an individual for experiencing and expressing concern and consideration for others, especially others whose situation is "different" from one's own. (Folger & Bush, 1994, pp. 15–16)

Folger and Bush (1994) stated that growth in these two dimensions is the "hallmark" (p. 16) of mature development from which a "higher state of being" (p. 20) will emerge.

Although interventions based on this framework have not been clearly defined (Franz, 1998), Folger and Bush (1994) argued that mediators should intervene by watching for specific turns of speech wherein they can "clarify parties' available choices . . . and encourage parties to deliberate among options." Mediators are also encouraged to

> reinterpret, translate, or reframe parties' statements and viewpoints . . . ask parties to acknowledge the value of such reformulations . . . encourage parties to consider how recognition of the other's perspective is central to the mediation process and to a productive response to conflict in general. (Folger & Bush, 1994, p. 18)

Folger and Bush (1994) argued that by following their transformative orientation, one will minimize mediators' controlling and influencing behaviors with their clients (cf. Menkel-Meadow, 1995). The authors did, however, acknowledge that their framework and interventions based on it have not yet been fully articulated.

This first type of scholarship using theory, namely theory building, is exciting. As these theories evolve, it will be important to design research that can operationalize the constructs so that interventions can be developed. Once the interventions are developed, they can then be empirically tested using appropriate research methodologies.

Process and Intervention Research

The second type of scholarship used in mediation combines process and intervention research. *Process research* is generally defined as research that strives to develop valid and generalizable knowledge about the process of providing a social intervention. *Intervention research* is generally defined as applied research that focuses on a particular social intervention or a set of interventions (Lowry, 1993). Quantitative methodological approaches are primarily used to conduct both types of research (Lowry, 1993; see the next section), with theory providing the foundation for developing the mediation interventions and the hypotheses to drive the research and the research questions.

Theory Providing the Foundation for Interventions

When theory is used to build interventions, it requires the operationalization of the theoretical constructs. Through empirical testing of these operationalized theories, we are beginning to learn more about mediation interventions; however, there is still much to be learned, particularly in refining the different theories and theoretical models to more appropriately fit the mediation context (Clement & Schwebel, 1993). Remember that these theories are often taken from other disciplines in social science and then applied to mediation. We also need to learn about the efficacy and effectiveness of different theoretical models when applied to mediation (Bickerdike, 1998; Bickerdike & Littlefield, in press; Kressel, 1985) and the circumstances or contexts under which one may be more effective than another (Bickerdike, 1998; Bickerdike & Littlefield, in press; Kressel, 1985).

Several conceptual scholars and empirical researchers have made significant strides in developing different models or interventions for mediation (e.g., Benjamin & Irving, 1992; Irving & Benjamin, 1989; A. I. Schewebel et al., 1994). Although not all researchers (Winslade, Monk, & Cotter, 1998) use a problem-solving orientation, most of them do (R. Fisher & Ury, 1981; R. Fisher et al., 1991; Menkle-Meadow, 1984, 1995), based on economic, labor negotiation, communications, social psychological, or family systems theories (Bickerdike, 1998; Black & Joffee, 1978; Campbell & Johnston, 1986; Coogler, 1978; Emery, 1994; Emery et al., 1987; J. M. Haynes & Charlesworth, 1996; J. Haynes & Haynes, 1989; Irving & Benjamin, 1995; Saposnek, 1983; A. I. Schwebel et al., 1994; Waldron, Roth, Fair, Mann, & McDermott, 1984).

An example of an intervention that is based on family systems theory is that of Irving and Benjamin. They developed *therapeutic family mediation* (TFM), which combines assessment, goal-directed therapy, mediation, and follow-up to assist disputants in solving their divorce-related issues and draws heavily from "communication (Bodin, 1981), structural (Aponte, 1981) and especially strategic (Stanton, 1981) models of family therapy" (Irving & Benjamin, 1995, p. 150). Potential clients first enter an assessment process that focuses on determining their readiness to enter into direct negotiations. Premediation is essentially goal-directed therapy that focuses on resolving relationship issues so that the clients are more ready and able to negotiate. Mediation is essentially the negotiation phase wherein agreements are developed and made. Follow-up by the mediator ensures compliance with the agreement and also ensures that the relationship issues are under control. Irving and Benjamin reported that assessment generally takes three or more sessions, and premediation four to eight sessions (Irving & Benjamin, 1995), often more sessions than court-sponsored programs allow for the entire case (Emery & Wyer, 1987a; Pearson et al., 1983; Pearson & Thoennes, 1985b). They also found that 20% of the clients who were assessed were contraindicated for mediation and were referred out to family therapy and/or judicial resolution of their cases; 50% of their clients needed goal-directed premediation sessions to be ready to mediate; and only 30% were ready to go directly into the mediation phase (Irving & Benjamin, 1995). Thus, according to this model, only a minority of clients are actually ready and able to enter mediation. This is an ominous statistic, given that the vast majority of mediation clients are seen in court-sponsored programs and do not receive this level of assessment and are not offered premediation sessions.

Although the model is theoretically developed and its proponents indicate high percentages of clients reaching agreement using this model, it has not been directly tested using efficacy designs (i.e., randomized controlled designs; see chapter 9). It is, therefore, unclear how it would fare as compared with other family-systems-based interventions, such as labor management interventions or litigation, or with shorter term interventions offered from court-based mediation programs.

Theory Providing the Hypotheses to Drive Research

Communications scholars and empirical researchers provide a good example of using theory to develop hypotheses that drive the research effort (e.g., Cobb, 1994a, 1994b, 1997; Cobb & Rifkin, 1991a, 1991b; Diez, 1984, 1986; Donohue et al., 1989, 1985, 1994; Donohue & Weider-Hatfield, 1988; Jones, 1985, 1988, 1994; Rifkin, 1994). These conceptual scholars and empirical researchers have combined communications theories and perspectives (Folger & Jones, 1994; Putnam & Folger, 1988) with a research methodology that focuses on moment-to-moment analysis of mediation process. This combination of theory and methodology has resulted in a rich and deep understanding of some of the issues involved in the process of mediation. These studies have microanalyzed disputant–disputant and mediator–disputant verbal exchanges to identify patterns in these exchanges (Jones, 1994). By developing an understanding of the dynamics, development, and escalation of conflict within mediation sessions, these scholars are then better able to predict disputant–disputant behaviors and the particular mediator behaviors that will lead to deescalation of conflict within sessions and to clients reaching an agreement (Jones, 1994). These scholars have also been able to highlight assumptions underlying the philosophy of mediation that are not valid for describing mediation in actual practice (i.e., neutrality-as-impartiality and neutrality-as-equidistancing; Cobb & Rifkin, 1991b). Although this work has contributed to understanding the actual process of mediation, it has been less effective in providing more comprehensive information about how to do mediation because it has been less effective in integrating other important theoretical concerns in mediation (e.g., the effects of interpersonal, social, cultural [Jones, 1994], and legal contexts on mediation processes and outcomes).

Integration of Approaches

Ideally, researchers should include both uses of theory, that is, developing interventions and developing hypotheses that drive the research (Emery, 1990; J. Haynes & Haynes, 1989; Irving & Benjamin, 1995; Kressel et al., 1989). Bickerdike's (1998) doctoral dissertation provides a good example of this type of approach. He accomplished what has been repeatedly argued as missing in the field: the integration of communication, negotiation, conflict (behavior and resolution), and family process theories as applied to mediation process and intervention strategies. Bickerdike is the only scholar thus far who has attempted this level of theoretical integration and sound empirical investigation. Bickerdike analyzed theories of conflict (R. Fisher et al., 1991; Levinger & Rubin, 1994; Rubin & Levinger, 1995; Rubin, Pruitt, & Kim, 1994), negotiation (Pruitt & Carnevale, 1993), and divorce process (Emery, 1994); applied them to two interventions grounded in different theoretical frameworks (i.e., labor management: J. Haynes & Haynes, 1989; J. M. Haynes & Charlesworth, 1996; TFM: Irving & Benjamin, 1995); derived propositions concerning client behavior in divorce mediation and mediation outcomes; developed hypotheses on the basis of these propositions; and then empirically tested them. He found a dominant influence of two variables: anger and the disparity in levels of attachment between the couple (i.e., one partner high, the other low). These two variables had serious consequences for both the process and outcome of mediation, although not to the extent argued by the therapeutic mediators (Bickerdike, 1998; Bickerdike & Littlefield, in press). In addition, these variables are complicated by who initiates the divorce and other gender-related factors (Bickerdike, 1998). This research is exciting because of the breadth of applicable theory that is incorporated into this work and the careful empirical methodology that is used. More of this level of detail is desperately needed.

Outcome-Based Evaluations

A third type of scholarship that is used in mediation studies evaluates mediation programs. *Outcome-based evaluation* is defined as "an immediate, responsive, service-oriented mode of inquiry, the aim of which is to assess the merit of the program" (Lowry, 1993, p. 92), and it is typically atheoretical. Outcome-based evaluation uses a variety of quantitative and qualitative methodologies (House, 1980; Lowry, 1993), although all major methodological approaches share the same logic: (a) establishing the criteria on which the program will be evaluated, (b) gathering data relevant to these criteria, and (c) making evaluative judgments of outcome on the basis of the criteria and data (Lowry, 1993). The questions usually addressed in outcome-based evaluation relate to program caseloads, how they change over time, how quickly the cases are processed, the number of cases that reach resolution, indicators of satisfaction, fairness, and the durability of agreements (Lowry, 1993). Relatively speaking, this is the easiest and cheapest type of analysis to conduct. Principal audiences for these studies are funding agencies, which do not seem to ask for nor wish to pay for anything more profound (Lowry, 1993).

The vast majority of mediation studies fall under this type of scholarship (Cauble et al., 1985; Dillon & Emery, 1996; Emery, Matthews, & Kitzmann, 1991; Emery, Matthews, & Wyer, 1991; Emery & Wyer, 1987a;

Fix & Harter, 1992; Irving & Benjamin, 1983, 1989, 1992; Irving et al., 1979, 1981; Kelly, 1989, 1990a, 1990b, 1991, 1995; Kelly & Duryee, 1992; Kelly & Gigy, 1989; Kelly et al., 1988; Kitzmann & Emery, 1994; Little et al., 1985; Lyon et al., 1985; Meierding, 1993; Pearson, 1981, 1991; Pearson & Thoennes, 1982, 1984b, 1985a, 1985b, 1986, 1988b, 1988c, 1989; Pearson et al., 1982, 1983; Thoennes & Pearson, 1985; Thoennes et al., 1991; Trost & Braver, 1987; Trost et al., 1988). Research findings from these studies to date can tell us the following: the number of people served in various programs; client reactions to mediation; the association between demographic variables and a decision to mediate; the number of people who reach agreements, comply with the agreements, and return to court; the variables associated with long- and short-term compliance; and sometimes what mediators report they do and do not do (Emery, 1994; Emery, Matthews, & Kitzmann, 1991; Emery, Matthews, & Wyer, 1991; J. Haynes & Haynes, 1989; Jones, 1994; Kelly, 1990a, 1990b, 1996; Kelly & Gigy, 1989; Kressel et al., 1989, 1994; McGillicuddy et al., 1987; Pearson & Thoennes, 1982, 1984b, 1989).[1] These studies are distinguished from the three other types of scholarship in that (a) theory building is not the focus, (b) theory is not used to develop an intervention or hypotheses, and (c) the focus of the study is not to analyze the intervention itself.

The largest and most famous program evaluation conducted to date is that of Pearson and Thoennes (1985a, 1985b, 1988b, 1989; Cauble et al., 1985; Little et al., 1985; Lyon et al., 1985). The focus of this evaluation was to compare clients who use court-based divorce mediation programs in three different states (Los Angeles, California; Hennepin County Minnesota; and 8 of the 13 courts in Connecticut) with a nonequivalent sample of clients who used the traditional adversarial system in Denver, Colorado, during similar years. The focus of the research was to (a) identify differences in the structure of the different mediation programs (e.g., referral sources, mediator training, hours of service, and numbers of sessions provided); (b) identify demographic and relationship characteristics of clients who mediate and those who refuse to mediate; (c) determine the percentages of clients who reach full or partial agreements either in mediation or after mediation but before trial; (d) assess levels of conflict between spouses and spouses and their children both in the short and long term; (e) determine rates and sources of satisfaction and dissatisfaction of clients with process and outcome of mediation; (f) determine relitigation rates; and (g) assess the litigants' costs associated with obtaining the divorce. Little information is provided on the models of mediation used at

---

[1] Another group of authors have drafted detailed descriptions of "how to" conduct mediation (Coogler, 1978; Coulson, 1983, 1996; J. Folberg & Taylor, 1984; Grebe, 1987, 1988; J. Haynes, 1994; J. M. Haynes, 1981; J. Haynes & Haynes, 1989; Irving & Benjamin, 1995; Kovach, 1994; Lemon, 1985; Mosten, 1997; Salius & Maruzo, 1988).

each site (Bickerdike, 1998), and there is no discussion of theories to structure the research or to choose the variables to study.

While the fact that most outcome evaluations in divorce mediation are atheoretical, they do not necessarily have to be. For example, Kitzmann and Emery (1993) conducted a study wherein theory was used to develop hypotheses to drive the outcome research. These scholars applied procedural justice theory (Lind & Tyler, 1988; Tyler, 1990) to the assessment of a divorce mediation program. They developed hypotheses about outcomes in divorce mediation on the basis of variables identified as important in procedural justice theory and then tested them. An important conclusion from this research is that the differences in the formal structure of the dispute resolution process (i.e., mediation vs. litigation) may be much less important to clients than the individual client's perception of the degree of conflict and hostility in their relationship and the negotiations, as well as the individual client's relative vantage points in the negotiation process (i.e., how likely they are to be awarded custody at trial; Kitzmann & Emery, 1993). Thus, procedural justice theory contributed to Kitzman and Emery's demonstration that assumptions concerning the importance attached to the construct of adversarialness were less important in this forum than it was originally believed to be.

Conceptual Critiques

A fourth type of scholarship is conceptual critiques of mediation. Related closely to Lowry's (1993) concept of social criticism, conceptual critiques question the "givens," subjects the conventional wisdom to intense scrutiny, and examines the ideological basis of programs proposed as reforms. These critiques are not concerned with determining the relative success of any particular intervention or program. Rather, the focus is on the premises and assumptions underlying the reform as a whole and on the historical and economic contexts within which the programs arose (Lowry, 1993). These critiques are generally offered from a particular theoretical perspective.

Gray (1994) and Esser's (1989) insightful critiques of the controlling theory and predominant research strategy used in alternative dispute resolution (ADR) as a whole, of which mediation is an important part, provide excellent examples of this approach. Gray (1994) provided a searing feminist critique of the core theoretical foundation of ADR: negotiation theory. Her analysis uses several feminist theories (i.e., standpoint, poststructuralist, nonessential and eco-feminism, and feminist liberalism) to provide the foundation for "an in-depth look at how the context of negotiations is structured . . . how this context influences negotiators' behavior" (Gray, 1994, p. 3), and how that behavior is interpreted by others. Her thesis is that the assumptions underlying negotiation theory and mediation practice that form the basis of studies in negotiation are gender-biased and systematically exclude feminine voices and concerns. The assumptions define not only the acceptable procedures for conducting negotiations but also the acceptable content of what is actually allowed to be addressed and the manner in which it is acceptable to address issues in negotiations. Gray argued that the central premises of negotiation theory and the scientific study of it enormously value socially constructed masculine characteristics such as "autonomy, rationality, objectivity, competitiveness and efficiency" (Gray, 1994, p. 4). In contrast, socially constructed feminine characteristics, such as "subjectivity, dependence, emotionality and connectedness," are in complete disfavor (Gray, 1994, p. 4); these issues are not allowed to be addressed. In addition, they are assumed to be unimportant and antithetical to attaining a quick and efficient result. Even the research designs focus on these male-oriented characteristic as variables of interest, whereas female-oriented variables are to be controlled or their effects eliminated from the scientific analysis. Gray argued that qualitative research designs that capture the stories, narratives, or voices of women are given little notice or credit. In these ways, the practice and scientific study of the process and of mediation negotiations are deeply rooted in gendered assumptions that systematically exclude the interests and voices of women (Cobb, 1993; Gray, 1994).

Another critique focuses on the research enterprise itself and argues that it has been misguided because of its lack of focus on theory. Esser (1989) argued that the framework guiding the conceptual scholarship, empirical research, and practice in the ADR movement as a whole has shifted the focus from *theory-driven* empirical research to *empirically driven* research in which data are supposed to eventually generate a theory. Esser's conceptual framework is as follows:

1. There are a small number of types of procedures (or programs) for resolving disputes that have distinct characteristics (e.g., unassisted negotiation, mediation, litigation, and arbitration).
2. These distinct characteristics make each procedure particularly good at resolving certain types of disputes (e.g., the relationship between disputants, nature of dispute, amount at stake, speed of processing, cost of processing, and power relationship between the parties). There is then an "ideal match" that can be made between type of procedure and type of dispute.
3. Every culture has a dispute processing system made up of several procedures having distinct boundaries (e.g., criminal, civil, minor civil further limited by amount at stake, or subject under dispute such as medical malpractice, consumer, employment, or family).

4. If the system is ineffective, reforms can be made to correct this ineffectiveness by applying a general theory of dispute processing.

Esser (1989) argued that this framework presupposes a period of theory-free program development followed by a period of evaluation to assess the procedures and produce the "definitive" typology of disputes and procedures. From these definitive typologies, it is reasoned that a general theory of dispute resolution will eventually emerge (Esser, 1989). Once this occurs, system administrators are to use the researchers' suggestions to modify the procedures offered, making the dispute resolution system more efficient. Practitioners are to provide the best interventions on the basis of the "recommended" typologies of procedures and disputes.

Unfortunately, the definitive typologies of procedures and dispute characteristics have proved elusive (Esser, 1989). For example, ADR procedures (e.g., mediation and arbitration) are not necessarily distinct; under some circumstances, mediators like arbitrators are ordered to make recommendations to the court, which are then generally followed. In this case, mediators are then more similar to quasi-arbitrators. Likewise, the well-ingrained dichotomy of mediation as totally distinct from litigation is misleading (Bush, 1989; Felstiner & Williams, 1980; Kressel, 1985). Furthermore, the assumption that mediation works the same for all clients is false for the reasons discussed earlier in this book (i.e., conflict-ridden couples, domestically abused spouses). Finally, mediation clients often use more than one type of procedure to resolve a dispute. At this point, it is unclear how to untangle the effects that one procedure might have on the other. Research has not proved whether one procedure (i.e., mediation, quasi-arbitration, or litigation) is the best for resolving all divorce disputes or which procedure is best for resolving divorce cases with which characteristics. Assuming that there are procedures and disputes with distinct characteristics has led scholars to continue the search for these characteristics, even in the face of strong evidence that no such clear distinctions exist (Esser, 1989).

Other critiques of divorce mediation focus specifically on a range of issues and some, but not all, either use theory to critique an important assumption or critique the theory used to support a procedure or intervention. For example, some critiques focus on whether the legal rights of parents should be the focus of mediation or protected in mediation (Bryan, 1992; Bush & Folger, 1994; Fineman, 1988; Folger & Bush, 1994). Other scholars focus on the underlying philosophy of mediation and question whether this philosophy gets implemented in actual mediation programs (Cobb, 1993; Cobb & Rifkin, 1991b; Dingwall, 1988; Dingwall & Greatbatch, 1991; Putnam, 1994; Rifkin et al., 1991; Winslade et al., 1998). Finally, the appropriateness of borrowing theoretical constructs from other fields has been criticized when careful thought was not given to the differences in social and relational contexts (Fineman, 1988; Leitch, 1986/1987; Regehr, 1994; Silbey & Merry, 1986). Family systems theory has been the focus of many of these critiques (e.g., Leitch, 1986/1987; Regehr, 1994).

In family systems theory, there is a focus on conceptualizing the family as an interrelated system of relationships rather than seeing each person as an individual. Each person is seen as playing a part in maintaining any problems that occur (i.e., circular causality). The history of a problem is ignored because the behaviors that may have begun a problem may not be the behaviors that are currently maintaining it (Fisch, Weakland, & Segal, 1982; Minuchin, 1974; Shoham & Rohrbaugh, 1997; Weakland & Fisch, 1992; Weakland, Watzlawick, Fisch, & Bodin, 1974), and assigning responsibility for particular behaviors leads to unproductive cycles of blaming. Systems theorists argue that this responsibility-free, nonblaming approach to defining problems can be a more productive approach to solving them (Bepko & Krestan, 1985; Rohrbaugh, Shoham, Spungen, & Steinglass, 1995). Feminist scholars, however, argue that when the history of a problem is ignored, individual responsibility for certain behaviors and gender inequality in families generally are also ignored (Regehr, 1994; Wheeler, 1985). For example, in cases of abuse, a particular person needs to be held responsible for his behavior, and including the victim as somehow coresponsible for the abuse is absurd (Leitch, 1986/1987; Regehr, 1994). Accepting this concept of circular causality is also particularly problematic when working with couples in mediation who have a history of physical or emotional abuse (Cobb, 1997; Regehr, 1994) or unequal negotiating power. Although most mediators agree that mediating cases when there has been severe physical violence is unadvisable, there is no general understanding or set of criteria of the behaviors that constitute severe domestic violence (Lerman, 1984) or unequal negotiating power; thus, as noted earlier in the book, it is unclear how to decide what level of domestic violence or disparity in negotiating power is too much. In addition, it is in cases with less obvious violence or cases wherein there exist more subtle differences in ability to negotiate that feminists argue a woman is perhaps most disadvantaged in mediation because her concerns are not given much merit (Regehr, 1994).

CONCLUSION

Although space limitations preclude our comprehensively reviewing the research that fits within the four types of scholarship, there are three overarching lessons to be learned from this literature. First, consistent throughout these literatures is an emphasis on the need to consider and account for the variety of contexts and variables that could affect mediation as researchers theorize about, conduct empirical studies of, and generalize about divorce mediation processes, interventions, and short- and long-term outcomes. *Contexts* seems to be a buzz word of the 1990s within discussions of mediation (Bush, 1989; Folger & Bush, 1994; Irving & Benjamin, 1995; Jones, 1994; Kramer, 1994; Winslade et al., 1998). Scholars and critics argue that all the necessary contexts and variables have not been accounted for in mediation research or practice. Examples of these contexts and variables include family development, couple/family interactions, sociocultural factors, ecological factors, and temporal contexts (Irving & Benjamin, 1995). Family development theories and research, for instance, indicate the importance of understanding the family's developmental stage when deciding on issues to focus on in mediation; different crises differentially affect families at different stages in their development. Couple interaction research provides clues to the communication patterns between family members before, during, and after the divorce. Family communication and developmental processes may vary greatly depending on socioeconomic and cultural backgrounds of the family members. A concern with ecological contexts and variables suggests the importance of addressing the influence that family members, social workers, and legal professionals have on the parties as they proceed through the process. Finally, attention to temporal factors naturally leads to a focus on both the many short- and long-term outcomes associated with divorce. The need for integration of these contexts and variables is critical.

A second important lesson from the four types of scholarship is that there has been a significant absence of programmatic research. Programmatic research generally occurs when scholars remain with a topic over time, focusing energy and resources on theory building, developing hypotheses and interventions, testing them, and returning to refine their theories. This type of research in divorce mediation is quite rare. There are, however, a couple of scholars who have been able to accomplish this, and Emery is one. He first developed a mediation intervention (Emery et al., 1987) based on the theoretical concepts of R. Fisher and Ury (1981) and D'Zurrilla and Goldfried (1971). This work would fit under the second type of scholarship, process and intervention research. Emery then developed a mediation program and conducted outcome-based studies to test its effectiveness (Emery & Jackson, 1989; Emery, Matthews, & Kitzmann, 1991; Emery, Matthews, & Wyer, 1991; Emery et al., 1987; Emery & Wyer, 1987a). This work would fit under the third type of scholarship, outcome-based evaluation. With his extensive experience in conducting research in divorce, he then returned to theory building and developed a cyclical theory of grief in divorce (Emery, 1994) as differentiated from traditional stage theories proposed by Bowlby (1969, 1973, 1979, 1980) and Kubler-Ross (1969). Although these latter theories may fit the grief process surrounding death, Emery found that these theories were less appropriate in the divorce context. This work would then fit into the first type of scholarship in mediation, theory building. Thus, Emery's work fits into the first three types of mediation scholarship, and he has added significantly to the general knowledge base in divorce process and mediation.

A third important lesson to be learned from the four types of scholarship is that although most of the empirical researchers' outcome studies appear to be divorced from the theory, we doubt seriously if they truly are. We suspect that the many researchers do not clearly define the ways in which theory is, in fact, driving their choices of variables to assess hypotheses and the intervention used in their outcome studies. This fact may be a result of the publication requirements or decisions of editors working for the journals publishing this work. It may also be the result of other context issues such as funding agency interests. Regardless of the reason, if researchers could make the connections among theory, research questions, interventions, and outcomes more clearly, we would be in a better position to refine both the theories and the interventions based on the feedback from the empirical investigations. Remember that these theories are often taken from other disciplines in social science and then applied to mediation; thus, there is a desperate need to refine them to better fit mediation.

In summary, the field would benefit greatly from four things: (a) careful attention to the variety of contexts and variables that could affect mediation; (b) more scholarly interest in conducting programmatic research, (c) more funding agency interest in funding programs of research in divorce mediation; and (d) clear statements relating theory to choices of research questions, methods, interventions, and outcome variables.

11

FUTURE MEDIATION THEORY

The importance of developing appropriate theoretical models to explain mediation practice and to predict under what conditions different mediation models will be most effective cannot be overemphasized. Thus, developing programmatic, theory-driven mediation research is essential for the future of this field. For readers to fully appreciate our argument, and also to guide future theory development, this final chapter considers why programmatic, theory-driven research is so valuable; what a good theory should look like; the kinds of theorizing that are needed to improve future mediation policy and practice; and the variables that are associated with this new theoretical perspective.

THE VALUE OF PROGRAMMATIC, THEORY-DRIVEN RESEARCH

There are several reasons why programmatic, theory-driven research is valuable. First, one-shot research and research conducted without the guidance of theory produce a significant amount of irrelevant information, which often obscure the relevant findings (Forscher, 1963). Unfortunately, without a theoretical perspective, there is no way to separate the irrelevant findings from the relevant ones in mediation scholarship.

Second, programmatic and theory-driven research would help us understand the causes for the inconsistent findings in the mediation literature.

For example, current research has found equivocal results for cost savings for courts and disputants, time needed to process cases, psychological functioning in parents undergoing mediation, rates of compliance with mediation and relitigation, and negotiation strategies of women versus men in mediation. It may be that one-shot studies do not provide enough depth or the longitudinal information necessary to sort out these inconsistencies. Important examples of the benefit of sustained, programmatic research come from Emery (1994; Emery, Matthews, & Kitzmann, 1991; Emery, Matthews, & Wyer, 1991; Emery & Wyer, 1987a) and Kelly (1989, 1990a, 1990b, 1991; Kelly et al., 1988).

Emery and his colleagues' data concerning feelings toward the outcomes of mothers in mediation versus in litigation caused quite a stir in the literature, with some claiming mediation was "bad" for women and "good" for men (e.g., Emery, 1994; Grillo, 1991). In comparing women and men who mediated and litigated, Emery and his colleagues found at Time 1 (5 weeks after settlement) that women and men who mediated were relatively close to one another on a variable asking them if they "won what you wanted" (Emery, 1994). However, means for mothers and fathers who litigated were far apart on this variable, with litigation mothers winning "quite a bit" and litigation fathers winning "a little" (Emery, 1994). Also, in a comparison of women who mediated with women who litigated, women who litigated won "quite a bit" whereas women who mediated won "somewhat." Emery (1994) argued that although the findings are clear, they ignore important aspects of the data.

First, mothers generally were satisfied with other measures of outcome, and the other study findings more strongly show men's disadvantage in litigation as opposed to women's disadvantage in mediation. Second, the precision of the item response choices is questionable. Winning "somewhat" of what they wanted in mediation may actually be a good outcome reflective of win–win solutions as opposed to win–lose solutions in litigation.

Kelly and her colleagues conducted a longitudinal study comparing clients of a voluntary, fee-for-service mediation program with couples litigating their divorces (Kelly, 1989, 1990a, 1990b, 1991; Kelly et al., 1988). Initial results indicated that mediation clients reported higher levels of cooperation during the divorce process and immediately postdivorce (Kelly et al., 1988). Interestingly, the difference still held at 1 year postdivorce; however, by 2 years postdivorce, the difference had disappeared (Kelly, 1990b). At 2 years postdivorce, the litigation group had increased slightly their levels of cooperation, whereas the mediation sample's level of cooperation slightly decreased. In other words, there was regression to a similar mean for these two groups. The same pattern held for several other variables: conflicts regarding the children, communication, satisfaction with support and property agreements, and compliance with child support orders

(Kelly, 1990b). Although the researchers concluded that the effects of mediation are primarily short-term rather than long-term, these effects occur at a time when emotional turmoil within the family is high and escalation of conflict is common, so the short-term calming effects of mediation are important (Kelly, 1990b). This research is significant because it gives us a clearer picture of the effects of mediation over time. It also explains why researchers collecting data at different points in time during and after the divorce may find different results.

Without the continued efforts by Emery, Kelly, and others, our understanding of satisfaction with outcomes, levels of conflict, parental cooperation and communication, and compliance with support orders in relation to time since divorce would still be limited and the findings would be inconsistent. Future programmatic research could be designed to test the theory-driven hypotheses for the causes for the disparate findings, as well as to integrate the array of variables inherent in mediation (e.g., individual client variables, couple interaction variables, mediator variables, in-session process variables, and outcome variables) that are likely to affect causal explanations (Bordens & Abbott, 1991; Irving & Benjamin, 1995).

Third, the results of programmatic, theory-driven research would allow governmental policymakers and program administrators to design more appropriate mediation policies and programs to meet the needs of divorcing couples and their children. Once the variables leading to desired outcome are better understood, there will be a base of knowledge from which program administrators and policymakers can draw, first, to prioritize the funding decisions for mediation, and second, to choose appropriate interventions to achieve those outcomes. Mediation practitioners would likewise be in a more informed position to provide relevant interventions to reach desired goals. Practitioners are often confused as to which intervention to use in a given situation (Jones, 1994; Kressel et al., 1989). Kressel et al. noted that at least in the psychotherapy arena, therapist interventions are typically rooted in theories of personality development and family dynamics. They also noted that in mediation, no such guiding theories are available to indicate appropriate mediation interventions. Thus, mediators are currently forced to respond to the immediate stimulus or a generalized preference for a particular style of mediation as opposed to any integrated view of the dynamics underlying the process of mediation.

WHAT SHOULD A GOOD THEORY LOOK LIKE?

Programmatic research is only part of the solution. The program of research will only be as good as the theory that it is focused on. Therefore, it is also important to understand what a theory is and what a good theory would consist of. Unfortunately, defining the term *theory* is always a bit hazardous because it is used in many different contexts and ways (Bordens & Abbott, 1991), with differing levels of specificity. For example, the *Webster's New World Dictionary, 2nd College Edition* (1984) defines *theory* as

1. . . . a mental viewing; contemplation
2. a speculative idea or plan as to how something might be done
3. a systematic statement of principles involved . . .
4. a formulation of apparent relationships or underlying principles of certain observed phenomena which has been verified to some degree
5. that branch of an art or science consisting in a knowledge of its principles and methods rather than in its practice; pure, as opposed to applied, science, etc.
6. popularly, a mere conjecture, or guess. (p. 1475)

Therefore, everything from a mere guess or conjecture to a formal set of propositional statements is considered a theory. In scientific writings, however, a narrower view of a theory typically prevails: "a series of propositions, each of which is a statement of some association between concepts" (Weis, 1998, p. 2; Babbie, 1995; Klein & White, 1996; Marx, 1963; Nye & Berardo, 1966, 1981; Reynolds, 1971); "a set of interrelated propositions (and corollaries to those propositions) that attempt to specify the relationship between a variable (or set of variables) and some behavior" (Bordens & Abbott, 1991, p. 496). Thus, theorizing is the process of systematically formulating and organizing ideas to understand a particular phenomenon, with no theory being intended to explain everything in the universe or everything about human beings.

Theories can be evaluated on their merit. For example, at a minimum, a good scientific theory must have correspondence with reality, have coherence, be parsimonious, and be falsifiable (Rosenthal & Rosnow, 1991). Theory also needs to be able to account for most of the existing data within a domain, predict novel events and behaviors, specify under what conditions those things will occur, be empirically testable (Bordens & Abbott, 1991), and have been tested to establish its validity (Popper, 1992a, 1992b).

Although some strides have been made in relation to theory building in mediation based on both existing theories developed outside the mediation context (Cobb, 1993, 1994a, 1994b; Cobb & Rifkin, 1991a; Winslade et al., 1998) and new theoretical approaches (Bush & Folger, 1994; Folger & Bush, 1994), these theories have not been evaluated for merit in terms of several of the conditions noted above. When researchers actually attempt to do so, they find that some of the criteria are unsatisfied.

For example, Cobb (1993, 1994a, 1994b) used existing narrative theory concepts, such as coherence (Agar & Hobbs, 1982), closure (Varela, 1979), and interdependence (White & Epston, 1990), to provide a theoretical base for her discussions of the complex verbal interactions that occur in mediation sessions between disputants and mediators. Cobb recognized that philosophically mediation is provided as an opportunity for disputants to "tell their stories" or to be heard by an authority and that these stories generally include descriptions of conflicts between the disputants and the disputants' "theory of responsibility" for the conflict (Cobb, 1994b). Cobb also found that these "conflict stories," or stories in which conflict is the focus, are constructed by creating logical and causal links between actors, their actions, and problematic outcomes.

The first narrative concept Cobb discussed, coherence, is defined as the degree to which the characters, the characters' actions, and the resulting outcomes in the disputant's stories fit together to create a story. Coherence can refer to both the fit in components within a given story and the fit in components between or across multiple stories. Cobb noted that in mediation the more coherent a story, the more likely it is to be the one that becomes the dominant story; the less coherent story is usually ignored, subsumed, or "marginalized." Cobb discussed each person's speech as a "web" of stories or narratives that is both reflected in and constructed by any particular story. Thus, any particular narrative is "nested" within a hierarchical structure of stories that provide meaning and context for shaping both old and new stories. She provided the example that when disputants come to mediation, each has a particular story with his or her version of a set of events, character roles, and themes. These stories are fit into a web of stories from each disputant's personal history, from stories told in the disputant's families and within his or her social networks, and from the disputant's cultural stories that serve to shape everyday stories (Cobb, 1994a). In terms of conflicts, Cobb argued that conflicts are the product of internarrative coherence—that is, the degree of coherence between the stories told by the two separate parties. As Cobb (1994a) noted, the "character roles in a disputant's story are contested and reformulated in the other's story, or the values celebrated in one story become values denigrated in another" (p. 54). The degree of coherence is never total; it also relies on the degree of narrative closure.

Cobb (1994a) defined the next concept, closure, as the notion that conflict stories often become rigid and difficult to change. In theory, conflict stories are open to infinite interpretations, but in practice Cobb noticed that most of the interpretations are extremely limited or closed. Thus, people reenact their conflicts by retelling their version of the story and not entertaining any new interpretations. Cobb asserted that there are particular points within the stories at which different interpretations could occur but they rarely do. She predicted that contests over the accuracy of any one story will occur around issues of causality, role relations, and values. For example, changes in plots can modify the chain of causality assigned to events and thus lead to different interpretations or new story lines.

Changes in the roles assigned to the characters can also modify stories. If the victim–victimizer roles assigned certain characters are changed, different stories will then be constructed. Changes in the moral frameworks or values from which the actions of characters are evaluated can lead to new interpretations of the characters and their actions.

There are two additional concepts that relate to closure or the stability of a particular story. First, the more "complete" a story, the less likely it will be modified or transformed by subsequent discussions or other versions of the story. Conversely, the less complete a story, the more ripe it is for modification and transformation because it is more open for interpretation. Second, variations in closure can be a function of cultural factors. For example, legal settings are generally governed by elaborate rules of procedure; thus, stories based on this rule-based logic are more effective in legal settings than are stories based on a relational logic (Conley & O'Barr, 1990). Stories based on relational logic focus on elaborating the interrelationships between people rather than the chain of events leading to an outcome (Bush & Folger, 1994; Folger & Bush, 1994).

The last narrative concept, interdependence, refers to the notion that patterns can be found in the way the characters are portrayed in the stories. The victim–victimizer roles often appear in mediation. The disputant telling the story constructs himself or herself as the victim while constructing the other disputant as the victimizer. The victimizer is attributed bad intent or given negative character traits and labels, whereas the victim is given a positive role and attributed good intent with positive character traits and labels (Cobb, 1994a). Within the narrative, then, the victim's role rests on the construction of the victimizer's role.

There is also an interdependence seen between stories told by each disputant. For example, accusations told in one disputant's stories are followed by justifications, denials, and excuses within the other disputant's story. Cobb (1994a) noted that the accusation/justification/denial/excuse pattern entrenches the parties and accounts for cycles of escalation in which conflicts are reenacted. She stated that this entrenched cyclical pattern of conflict is the justification for third-party intervention in conflicts. As opposed to moving forward to solve the conflict, the parties inside the conflict reenact their entrenched pattern. Intervention of a third party can alter the disputants' entrenched positions and generate new patterns of interaction and interdependence.

There are several important contributions made by Cobb's theoretical work. She provided theoretical mechanisms through which research findings in mediation can be explained, and she provided theoretical responses to the arguments that argue that mediators should only control the process of mediation and not the content of what is discussed or decided in mediation. She argued that the act of providing a process for disputants to "tell their stories" (e.g., "venting and listening, regulating speaking turns, scheduling public and private sessions, exploring alternatives, creating options, and building an agreement"; Cobb, 1994a, pp. 58–59) is in fact much more than merely regulating the process of mediation. The "telling" is in fact a constructive process wherein the content allowed to be discussed and elaborated by mediators has a profound impact on the resulting agreements produced.

This argument has relevance for agreements negotiated in mediation. As noted earlier, stories that are less coherent, complete, and culturally resonant tend to be dominated, ignored, or marginalized by the more coherent stories. The disputant with the less-coherent story tends to become entrenched in a particular role in the prevailing story and is not allowed to redefine himself or herself with a more legitimate position in construction of the new story. Cobb suggested that the ability of the disputants to define themselves in a coherent manner and resist the negative characterizations that others have of them is critical. The redefinition occurs by the less-coherent storyteller being encouraged and allowed to elaborate her or his story. Without this elaboration, the dominant story will prevail. The result is that the parties will reenact their conflict, and the construction of any mediation agreement will not reflect the input from the less-coherent storyteller. Without both positions represented, the agreement will be unfair to one of the parties. The degree to which those self-definitions are elaborated by the mediator will assist the disputants in constructing a less conflictual story, fairer agreement, and better relationship. Recognition of the fact that mediators must control or "manage" the content of mediation stories is contrary to the popular belief that mediators must regulate the process only. In fact, mediators must also "manage the construction of content" to be effective (Cobb, 1994a, p. 60).

Cobb also provided a theoretical framework for understanding why some people do not succeed in mediation. She suggested, contrary to the mediation philosophy, that the "telling of stories" will help clients resolve their conflict, that the telling of stories can reproduce rather than resolve a conflict in some cases. The stories that are told have varying degrees of coherence and closure, and to varying degrees the characters within the stories are entrenched in particular roles (e.g., victim–victimizer). She predicted that the stabilization of stories occurs before the mediation actually takes place as the parties rehearse their stories to their own social network. Thus, merely telling one's story offers no assurance that the conflict can be resolved. Without the particular types of interventions on the part of the mediator outlined above, clients will reinvent the conflict in mediation.

Cobb also predicted that this marginalization of stories may differentially affect women and men in mediation. Cobb and others argue that studies have consistently shown that the stories women tell generally are much less coherent, less complete, and more relational (as opposed to rule-based) than stories told by men (Conley & O'Barr, 1990; Gilligan, 1982; Gray, 1994). The important prediction from this research for mediation is that then the stories constructed within mediation sessions by verbal exchanges by disputants and mediators and any agreements produced therein may be less likely to reflect women's beliefs and interests. Women are likely to feel they were not allowed to fully participate in mediation by the mediator or the other party because their stories are less likely to be elaborated and less likely to add significantly to the new stories being constructed in mediation. Also, any agreements produced are less likely to address the women's concerns.

To combat the problem of inclusion of all disputants' stories regardless of coherence, completeness or logic, Cobb suggested several different interventions that mediators should use. She suggested that mediators should not have one disputant and then the other tell their entire story uninterrupted. Rather, the mediator should develop sets of questions to be asked of both disputants, so the story emerges. She further argued that the mediator must elaborate the stories of both parties during this questioning process regardless of the coherence, completeness, and cultural resonance of the story given. Without doing so, one story will predominate and guide any agreement reached. Mediators must intervene and assist disputants to open up their formerly closed conflict stories to new interpretations. Cobb noted that creation of new stories is accomplished by destabilization of the old. Furthermore, she noted that "destabilization can be accomplished via the use of circular questions (Fleuridas, Nelson, & Rosenthal, 1986; Tomm, 1987), reframing (Putnam & Holmer, 1992; Watzlawick, Weakland, & Fisch, 1974), positive connotation (Selvini-Palazzoli, Boscolo, Ceechin, & Prata, 1980; Shoham-Salomon & Rosenthal, 1987), and externalization (White & Epston, 1990)" (Cobb, 1994a, p. 60). Although she stated that these therapeutic techniques are necessary, she does not elaborate how to use them effectively.

In looking at Cobb's theorizing in relation to the criteria noted above for evaluating theories (i.e., correspondence with reality; coherence; parsimony; specific conditions noted when behaviors and events will and will not occur; ability to predict novel events; coverage of existing data; and whether it is falsifiable, testable, rejectable, and has been tested), some of these conditions are met. Unfortunately, Cobb's theory has not yet been operationalized and empirically tested, so several of these criteria await further analysis. In the first criterion, correspondence with reality, her interpretation of narrative theory appears to have good correspondence with the reality of mediation sessions. Clients are invited to "tell their stories," and they do so with varying degrees of coherence, closure, and interrelatedness as Cobb used these concepts. Unfortunately, without detailed empirical analysis, it is difficult to state this with conviction. For example, the prediction has yet to be tested that less coherent stories will be subsumed by the more coherent, and that resulting agreements in these cases, if any, will be less likely to reflect the concerns of both parties. In addition, the mediation interventions she outlined as productive for elaborating the less coherent story have not been clearly defined, operationalized, and empirically tested. And whether or not her suggested interventions can prevent the abuses noted in her theorizing has yet to be tested.

The coherence of Cobb's theory is significant because it is based on a long tradition of narrative theory and research in communications (Agar & Hobbs, 1982; Kolb, 1995; Varela, 1979; White & Epston, 1990). She captured the narrative theory concepts well for the mediation domain and related them to specific behaviors of both mediators and disputants. Her theory is complex, while much of mediation philosophy or ideology has been criticized for being too simplistic (Ellis, 1990; W. L. F. Felstiner & Williams, 1980; Levy, 1984). Thus, parsimony is relative to the complexity of the behaviors it is used to explain. Again, without further empirical testing, it is difficult to say if modifications could be made to the theory that would render it more parsimonious. The remaining criteria (i.e., specific conditions noted when behaviors and events will and will not occur, ability to predict novel events, coverage of existing data, falsifiability, testability, and rejectability) cannot be assessed without further operationalization of the specific concepts (i.e., coherence, closure, and interrelatedness) and interventions (i.e., circular interviewing, circular questions, reframing, positive connotation, and externalization), as well as empirically sound research conducted testing these constructs and interventions. Cobb had, however, laid the theoretical groundwork for a significant program of research in this area, and one from which mediation would greatly benefit.

Similar arguments can be made about the other major theoretical initiatives in mediation (Bush & Folger, 1994; Winslade & Cotter, 1997; Winslade et al., 1998). For example, Winslade et al. (1998) and Winslade and Cotter (1997) also capitalized on narrative theory and discussed its applicability to divorce mediation, although they do so on a different level than Cobb did. Although Cobb focused on theory building through applying existing narrative theory to divorce mediation, Winslade and his colleagues focused on using existing narrative psychotherapeutic interventions to design a new mediation intervention. They developed a seven-point summary of the features of a narrative-based intervention for divorce mediation. Cobb focused on theoretical mechanisms and explanations for why a narrative-based intervention should work, whereas Winslade focused on designing the intervention. Unfortunately, the intervention designed by Winslade et al. (1998), like the theory-building efforts of Cobb, has not been operationalized and empirically tested; thus, again, many of the criteria for evaluating a theory cannot be addressed in assessing this work. An interesting strategy might be to combine the efforts of Cobb and Winslade et al. At least some of the theoretical constructs proposed by Cobb could be tested using the intervention designed by Winslade et al. for, in fact, Winslade et al. (1998; Winslade & Cotter, 1997) based much of their work on Cobb's analysis of narrative theory.

Instead of using theory from other disciplines as a starting point as Cobb did, Bush and Folger developed a new theory of mediation, and these theory-building efforts begin with what they defined as the central goal of mediation: "engendering moral growth and transforming human character, toward both greater strength and greater compassion" (Bush & Folger, 1994, p. 27; Menkel-Meadow, 1995). This goal appears to be in service of "the ultimate goal of moral development" (Bush & Folger, 1994, p. 27). The authors preferred these goals to others, including social justice and system efficiency, because they saw them as "sounder, more coherent and more justifiable" (Bush & Folger, 1994, p. 28; Mendel-Meadow, 1995).

Bush and Folger (1994) argued that parties come to disputes "typically unsettled, confused, fearful, disorganized, and unsure of what to do" (p. 85). Through mediation, parties become empowered and "grow calmer, clearer, more confident, more organized and more decisive" and regain strength to take control of their situation (Bush & Folger, 1994, p. 85). "Growth in *recognition* involves realizing and strengthening one's capacity as an individual for experiencing and expressing concern and consideration for others, especially others whose situation is 'different' from one's own" (Folger & Bush, 1994, pp. 15–16). The authors argued that parties also come to mediation feeling "threatened, attacked, and victimized . . . defensive, suspicious, and hostile . . . and almost incapable of looking beyond their own needs" (Bush & Folger, 1994, p. 89). Through transformative mediation, parties can "voluntarily choose to become more open, attentive, sympathetic, and responsive to the situation of the other party," thus appreciating the other party's position (Bush & Folger, 1994, p. 89). Bush and Folger (1994) stated that growth in these two dimensions is the "hallmark" of mature development and a "higher state of being." They argued that instead of trying to solve "the problem" or change the situation between the parties, their proposed interventions can instead transform the parties themselves as human beings (Bush & Folger, 1994).

The interventions suggested by Bush and Folger (1994) are based on three strategies: (a) microfocusing on parties' contributions, (b) encouraging parties' deliberation and choice making, and (c) encouraging perspective taking. Microfocusing on parties' contributions is described as scrutinizing the "parties' individual moves—their statements, challenges, questions, narratives—for possibilities each affords for transformative opportunities" (Bush & Folger, 1994, p. 100), such as points at which parties can be encouraged to recognize another's perspective. Encouraging parties' deliberation and choice making is defined as encouraging the parties to consider, reflect, and deliberate about their options, goals, and resources. Under the transformative approach, mediators cannot, however, mold issues, make proposals, or define terms for settlement. In transformative mediation, the focus is clearly not on reaching settlements. Mediators are discouraged from ever pressing the parties to draft a settlement agreement. Encouraging perspective taking is defined as looking for places in each party's statements that allow one party to consider the other's situation or perspective. Mediators are encouraged to "reinterpret, translate, and reframe parties' statements—not to shape issues or solutions" but to make the message more comprehensible to the other party (Bush & Folger, 1994, p. 101). Mediators are also encouraged to pay attention to relational issues and include in any agreements statements about misunderstandings that have been cleared up or changes in views of the other party that have occurred as a result of the mediation. Beyond this general description, the interventions based on this framework have not yet been clearly defined (Franz, 1998).

The importance of Bush and Folger's work is in their straightforward statement regarding their goals (Menkel-Meadow, 1995). Rarely do mediation theorists, researchers, or practitioners clearly state what it is they hope to accomplish. Their second major contribution to family mediation is that they focus the field on questioning whether settlement rates are an adequate criterion against which to judge the success of mediation. As just noted, Bush and Folger are most concerned with the moral development of the parties rather than on the quick attainment of a settlement agreement. Unfortunately, in terms of the criteria to evaluate a theory (i.e., correspondence with reality, coherence, parsimony, specific conditions noted when behaviors or events will and will not occur, ability to predict novel events, coverage of existing data, falsifiable, testable, rejectable, and has been tested), transformative mediation has not been defined with enough precision to assess many of these criteria.

For example, in terms of correspondence with reality, Bush and Folger proposed transformative mediation as a general theory of mediation as opposed to a specific intervention for family mediation. It is unclear what these authors would modify, if anything, for the divorce context. Thus, transformative mediation's correspondence with reality in the legal context is, at best, tenuous. Although parties can voluntarily hire a private mediator to assist them in resolving their dispute and pay for as many sessions as they deem necessary, the vast majority of mediation clients are mandated to attend court-sponsored mediation by either state statute or local court rules. Mediation, as defined in state and local law, is a process to resolve conflict and reach agreements on custody and visitation issues (Rogers & McEwen, 1994). The goals in transformative mediation of empowerment, recognition, and higher moral development, while laudable and desirable, are not the most important ones as defined by this law. Thus, the goals of transformative mediation and the legal context of divorce mediation appear to be at odds.

In addition, Bush and Folger (1994) stated that they wish to change individuals, not just the interpersonal environment or situations (Bush & Folger, 1994). First, as noted in earlier sections of this book having to do with marital therapy, changing individuals is a long and difficult process even if both parties are ready and willing to work toward change in their relationship (Jacobson et al., 1987). Rarely are couples who are seeking or mandated to attend divorce mediation willing or able to put forth the financial resources or the emotional effort that would be necessary for meaningful change to occur and be sustained in their relationship. Instead, most clients are focused on resolving the immediate conflict, negotiating a settlement agreement, and getting on with their lives. Second, changing individuals is not realistic in the legal context because many court-connected programs simply do not have the funding to pay for the resources necessary to allow parties to mediate indefinitely in hopes that they will eventually evolve to a "higher state of being" (Folger & Bush, 1994, p. 20; see also Fleischer, 1996). There are often limits placed on the number of sessions or the issues that can be addressed in mediation, and the funding sources often base decisions about continued support for the program on rates of agreement. A theory-driven intervention with the combination of a vague focus on moral development, potentially requiring many mediation sessions, and a lack of focus on solving problems and drafting agreements is not realistic in the publicly funded legal system.

In terms of coherence and parsimony, transformative mediation as it is currently defined is vague (Menkel-Meadow, 1995). Bush and Folger (1994) defined neither low nor high moral development. Thus, the criteria of coherence is not met because it is not clear what is being transformed or how it is being done (Menkel-Meadow, 1995). And because the theory is not yet coherent, the criteria of parsimony are also impossible to assess.

In terms of empirical evaluation, "[i]f we cannot clearly articulate what it is we are transforming, how can we evaluate what we have done?" (Menkel-Meadow, 1995, p. 237). This is an essential problem for meeting the remaining criteria of a good theory (i.e., specific conditions noted when behaviors and events will and will not occur and ability to predict novel events). As one critic (Menkel-Meadow, 1995) argued, transformative mediation may be possible, "but only if we define our terms more clearly, state our goals more modestly and inclusively, and remain sensitive to the social and political situations and institutions in which we do our work" (p. 239). In Bush and Folger's defense, they clearly stated that in their work they are taking only the first step toward providing a new theory of mediation. In essence, they see themselves as the visionaries of a new approach; they assume others can then "refine, study, and follow it" (Bush & Folger, 1994, p. 112).

Both uses of theory outlined above—the use of existing theory in a new way (e.g., Cobb) and building a new theory (e.g., Bush and Folger)

—are in the early stages. Neither has been subjected to detailed empirical analysis in the family mediation context. Although it will be exciting to watch as these approaches grow and develop, neither as yet can meet many of the criteria for evaluating a good theory.

WHAT KIND OF THEORIZING IS NEEDED NOW?

So where should future theory-building efforts begin? Should they simply build on existing theoretical excursions, or should a different approach be used? We believe that future theory development must start with a new direction—that is, defining goals for mediation. Why? Because mediation has been promoted and touted as achieving a variety of different goals, some of which are inconsistent and contradictory (Luban, 1989). For example, to label fiscal and temporal efficiency in judicial administration as the most important goal of mediation would conflict with a goal of quasi-therapy for mediation in which success in quasi-therapy may require the expenditure of more time and greater resources (Irving & Benjamin, 1995; Rogers & McEwen, 1994). Bush and Folger did not consider this point and solely focused on the one goal: quasi-therapy (i.e., transformation of individuals and relationships). Thus, we need to identify the law's goals for mediation and develop both theory and evaluation strategies to specifically measure the conditions under which these goals are likely to be achieved.

Once these disparate goals are clearly identified, then the second level of theory development is to reason backward to derive the combination of variables and context-specific influences, which would logically lead to achieving each separate goal (Bush, 1989). In developing these causal models, researchers can integrate existing theories. For example, conflict theories, negotiation and bargaining theories, family systems, social exchange theory, game theory, justice theories, and communications theories will provide guidance regarding the relationships between the variables as well as the relationships between the variables and the desired outcomes.

This process will then provide a strong theoretical base for mediation research that will lead to empirical studies wherein the models are refined and relationships between variables clarified. Once the variables leading to each specific desired outcome are thoroughly understood, there will be a theoretical base from which program administrators and policymakers can draw on to prioritize the conflicting goals of mediation and choose appropriate interventions to achieve those goals. This sequence is essential because researchers, program administrators, and policymakers often fall into "[t]he politically attractive option of embracing multiple, contradictory goals" (Rogers & McEwen, 1994, pp. 27–28). Unfortunately, embracing noncommensurate goals "prevents clear thinking about the potential risks, as well as benefits of mediation" (Rogers & McEwen, 1994, pp. 27–28). Without clear thinking about goals and the causal models underlying them, scholars and researchers cannot develop a sound base for the discipline.

Unfortunately, mediation is plagued by legitimate, noncommensurate goals that reflect the different vantage points from which mediation is viewed (Tyler, 1989). For example, as central players in the legal system, legislators, judges, court administrators, and mediation program managers are generally supportive of the structure in which they work and their roles require that they be concerned with issues of fiscal and temporal efficiency in processing cases (Tyler, 1989). Vendors of mediation services, both private and court-sponsored, need clients for business, so they also focus on these benefits relative to litigation (Luban, 1989). Thus, from the vantage point of key players within the legal system, the goal of system efficiency is clearly important. From the vantage point of mediation practitioners, particularly practitioners who are trained in mental health fields, often their roles encourage them to see mediation as a means to change the existing relationship between disputants (i.e., to explore and resolve the root causes of conflicts, to increase psychological functioning of parents, and to teach disputants skills in coparenting and dispute resolution). Thus, from the vantage point of mental health trained mediation practitioners, quasi-therapy is clearly an important goal. From the vantage point of lawyers, feminist scholars, and community activists, protecting the legal rights and safety of disputants and gaining access to the legal system for those who have been traditionally denied access are clearly important goals. By participants' airing their concerns in front of neutral parties, resolving their own conflicts, and thus reducing their dependence on professionals, a "better justice" is attained (Abel, 1982; Luban, 1989). Thus, for these people, individual rights and social justice are much more compelling goals than either quasi-therapy or system efficiency. Moreover, we can classify the goals of mediation on the basis of these divergent perspectives into the three general categories noted above: system efficiency, quasi-therapy, and justice.[1]

System Efficiency

One of the key incentives for creating legislation and local court rules authorizing or mandating divorce mediation was to relieve pressure on the courts and make them more efficient in handling divorce disputes (Fix & Harter, 1992; Irving & Benjamin, 1995; McIsaac, 1981; Pearson, 1981; Pearson & Thoennes, 1982). After passage of the no-fault divorce laws in the 1960s, courts experienced a sharp rise in the number of divorce cases filed, many of which returned again and again for reprocessing. Judges be-

---

[1] There are others who have defined the goals and subgoals of mediation (see Bush & Folger, 1994; Esser, 1989; Luban, 1989; Menkel-Meadow, 1995; Silbey & Merry, 1986; Tyler, 1989).

came increasingly frustrated as the cases clogged their calendars. Court administrators became concerned about how to stretch existing court resources to meet the increasing demand. Cases in other areas of law were not able to be processed because of the tremendous caseload in family law. Although only a fraction of the total cases have contests over custody or visitation at the time of divorce, this number seriously underestimated the number of cases that eventually returned to the court for additional hearings (Emery, 1994). In the 1970s, approximately 33% of all divorced parents legally disputed custody *at some point after* the divorce (Emery, 1994; Foster & Freed, 1973). By the 1980s, more than 40% of the postdivorce population in the United States failed to comply with support and custody orders (Kelly, 1990b, 1991). Judges, lawyers, court personnel, and lawmakers began asking if there was a better way (Burger, 1982). Thus, it is not surprising that most of the empirical research surrounding the goals of mediation has focused on the goal of system efficiency (e.g., speed, cost, and relitigation).

Quasi-therapy

A second key reason mediation was developed was to more adequately address the emotionally charged nature of the divorce process. Judges, lawyers, court personnel, and disputants recognized that there were often significant emotional problems in divorce that were not adequately addressed and that caused disputants problems getting through the legal system. The difference between the legalities of divorce and the emotions that go along with obtaining a divorce is described in terms of the difference between obtaining a "legal divorce" and an "emotional divorce" (Griffiths, 1986; Sarat & Felstiner, 1986). Although a signed agreement signifies successful resolution of the legal divorce, it signifies nothing about the resolution of emotional issues. In addition, if one of the parties has significant emotional issues that are not being addressed, the legal process of divorce can become a weapon to harass and punish the other parent. In fact, clinicians argue that emotional conflict can be significantly increased when couples become involved in the adversarial structure of the court because it increases negative feelings between spouses by emphasizing individual positions, opposition, and confrontation, as opposed to emphasizing shared feelings, common goals, and values (Coogler, 1978; Emery, 1994; Irving & Benjamin, 1995; Kressel, 1985). The resolution of emotional conflicts is a long process and can take the active intervention of a mental health professional and a substantial amount of work on the parents' part, and many parents refuse to seek this help. Thus, judges are caught in the middle of an emotional struggle between disputants without the clinical skills or training to adequately deal with these issues. Mediation was proposed by many to assist the parties not only in resolving issues involved in the legal divorce but also in simultaneously addressing the emotional issues so that the legal process did not become a forum for disputants "acting-out" their anger and other psychological motives.

Indeed, embedded in state statutes and local court rules authorizing mediation are statements concerning the ability of mediation to reduce acrimony between parties and to minimize stress and anxiety (North Carolina, 1999). Mediation scholars also emphasize its ability to address bitterness, anger, and tension; resolve lingering attachments; increase communication; and focus on the emotional needs of the family (Dillon & Emery, 1996; Irving & Benajmin, 1995). "Mediation is thought by many to reduce hostility and stress, improve the communication and cooperation of the participants, accelerate the psychological adjustment to divorce, result [sic] in higher levels of satisfaction with the result" (Kelly et al., 1988, p. 453). Advocates of mediation argue that emotionally charged and difficult cases are referred, through mediation processes, out of the traditional court processes to another agency with specialized processes and personnel specifically trained to manage them (Gerber, 1990). Mediation has been traditionally conducted by mental health professionals or other professionals with training in family conflict and dispute resolution, whereas courtroom disputes are argued by attorneys and monitored by judges, most of whom have no training in mental health issues, family conflict, or alternative dispute resolution methods. Some argue that solving disputants' legal problems is frequently not possible without first addressing individual or relationship level emotional issues (Irving & Benjamin, 1995).

Justice

If people obey the law because they perceive its procedures as just (Tyler, 1990), then divorce litigation should be procedurally just. But this is not always the case. Feminist scholars have noted that women often enter the divorce arena substantially less knowledgeable than their husbands about the law and the courts, less financially capable of hiring attorneys equal in knowledge to those representing their husbands, and inappropriately more trusting of their husbands' good intentions and goodwill than is warranted. The result is a system that has been perceived in many cases as unjust because it is biased against women in society. Thus, a concern with justice has become important in feminist scholarship in general and in divorce litigation in particular.

Mediation has been seen by some as providing one opportunity for redressing this imbalance. During mediation, parties can be taught to clearly identify and articulate their own goals for the divorce and have an opportunity to work with a neutral third party to reach a settlement that represents the woman's interests as much as the man's.

These issues are not indigenous necessarily to women but may reflect the broader problem of people facing the termination of a relationship with substantial emotional baggage driving their view of what an appropriate outcome should be. Thus, whether it be the man or the woman, or both, the parties often burden the courts with unrealistic and inappropriate expectations for resolving what is not just a legal dilemma for them, but an emotional one (Griffiths, 1986; Sarat & Felstiner, 1986).

Mediation has been seen as a solution for these people as well. The use of a neutral mediator, the opportunity for both parties to fully air concerns, and the use of a less adversarial context are all seen by some as providing the necessary opportunity for just solutions to emerge and for justice to be served. Justice in this case does not necessarily rely on procedural matters but also incorporates the opportunity for people to feel satisfaction in being able to tell their complete story, have the other party hear it, and feel satisfaction with an outcome that they mutually shared in drafting.

Moreover, it can be argued that a major difference between mediation and litigation is that in mediation the disputants' *perceptions* of what is just can actually be used to shape the mediation, including the process and the drafting of the settlement agreement. This focus on individual perceptions should affect the ultimate satisfaction of the parties with it. As Finkel (1995) noted, people's common-sense perceptions of justice often differ dramatically from the law's edicts. Mediation under this view thus can provide an opportunity for common-sense justice to merge with a legal outcome. Litigation is less likely to achieve this result, according to this logic, because the courts are bounded by traditional rules of evidence, with the judge imposing his or her view on an appropriate result for the parties.

Finally, perceptions are often shaped by the information one has available. Concerns with justice in divorce litigation have centered around fears that one or both of the parties in the traditional divorce litigation are denied access to relevant information that could shape their desires and goals for the outcome. Mediation has been seen as a mechanism for minimizing this inadequacy in the flow of information and thereby increasing the justice of the system. Mediators, unlike judges, have the ability and opportunity to discuss with the disputants the options, procedures, and settlement outcomes that have been used in the past by other parties that may be of value for the current disputants to consider in framing their desired outcomes. Thus, mediation can promote distributive justice (Deutsch, 1985), procedural justice (Tyler, 1990), and common-sense justice (Finkel, 1995).

VARIABLES ASSOCIATED WITH EACH GOAL OF MEDIATION

After we understand the goals, any good theory must be able to identify the variables associated with that goal and the causal relationships between those variables. Ultimately, it is these causal models that define the theory of mediation associated with each goal. It is beyond the scope of this book to comprehensively model each of the three goals for mediation. Rather, our intent is to prove the value of our recommended direction for future mediation research. What is needed, which the remainder of this chapter now does, is to identify variables associated with one of mediation's goals and present a preliminary model for explaining the causal relationships between these variables and the ultimate goal.

We say "preliminary" advisedly because future researchers including ourselves will need to more precisely specify alternative models, collect data, and test these models using statistical techniques such as causal modeling. Through programmatic research following this paradigm, the appropriate model or models to explain each goal will be refined over time, and practitioners and policymakers will be better able to understand which approaches and what factors will make their programs more likely to achieve the goal or goals they specify. For the purposes of this chapter, we arbitrarily chose the goal of system efficiency to model.

System Efficiency Variables

One of the key incentives for creating legislation and local court rules authorizing or mandating divorce mediation was to relieve pressure on the courts (Fix & Harter, 1992; Irving & Benjamin, 1995; McIsaac, 1981; Pearson, 1981; Pearson & Thoennes, 1982). Judges and court administrators became increasingly frustrated with the burgeoning caseload without a commensurate increase in resources to respond to this new workload. Thus, it is not surprising that most of the empirical research surrounding the goals of mediation has focused on the goal of system efficiency (e.g., speed, cost, and resources).

In terms of ease of evaluating mediation programs, cost, speed, and compliance with court decisions (e.g., relitigation rates) are seen as ideal criteria against which to evaluate dispute resolution programs (Tyler, 1989). At first glance, these efficiency goals appear deceptively clear and concrete with compelling face validity (Bush, 1989; Tyler, 1989); however, as noted in chapter 8, the empirical research is equivocal on the issues of cost, speed, and rates of relitigation. This is understandable because there is little consensus in the literature in defining these variables. To make matters more problematic, there are a complex set of relevant variables that are rarely considered together in approaching this issue. Thus, one of the first steps in the process of defining a model of system efficiency is to impose a structure on the range of relevant outcome goals and possible causal variables by identifying them and then by grouping them into categories. These categories of variables can then be considered in more detail. In our model of system efficiency, the categories include dispute–

participant variables, divorce process variables, and divorce outcome variables. Outcomes include first-level system cost outcomes (e.g., costs to disputants at the end of initial mediation or divorce) and ultimate system cost outcomes (e.g., costs to disputants including postlitigation legal costs if any).

Dispute–Participant Variables

Couples come to the legal system with a history, and this history can play an important part in the cost of resources needed to process their case. For example, consider a cooperative, lower socioeconomic status (SES) couple with little personal or real property and no children, who have no experience with the legal system, who have hired attorneys, and whose goal is to have an equitable division of assets. Compare them with an angry, high-SES couple who have a good deal of assets and several children, who both have experience with litigation and mediation, who have hired attorneys, who have a long history of conflict-ridden interactions, and whose goal is to punish each other by contesting visitation and custody. These two types of couples likely generate significantly different resource pressures. This example also illustrates several important sets of dispute–participant variables.

First, understanding the participant characteristics in terms of demographics (e.g., age, length of marriage; age of children, if any; amount of assets; and SES), personality variables (e.g., level of anger, willingness to take risks, and current mental health), and relationship variables (e.g., disparity in levels of attachment, pattern of couple communication and interaction, goals of parties, and knowledge of family finances) is important for understanding and predicting costs of processing these cases. For example, demographics are important in that they will likely predict the number of and complexity of issues that will need to be resolved and thus the number of system resources needed to address them. The longer a couple are married (at least up to some asymptote), the more likely they will have children and have accumulated assets. The presence of both assets and children leads to more complicated divorce proceedings (Sales et al., 1993a, 1993b) and possibly the need for more legal system resources to resolve them. For example, for a couple from the lower SES income bracket who are married a long period, have several children, and cannot agree to custody and visitation arrangements, referral to public-sponsored mediation or a publicly funded custody evaluation may be necessary to resolve these issues.

Second, personality and relationship variables are also likely to predict *how* a couple will likely resolve their divorce and also *how likely* it will be for the couple to need resources. For example, high levels of anger and an antagonistic pattern of interaction are associated with both poor mediation processes (Bickerdike, 1998) and poor mediation outcomes (Bickerdike, 1998; Irving & Benjamin, 1992). Bickerdike found that couples with high levels of anger prior to entering mediation are likely to engage in higher levels of contentious behaviors and lower levels of problem solving during the mediation sessions, which in turn leads to more sessions and poorer outcomes. Bickerdike concluded that for some couples even the intervention of highly trained and skilled mediators was not enough to overcome the effects of preexisting levels of anger. Instead of providing a less adversarial forum to air their concerns and develop an agreement, mediation provides for these antagonistic couples the opportunity to recapitulate their pattern of couple communication and interaction (e.g., abusing and attacking one another). In these cases, traditional face-to-face negotiation is not productive, and greater resources may be needed than with couples who are cooperative. Once the causal mechanisms associated with this pathway are understood, the legal system can suggest alternative and more cost-effective options for these couples. For example, an option is for the participants to receive premediation treatment to modify the level of conflict prior to the initiation of mediation (Irving & Benjamin, 1995; A. I. Schwebel et al., 1993).

Third, type of dispute is important in that different historical patterns may suggest different methods for handling a case to minimize ultimate costs to the legal system. For example, whether the current case is an initial divorce, a postdecree action contesting some part of the decree, or merely a formality to apprise the court of agreed-to change the couple is making in arrangements regarding the children could influence costs and be causally related to the best method for handling a dispute to reduce those costs. For example, several ancillary programs (e.g., special masters, case managers, and family court advisors) and specialized mediation programs have been suggested as more cost-effective in dealing with couples who continually relitigate provisions of the decree or are unable to meet the demands of the court (Campbell & Johnston, 1986; Johnston & Campbell, 1988). Instead of processing these cases through the litigation system or mandating them to attend general mediation, it might be that bypassing these systems and assigning the cases to the ancillary programs is ultimately more cost-effective.

Divorce Process Variables

There are several categories of divorce process variables that affect the ultimate costs of processing cases. Those include level of attorney involvement, local legal culture, and nature of the process.

Not all disputants hire attorneys, and, if they do, some clients hire attorneys only as advisors for particular portions of the case. If, on the one hand, attorneys are involved and are able to resolve some or all of the divorce issues without significant involvement of the courts, the costs of resolving the dispute to the couple are higher but the costs for the legal system are significantly reduced (Fix & Harter, 1992). If, on the other hand, attorneys file a number of motions with the court that require hearings to resolve points of contention between the spouses, the costs for both the parties and the legal system are significantly increased. Disputants who do not have attorneys often require many more court resources. To a large extent, these parents rely extensively on court services and child support agencies for answers to their family law problems (Pearson, 1993). Personnel in these agencies are not lawyers and are not necessarily willing or able to advocate for the parents in an effective way (Pearson, 1993). Alternatively, litigants may rely on divorce kits containing the legal paperwork necessary to file for and complete a divorce, as they did in the Maricopa County study noted earlier (Sales et al., 1993a, 1933b). Despite the fact that the Maricopa County pro se litigants often relied on these kits, nearly one third still had problems with the legal process, the legal forms, or both, and nearly half of these litigants were not able to find solutions for these problems (Sales et al., 1993a, 1993b).

The local legal culture will also affect the ultimate cost of processing divorce cases. The rules of civil procedure dictate how and when cases are referred to mediation. If there are hearings required prior to a case being referred out, or if referral depends on judicial discretion, more court resources will be expended prior to that determination. In addition, attorney billing practices (e.g., whether attorneys bill on an hourly basis or a flat fee) will make a difference in terms of overall costs to both the parties and the legal system.

The setting where the service is provided (i.e., court-sponsored vs. private) can also affect costs for both the clients and the legal system. Costs of court-sponsored programs are mostly borne by the legal system in that the services are generally free to the clients. Although rare, some large court-sponsored programs charge clients on a sliding-fee scale. Counties that keep a roster of approved mediators and refer clients to private, fee-for-service programs are likely to cost the clients a great deal more but the legal system less.

In addition, voluntariness (i.e., mandatory, voluntary, or at judicial discretion) of participation in the mediation program is likely to affect the costs to the legal system of providing the service. Mandatory court-sponsored programs are likely to cost the legal system a great deal to staff, operate, and maintain. By maintaining these large programs, there may be reductions in other programs, such as costs of maintaining the litigation program, but to date there are no consistent or comprehensive data gathered that clearly indicate this cost savings. On the other hand, large court-sponsored programs that process many mandated cases can do so at a lower cost than those programs that only process a few clients who are self-referred.

Other parts of the legal culture will be causally related to resource outcomes. For example, the level of training of the third party (e.g., degrees and specialized training) is likely to affect costs both for the clients and the legal system. More highly trained mediators with advanced degrees are likely to cost the legal system more if they are hired to work in court-sponsored programs. They are likely to cost the clients more if they are providing services through private, fee-for-service programs. The model of mediation provided can significantly affect the costs of services provided. Models that use a team of mediators for each case, assess, and then address emotional issues by offering premediation therapy or addressing all divorce issues are likely to require many more sessions than models that use only one mediator, ignore or only minimally acknowledge emotional issues, and restrict the focus to custody/visitation disputes. Restrictions on the number of sessions and number of mediators that can be provided in each case, or that can be provided at no cost to the legal system (i.e., referral to private, fee-for-service programs), will directly affect the ultimate costs borne by the legal system.

Divorce Outcome Variables

When a party proceeds through the process to resolve their case, there are several possible outcomes. In the litigation system, once a case settles prior to trial or includes a trial, an agreement is drafted and filed with the court, or a court ruling is made and the current case ends.

When mediation is involved, there are several possible outcomes. For example, couples can reach a full agreement in mediation or have either one of the attorneys or the mediator draft the agreement. Couples can also reach a partial or no agreement in mediation. Couples reaching partial agreement in mediation can settle the remaining issues between themselves prior to any further involvement with the court or proceed to a court hearing where the judge makes a final decision. Couples can reach no agreement in mediation and require processing of their entire case by the litigation system. These couples can then require hearings and/or custody evaluations to settle their cases, at considerable cost to the legal system.

First-Level System Cost Outcomes

At this point, where cases end, the variables associated with the costs of processing cases can be considered. The variables described thus far address costs for processing an initial divorce. In considering these first-level system efficiency cost outcomes, one needs to consider several pieces of information. For example, cost-effectiveness can relate to both costs to the government and costs to the disputants. Costs to the government include costs of maintaining the litigation system. Personnel costs (e.g., judges, administrative staff, and clerical support staff), physical resource costs (e.g., overhead including building and maintenance of courthouses, heating/cooling), and miscellaneous operating costs (e.g., office supplies, computer equipment) are all required to maintain this system. All these governmental costs relate equally to maintaining a third-party system if it is public and court-sponsored. If the third-party system entails only maintenance of an approved roster of community mediators, with the sessions held at the mediators' private offices and session fees borne by the clients, a much different level of costs is associated with this third-party system. In addition, there are costs to the disputants (e.g., professional fees and court costs).

There is a complex relationship between the costs borne by the governmental entities and those borne by the disputants. Often cost savings found for one entity can be offset by increasing costs for another. For example, one study of arbitration, whose findings could generalize to mediation, found that while court-annexed arbitration reduced the cost of processing cases for the disputants and the counties where the cases were filed, it simultaneously increased the cost for the state (Hensler, 1986; Hensler, Lipson, & Rolph, 1981). Lower attorney fees for clients and reduced use of local courts were offset by increases in costs for the state in maintaining the arbitration program. A second study found that in attorney-negotiated divorce cases, the majority of clients had not been before a judge before serious settlement negotiations were initiated, whereas in mediated cases, the vast majority of clients had been before a judge one or more times prior to mediation (Fix & Harter, 1992). Thus, attorney-negotiated cases may be more costly for the disputants but are likely to be less expensive for the courts. Therefore, in the issue of fiscal efficiency, an important consideration is cost efficiency for whom (i.e., federal, state or local government, or disputants) and how the outcomes that change costs for one entity may affect another.

Ultimate System Outcomes

Finally, many cases require reprocessing or are contested and relitigated. These cases enter the legal system with a different history and set of characteristics that may be best handled in an alternative fashion. Special ancillary programs for special needs families have been recently developed (e.g., special masters, case managers, family court advisors, and divorce arbitration; Arizona, 1998a; Coconino County, Arizona, 1996). There is some research to support handling these cases separately and providing separate intervention options for containing the conflicts (Campbell & Johnston, 1986; Johnston & Campbell, 1988; Heister, 1985). There are, however, costs associated with then maintaining these court-sponsored ancillary programs (e.g., personnel costs). The ultimate costs of maintaining a legal system for processing divorce-related cases that involve postdecree actions need to include all divorce and postdecree legal costs.

CONCLUSION

Thinking about developing a theory of mediation that identifies desired outcomes within major goals, and the causal variables and mechanisms associated with those outcomes and ultimate goals, will lead to an understanding of mediation that is far more comprehensive and instructive than we have experienced in the field to date. The examples contained in this chapter are illustrative only. This is important to understand inasmuch as the examples are only pieces of the ultimate causal model of system efficiency that will need to be developed and empirically supported, and of the approach that modeling the other mediation goals will need to mimic. The actual modeling and research designs, for example, will need to include not only hypothesized direct pathways but also the mediator and moderator variables within those pathways. Once this is accomplished, the analysis and recommended directions that this book has provided should ultimately and significantly improve the way divorce and family mediation in this and other countries evolve and operate.

REFERENCES

Abel, R. L. (1982). The contradictions of informal justice. In R. L. Abel (Ed.), *The politics of informal justice: The American experience* (Vol. 1, pp. 267–311). New York: Academic Press.

Agar, M., & Hobbs, J. (1982). Interpreting discourse: Coherence and the analysis of ethnographic interviews. *Discourse Process, 5*, 1–32.

Ahrons, C. R. (1994). *The good divorce.* New York: HarperPerrennial.

Ahrons, C. R., & Rodgers, R. H. (1987). *Divorced families: A multidisciplinary developmental view.* New York: Norton.

Akister, J. (1993). The spouse subsystem in the family context: Couple interaction categories. *Journal of Family Therapy, 15*, 1–21.

Alaska Judicial Council. (1992, February). *Alaska child visitation mediation pilot project: Report to the legislature.* Anchorage, AK: Author.

Alfini, J. J. (1991). Symposium: Trashing, bashing, and hashing it out: Is this the end of "good mediation"? *Florida State University Law Review, 19*, 47–75.

Allport, G., & Postman, L. (1975). *The psychology of rumor.* New York: Henry Holt.

American Bar Association. (1986). *Divorce and family mediation: Standards of practice* (Task Force on Mediation, Section of the Family Law). Chicago: Author.

American Psychiatric Association. (1994). *Diagnostic and statistical manual of mental disorders* (4th ed.). Washington, DC: Author.

American Psychiatric Association, Guidelines Steering Committee and the Office of Research. (1993). *Development of a psychiatric practice research network: Overview of the purpose and a proposal approach.* Unpublished manuscript.

American Psychological Association, Division 12 (Clinical Psychology) Task Force on Promotion and Dissemination of Psychological Procedures. (1995). Training in dissemination of empirically-validated psychological treatments: Report and recommendations. *Clinical Psychologist, 48*, 3–23.

American Psychological Association Task Force on Psychological Intervention Guidelines. (1995). *Template for developing guidelines: Interventions for mental disorders and psychological aspects of physical disorders.* Washington, DC: American Psychological Association.

Aponte, H. J. (1981). Structural family therapy. In A. S. Gurman & D. P. Kniskern (Eds.), *Handbook of family therapy* (pp. 310–360). New York: Brunner/Mazel.

Arizona. (1998a). Arizona revised statutes Section 25-405 and Section 25-410 (authorizes and defines Family Court Advisors and Special Masters).

Arizona. (1998b). Arizona revised statutes, Sections 25-901 to 25-906 (authorizes and defines Covenant Marriages).

Arizona Dispute Resolution Association. (1996). *Rules for certification of mediators.* Phoenix: Author.

Babbie, E. (1995). *The practice of social research* (7th ed.). Belmont, CA: Wadsworth.

Bahr, S. (1981). An evaluation of court mediation: A comparison in divorce cases with children. *Journal of Family Issues, 2,* 39–60.

Bargh, J. A., Chaiken, S., Govender, R., & Pratto, F. (1992). The generality of the automatic attitude activation effect. *Journal of Personality and Social Psychology, 62,* 893–912.

Barlow, D. H. (1996). Health care policy, psychotherapy research, and the future of psychotherapy. *American Psychologist, 51,* 1050–1058.

Barsky, A., Este, D., & Collins, D. (1996). Cultural competence in family mediation. *Mediation Quarterly, 13,* 167–178.

Baucom, D. H., Shoham, V., Mueser, K. T., Daiuto, A. D., & Stickle, T. R. (1998). Empirically supported couple and family interventions for marital distress and adult mental health problems. *Journal of Consulting and Clinical Psychology, 66,* 53–88.

Bautz, B. J. (1988). Divorce mediation: For better or for worse? *Mediation Quarterly, 22,* 51–60.

Bautz, B. J., & Hill, R. M. (1989). Divorce mediation in New Hampshire: A voluntary concept. *Mediation Quarterly, 7,* 33–40.

Beck, C. J. A., & Sales, B. D. (2000). A critical reappraisal of family mediation. *Psychology, Public Policy, and Law, 6.*

Beck, C. J. A., Sales, B. D., & Benjamin, B. A. H. (1996). Lawyer distress: Alcohol-related problems and other psychological concerns among a sample of practicing lawyers. *Journal of Law and Health, 10,* 1–60.

Bell, C. R. (1962). Personality characteristics of volunteers for psychological studies. *British Journal of Social and Clinical Psychology, 1,* 81–95.

Benjamin, M., & Irving, H. H. (1992). Toward a feminist-informed model of therapeutic family mediation. *Mediation Quarterly, 10,* 129–154.

Benjamin, M., & Irving, H. H. (1995). Research in family mediation: Review and implications. *Mediation Quarterly, 13,* 53–82.

Bepko, C., & Krestan, J. (1985). *The responsibility trip: A blueprint for treating the alcoholic family.* New York: Free Press.

Bergin, A. E., & Garfield, S. L. (Eds.). (1994). *Handbook of psychotherapy and behavior change* (4th ed.). New York: Wiley.

Bernard, S. E., Folger, J. P., Weingarten, H. R., & Sumeta, Z. R. (1984). The neutral mediator: Value dilemmas in divorce mediation. *Mediation Quarterly, 4,* 61–74.

Beutler, L. E. (1983). *Eclectic psychotherapy: A systematic approach.* Elmsford, NY: Pergamon.

Beutler, L. E. (1998). Identifying empirically supported treatments: What if we didn't? *Journal of Consulting and Clinical Psychology, 66,* 113–120.

Beutler, L. E., & Clarkin, J. F. (1990). *Systematic treatment selection: Toward targeted therapeutic interventions.* New York: Brunner/Mazel.

Bickerdike, A. J. (1998). *Conflict resolution in divorce mediation: The impact of the divorce adjustment process and negotiation behaviour on mediation outcome.* Unpublished doctoral dissertation, La Trobe University, Bundoora, Victoria, Australia.

Bickerdike, A., & Littlefield, L. (in press). Divorce adjustment and mediation: Theoretically grounded process research. *Mediation Quarterly.*

Bienenfeld, F. (1983). *Child custody mediation.* Palo Alto, CA: Science & Behavior Books.

Black, M., & Joffee, W. (1978). A lawyer/therapist team approach to divorce. *Conciliation Courts Review, 16,* 1–5.

Bloom, B. L., Asher, S. J., & White, S. W. (1978). Marital disruption as a stressor: A review and analysis. *Psychological Bulletin, 85,* 867–894.

Bodin, A. M. (1981). The interactional view: Family therapy approaches of the Mental Health Institute. In A. S. Gurman & D. P. Kniskern (Eds.), *Handbook of family therapy* (pp. 267–309). New York: Brunner/Mazel.

Bordens, K. S., & Abbott, B. B. (1991). *Research design and methods: A process approach* (2nd ed.). Mountain View, CA: Mayfield.

Borkovec, T. D., & Castonguay, L. G. (1998). What is the scientific meaning of empirically supported therapy? *Journal of Consulting and Clinical Psychology, 66,* 136–142.

Bowlby, J. (1969). *Attachment and loss: Vol. 1. Attachment.* London: Hogarth Press.

Bowlby, J. (1973). *Attachment and loss: Vol. 2. Separation.* London: Hogarth Press.

Bowlby, J. (1979). *The making and breaking of affectional bonds.* London: Tavistock.

Bowlby, J. (1980). *Attachment and loss: Vol. 3. Loss.* London: Hogarth Press.

Braver, S. L., Fitzpatrick, P. J., & Bay, R. C. (1991). Noncustodial parent's report of child support payments. *Family Relations, 40,* 180–185.

Braver, S. L., Wolchik, S. A., Sandler, I. N., Fogas, B. S., & Zvetina, D. (1991). Frequency of visitation by divorced fathers: Differences in reports by fathers and mothers. *American Journal of Orthopsychiatry, 61,* 448–454.

Braver, S. L., Wolchik, S. A., Sandler, I. N., Sheets, V. L., Fogas, B. S., & Bay, R. C. (1993). A longitudinal study of noncustodial parents: Parents without children. *Journal of Family Psychology, 7,* 9–23.

Brodsky, S. L. (1990). Professional ethics and professional morality and the assessment of competence for execution: A response to Bonnie. *Law and Human Behavior, 14,* 91–97.

Brown, D. G. (1982). Divorce and family mediation: History, review, future directions. *Conciliation Courts Review, 20*(2), 1–44.

Brown, E. M. (1988). Divorce mediation in a mental health setting. In J. Folberg & A. Milne (Eds.), *Divorce mediation: Theory and practice* (pp. 127–141). New York: Guilford Press.

Bryan, P. E. (1992). Killing us softly: Divorce mediation and the politics of power. *Buffalo Law Review, 40,* 441–523.

Bryan, P. E. (1994, Summer). Reclaiming professionalism: The lawyer's role in divorce mediation. *Family Law Quarterly*, 177–222.

Burger, W. E. (1982). Isn't there a better way? *American Bar Association Journal*, 68, 274–277.

Bush, R. A. B. (1989). Defining quality in dispute resolution: Taxonomies and anti-taxonomies of quality arguments. *Denver University Law Review*, 66, 335–380.

Bush, R. A. B., & Folger, J. P. (1994). *The promise of mediation: Responding to conflict through empowerment and recognition*. San Francisco: Jossey-Bass.

California. (1999). California Family Code, Chapter 11, Article 2, Section 3170(a).

Campbell, L. E. G., & Johnston, J. R. (1986). Impasse-directed mediation with high conflict families in custody disputes. *Behavioral Sciences and the Law*, 4, 217–241.

Camplair, C. W., & Stolberg, A. L. (1990). Benefits of court sponsored divorce mediation: A study of outcomes and influences on success. *Mediation Quarterly*, 7, 199–213.

Cauble, A. E., Thoennes, N., Pearson, J., & Appleford, R. (1985). A case study: Custody resolution counseling in Hennepin County, Minnesota. *Conciliation Courts Review*, 23(2), 27–35.

Cavanaugh, R. C., & Rhode, D. L. (1976). Project: The unauthorized practice of law and pro se divorce: An empirical analysis. *Yale Law Journal*, 86, 104–184.

Chambless, D. L. (1996). In defense of dissemination of empirically supported psychological interventions. *Clinical Psychology: Science and Practice*, 3, 230–235.

Chambless, D. L., & Hollon, S. D. (1998). Defining empirically supported therapies. *Journal of Consulting and Clinical Psychology*, 66, 7–18.

Chambless, D. L., Sanderson, W. C., Shoham, V., Johnson, S. B., Pope, K. S., Crits-Christoph, P., Baker, M., Johnson, B., Woody, S. R., Sue, S., Beutler, L., Williams, D. A., & McCurry, S. (1996). An update on empirically validated therapies. *Clinical Psychologist*, 49, 5–14.

Christensen, A. (1987). Detection of conflict patterns in couples. In K. Hahlweg & M. J. Goldstein (Eds.), *Understanding major mental disorders: The contribution of family interaction research* (pp. 250–265). New York: Family Process Press.

Christensen, A. (1988). Dysfunctional interaction patterns in couples. In P. Noller & M. A. Fitzpatrick (Eds.), *Perspectives on marital interaction* (pp. 31–52). Clevedon, England: Multilingual Matters.

Clement, J. A., & Schwebel, A. I. (1993). A research agenda for divorce mediation: The creation of second order knowledge to inform legal policy. *Ohio State Journal on Dispute Resolution*, 9, 95–113.

Cobb, S. (1993, July). Empowerment and mediation: A narrative perspective. *Negotiation Journal*, 245–259.

Cobb, S. (1994a). A narrative perspective on mediation: Toward the materialization of the "storytelling" metaphor. In J. P. Folger & T. S. Jones (Eds.), *New directions in mediation: Communication research and perspectives* (pp. 48–63). Thousand Oaks, CA: Sage.

Cobb, S. (1994b). "Theories of responsibility": The social construction of intentions in mediation. *Discourse Processes, 18*, 165–186.

Cobb, S. (1997). The domestication of violence in mediation. *Law & Society Review, 31*, 397–440.

Cobb, S., & Rifkin, J. (1991a). Neutrality as a discursive practice: The construction and transformation of narratives in community mediation. *Studies in Law, Politics and Society, 11*, 69–91.

Cobb, S., & Rifkin, J. (1991b). Practice and paradox: Deconstructing neutrality in mediation. *Law and Social Inquiry, 16*(1), 35–62.

Coconino County, Arizona. (1996). *Rule XX, Local Rule of Practice, and Rule 53, Rules of Civil Procedure* (authorizes and defines special master program).

Cohen, I. (1998). Postdecree litigation: Is joint custody to blame? *Family and Conciliation Courts Review, 36*(1), 41–53.

Cohen, S. (1982). *The diversion study: A preliminary report* [Unpublished report]. Oregon City, OR: Clackamas Circuit Court.

Cohen, S. (1988). *Statistical power analysis in the behavioral sciences* (2nd ed.). Hillsdale, NJ: Erlbaum.

Colorado Revised Statutes. (1998). C.R.S. 13-22-311 and C.R.S. 14-10-124(8).

Conley, J. M., & O'Barr, W. M. (1990). *Rules versus relationships: The ethnography of legal discourse.* Chicago: University of Chicago Press.

Coogler, O. J. (1978). *Structured mediation in divorce settlement: A handbook for marital mediators.* Lexington, MA: D.C. Heath.

Corcoran, K., & Melamed, J. (1990). From coercion to empowerment: Spousal abuse and mediation. *Mediation Quarterly, 7*, 303–316.

Coulson, R. (1969). Family arbitration—An exercise in sensitivity. *Family Law Quarterly, 3*, 22–30.

Coulson, R. (1983). *Fighting fair: Family mediation will work for you.* New York: Free Press.

Coulson, R. (1996). *Family mediation: Managing conflict, resolving disputes* (2nd ed.). San Francisco: Jossey-Bass.

Cox, S., & Dwyer, M. (1987). *Self-help law: Its many perspectives* (Research report prepared for the American Bar Association, Chicago). Chicago: American Bar Association.

Crits-Christoph, P., & Mintz, J. (1991). Implications of therapist effects for the design and analysis of comparative studies of psychotherapies. *Journal of Consulting and Clinical Psychology, 59*, 20–26.

Danzig, R. (1973). Toward the creation of a complementary, decentralized system of criminal justice. *Stanford Law Review, 26*, 1–54.

Davis, G., & Roberts, M. (1988). *Access to agreement.* Milton Keyes, UK: Open University Press.

Davison, G. C., & Lazarus, A. A. (1995). The dialectics of science and practice. In S. C. Hayes, V. M. Follette, R. M. Dawes, & K. E. Grady (Eds.), *Scientific standards of psychological practice: Issues and recommendations* (pp. 95–120). Reno, NV: Context Press.

Depner, C. E., Cannata, K., & Ricci, I. (1995). Report 4: Mediated agreements on child custody and visitation: 1991 California Family Court Services Snapshot Study. *Family and Conciliation Courts Review, 33,* 87–109.

Depner, C., Cannata, K. B., & Simon, M. B. (1992). Building a uniform statistical reporting system: A snapshot of California Family Court Services. *Family and Conciliation Courts Review, 30,* 185–206.

Derogatis, L. (1977). *The SCL–90 Manual I: Scoring, administration, scoring and procedures for the SCL–90.* Baltimore: John Hopkins School of Medicine, Clinical Psychometric Research Unit.

Deutsch, M. (1969). Conflicts: Productive and destructive. *Journal of Social Issues, 25,* 7–41.

Deutsch, M. (1973). *The resolution of conflict.* New Haven, CT: Yale University Press.

Deutsch, M. (1985). *Distributive justice.* New Haven, CT: Yale University Press.

Diez, M. (1984). Communicative competence: An interactive approach. In R. Bostrom (Ed.), *Communication yearbook* (Vol. 8, pp. 56–79). Beverly Hills, CA: Sage.

Diez, M. (1986). Negotiation competence: A conceptualization of the rules of negotiation interaction. In D. Ellis & W. Donohue (Eds.), *Contemporary issues in language and discourse processes* (pp. 223–237). Hillsdale, NJ: Erlbaum.

Dillon, P. A., & Emery, R. E. (1996). Divorce mediation and resolution of child custody disputes: Long-term effects. *American Journal of Orthopsychiatry, 66,* 131–140.

Dingwall, R. (1988). Empowerment or enforcement? Some questions about power and control in divorce mediation. In R. Dingwall & J. M. Eekelaar (Eds.), *Divorce, mediation and the legal process* (pp. 150–167). Oxford, England: Clarendon.

Dingwall, R., & Eekelaar, J. (1988). A wider vision. In R. Dingwall & J. Eekelaar (Eds.), *Divorce mediation and the legal process* (pp. 168–182). Oxford, England: Clarendon.

Dingwall, R., & Greatbatch, D. (1991). Behind closed doors: A preliminary report on mediator/client interaction in England. *Family and Conciliation Courts Review, 29,* 291–303.

Dobson, K. S. (1989). A meta-analysis of the efficacy of cognitive therapy for depression. *Journal of Consulting and Clinical Psychology, 57,* 414–419.

Doherty, W. J., Boss, P. G., LaRossa, R., Schumm, W. R., & Steinmetz, S. K. (1993). Family theories and methods: A contextual approach. In P. G. Boss, W. J. Doherty, R. LaRossa, W. R. Schumm, & S. K. Steinmetz (Eds.), *Sourcebook of family theories and methods: A contextual approach* (pp. 3–30). New York: Plenum.

Donohue, W. A. (1991). *Communication, marital dispute and divorce mediation*. Hillsdale, NJ: Erlbaum.

Donohue, W. A., Allen, M., & Burrell, N. (1985). Communication strategies in mediation. *Mediation Quarterly, 10*, 75–89.

Donohue, W. A., Drake, L., & Roberto, A. J. (1994). Mediator issue intervention strategies: A replication and some conclusions. *Mediation Quarterly, 11*, 261–274.

Donohue, W. A., Lyles, J., & Rogan, R. (1989). Issue development in divorce mediation. *Mediation Quarterly, 24*, 19–28.

Donohue, W. A., & Weider-Hatfield, D. (1988). Communication strategies. In J. Folberg & A. Milne (Eds.), *Divorce mediation: Theory and practice* (pp. 297–315). New York: Guilford Press.

Downing, J. W., Judd, C. W., & Brauer, M. (1992). Effects of repeated expressions on attitude extremity. *Journal of Personality and Social Psychology, 63*, 17–29.

Doyle, P. M., & Caron, W. A. (1979). Contested custody intervention: An empirical assessment. In D. H. Olson, M. Cleveland, P. Doyle, M. F. Rockcastle, B. Robinson, R. Reimer, J. Minton, W. Caron, & S. Cohen (Eds.), *Child custody: Literature review and alternative approaches* (Monograph for the McKnight Foundation, pp. 137–190). St. Paul, MN: Hennepin County Domestic Relations Division.

Dukes, F. (1993, January). Public conflict resolution: A transformative approach. *Negotiation Journal*, 45–57.

Duryee, M. A. (1995). Guidelines for family court services intervention when there are allegations of domestic violence. *Family and Conciliation Courts Review, 33*, 79–86.

Dutton, D. G., & Browning, J. J. (1988). Concern for power, fear of intimacy, and aversive stimuli for wife assault. In G. Hotaling, D. Finkelhor, J. T. Kirkpatrick, & M. A. Straus (Eds.), *Family abuse and its consequences: New directions in research* (pp. 163–175). Newbury Park, CA: Sage.

D'Zurrilla, T., & Goldfried, M. (1971). Problem solving and behavior modification. *Journal of Abnormal Psychology, 78*, 107–126.

Elkin, I., Shea, M. T., Watkins, J. T., Imber, S. D., Sotsky, S. M., Collins, J. F., Glass, D. R., Pilkonis, P. A., Leber, W. R., Docherty, J. P., Fiester, S. J., & Parloff, M. B. (1989). National Institute of Mental Health treatment of depression collaborative research program: General effectiveness of treatments. *Archives of General Psychiatry, 46*, 971–982.

Ellis, D. (1987). Post-separation woman abuse: The contribution of lawyers as "barracudas," "advocates," and "counselors." *International Journal of Law and Psychiatry, 10*, 403–411.

Ellis, D. (1990). Marital conflict mediation and post-separation wife abuse. *Law and Inequality Journal, 8*, 317–339.

Ellis, D., Ryan, J., & Choi, A. (1988). *Lawyers, mediators and the quality of life among separated and divorced women* (Report No. 25). North York, Ontario,

Canada: York University, LaMarsh Research Programme on Violence and Conflict Resolution.

Elson, H. M. (1988). Divorce mediation in a law office setting. In J. Folberg & A. Milne (Eds.), *Divorce mediation: Theory and practice* (pp. 143–162). New York: Guilford Press.

Emery, R. E. (1990). Divorce mediation: A practice in search of a theory [Review of the book *Divorce mediation: Theory and practice*]. *Contemporary Psychology, 35*, 373–374.

Emery, R. E. (1994). *Renegotiating family relationships: Divorce, child custody, and mediation.* New York: Guilford Press.

Emery, R. E., & Jackson, J. A. (1989). The Charlottesville Mediation Project: Mediated and litigated child custody disputes. *Mediation Quarterly, 24*, 3–18.

Emery, R. E., Matthews, S. G., & Kitzmann, K. M. (1991). Child custody mediation and litigation: Parents' satisfaction one year after settlement. *Journal of Consulting and Clinical Psychology, 62*, 124–129.

Emery, R. E., Matthews, S. G., & Wyer, M. M. (1991). Child custody mediation and litigation: Further evidence on the differing views of mothers and fathers. *Journal of Consulting and Clinical Psychology, 59*, 410–418.

Emery, R. E., Shaw, D. S., & Jackson, J. A. (1987). A clinical description of a model of child custody mediation. In J. P. Vincent (Vol. Ed.), *Advances in family intervention, assessment, and theory* (Vol. 4, pp. 309–333). Greenwich, CT: JAI Press.

Emery, R. E., & Wyer, M. M. (1987a). Child custody mediation and litigation: An experimental evaluation of the experience of parents. *Journal of Consulting and Clinical Psychology, 55*, 179–186.

Emery, R. E., & Wyer, M. M. (1987b). Divorce mediation. *American Psychologist, 42*, 472–480.

Engram, P. S., & Markowitz, J. R. (1985). Ethical issues in mediation. *Mediation Quarterly, 8*, 19–32.

Erickson, S. K., & McKnight, M. S. (1990). Mediating spousal abuse divorces. *Mediation Quarterly, 7*, 377–388.

Esser, J. (1989). Evaluations of dispute processing: We do not know what we think and we do not think what we know. *Denver University Law Review, 66*, 499–562.

Fairburn, C. G., Jones, R., Peveler, R. C., Hope, R. A., & O'Connor, M. (1993). Psychotherapy and bulimia nervosa: Longer-term effects of interpersonal therapy. *Archives of General Psychiatry, 50*, 419–428.

Fazio, R. H. (1986). How do attitudes guide behavior? In R. M. Sorrentino & E. T. Higgins (Eds.), *Handbook of motivation and cognition: Foundations of social behavior* (pp. 204–243). New York: Guilford Press.

Feer, M. (1992). On "Toward a New Discourse for Mediation: A Critique of Neutrality." *Mediation Quarterly, 10*, 173–177.

Felstiner, W. F. (1974). Influences of social organization on dispute processing. *Law & Society Review, 9*, 63–94.

Felstiner, W. F. (1975). Avoidance as dispute processing: An elaboration. *Law & Society Review, 10*, 695–706.

Felstiner, W. L. F., & Sarat, A. (1992). Symposium: Enactments of power: Negotiating reality and responsibility in lawyer–client interactions. *Cornell Law Review, 77*, 1447–1498.

Felstiner, W. L. F., & Williams, L. A. (1978). Mediation as an alternative to criminal prosecution: Ideology and limitations. *Law and Human Behavior, 2*, 223–244.

Felstiner, W. L. F., & Williams, L. A. (1980). *Community mediation in Dorchester, Massachusetts*. Washington, DC: U.S. Department of Justice, National Institute of Justice.

Fensterheim, H., & Raw, S. D. (1996). Empirically validated treatments, psychotherapy integration, and the politics of psychotherapy. *Journal of Psychotherapy Integration, 6*(3), 207–215.

Fineman, M. (1988). Dominant discourse, professional language, and legal change in child custody decision making. *Harvard Law Review, 101*, 727–774.

Finkel, N. J. (1995). *Commonsense justice: Jurors' notions of the law*. Cambridge, MA: Harvard University Press.

Fisch, R., Weakland, J. H., & Segal, L. (1982). *The tactics of change*. San Francisco: Jossey-Bass.

Fischer, K., Vidmar, N., & Ellis, R. (1993). The culture of battering and the role of mediation in domestic violence cases. *Southern Methodist University Law Review, 46*, 2117–2174.

Fisher, L. (1995). An empirically derived typology of families: I. Relationships and adult health. *Family Process, 34*, 161–182.

Fisher, R., & Ury, W. (1981). *Getting to yes: Negotiating agreement without giving in*. Boston: Houghton Mufflin.

Fisher, R., Ury, W., & Patton, B. (1991). *Getting to yes: Negotiating agreement without giving in* (2nd ed.). New York: Penguin.

Fitzpatrick, M. A. (1988). *Between husbands and wives: Communication in marriage*. Newbury Park, CA: Sage.

Fix, M., & Harter, P. (1992). *Hard cases, vulnerable people: An analysis of mediation programs at the multi-door courthouse of the Superior Court of the District of Columbia*. Washington, DC: The Urban Institute, State Justice Institute.

Fleischer, J. M. (1996). Directing and administrating a mediation program: The transformative approach. *Mediation Quarterly, 13*, 295–304.

Fleuridas, C., Nelson, T., & Rosenthal, C. (1986). The evolution of circular questions. *Journal of Marriage and Family Therapy, 12*, 113–127.

Folberg, H. J. (1974). Facilitation agreement: The role of counseling in the courts. *Conciliation Courts Review, 12*, 17–20.

Folberg, J. (1983). A mediation overview: History and dimensions of practice. *Mediation Quarterly, 1*, 3–13.

Folberg, J., & Milne, A. (1988). *Divorce mediation: Theory and practice*. New York: Guilford Press.

Folberg, J., & Taylor, A. (1984). *Mediation: A comprehensive guide to resolving conflicts without litigation*. San Francisco: Jossey-Bass.

Folger, J. P., & Bernard, S. E. (1985). Divorce mediation: When mediators challenge divorcing parties. *Mediation Quarterly, 10*, 5–23.

Folger, J. P., & Bush, R. A. B. (1994). Ideology, orientations to conflict, and mediation discourse. In J. P. Folger & T. S. Jones (Eds.), *New directions in mediation: Communication research and perspectives* (pp. 3–25). Thousand Oaks, CA: Sage.

Folger, J. P., & Jones, T. S. (1994). *New directions in mediation: Communication research and perspectives*. Thousand Oaks, CA: Sage.

Forester, J., & Stitzel, D. (1989, July). Beyond neutrality: The possibilities of activist mediation in public sector conflicts. *Negotiation Journal*, 251–264.

Forscher, B. K. (1963). Chaos in the brickyard. *Science, 42*, 591–598.

Foster, H. H., & Freed, D. J. (1973). Divorce reform: Breaks on breakdown. *Journal of Family Law, 74*, 443–493.

Fowers, B. J. (1996). Predicting marital success for premarital couple types based on PREPARE. *Journal of Marital and Family Therapy, 22*, 103–119.

Franz, P. L. (1998). Habits of highly effective transformative mediation programs. *Ohio State Journal on Dispute Resolution, 13*, 1039–1070.

French, J., & Raven, B. (1959). The bases of social power. In D. Cartwright (Ed.), *Studies in social power* (pp. 150–167). Ann Arbor: University of Michigan Press.

Fuller, L. L. (1970). Mediation—Its forms and functions. *Southern California Law Review, 44*, 305–339.

Fuller, L. L. (1978). The forms and limits of adjudication. *Harvard Law Review, 92*, 353–409.

Fuller, R. M., Kimsey, W. D., & McKinney, G. C. (1992). Mediator neutrality and storytelling order. *Mediation Quarterly, 10*, 187–192.

Gaffan, E. A., Tsaousis, I., & Kemp-Wheeler, S. M. (1995). Researcher allegiance and meta-analysis: The case of cognitive therapy for depression. *Journal of Consulting and Clinical Psychology, 63*, 966–980.

Garfield, S. (1998). Some comments on empirically supported treatments. *Journal of Consulting and Clinical Psychology, 66*, 121–125.

Gerber, R. J. (1990). Recommendation on domestic relations reform. *Arizona Law Review, 32*, 9–19.

Gilligan, C. (1982). *In a different voice: Psychological theory and women's development*. Cambridge, MA: Harvard University Press.

Girdner, L. K. (1990). Mediation triage: Screening for spouse abuse in divorce mediation. *Mediation Quarterly, 7*, 365–376.

Goerdt, J. A. (1992). *Divorce courts: Case management, case characteristics, and the pace of litigation in 16 urban jurisdictions.* Williamsburg, VA: National Center for State Courts/State Justice Institute.

Goldfried, M. R., & Wolfe, B. E. (1998). Toward a more clinically valid approach to therapy research. *Journal of Consulting and Clinical Psychology, 66,* 143–150.

Goldschmidt, J. (1997, May). *How are judges and courts coping with pro se litigants?: Results from a survey of judges and court managers.* Paper presented at the Annual Meeting of the Law and Society Association, St. Louis, MO.

Gottman, J. M. (1993). The roles of conflict engagement, escalation, and avoidance in marital interaction: A longitudinal view of five types of couples. *Journal of Consulting and Clinical Psychology, 61,* 6–15.

Gottman, J. M. (1994). *What predicts divorce? The relationship between marital process and marital outcomes.* Hillsdale, NJ: Erlbaum.

Gottman, J. M., & Krokoff, L. J. (1989). The relationship between marital interaction and marital satisfaction: A longitudinal view. *Journal of Consulting and Clinical Psychology, 53,* 151–160.

Gray, B. (1994). The gender-based foundations of negotiation theory. *Research on Negotiations in Organizations, 4,* 3–36.

Greatbatch, D., & Dingwall, R. (1989). Selective facilitation: Some preliminary observations on a strategy used by divorce mediators. *Law & Society Review, 23,* 613–641.

Grebe, S. C. (1987). The rules of structured mediation. *Conciliation Courts Review, 25,* 37–51.

Grebe, S. C. (1988). Structured mediation and its variants: What makes it unique. In J. Folberg & A. Milne (Eds.), *Divorce mediation: Theory and practice* (pp. 225–248). New York: Guilford Press.

Griffiths, J. (1986). What do Dutch lawyers actually do in divorce cases? *Law & Society Review, 10,* 135–175.

Grillo, T. (1991). The mediation alternative: Process dangers for women. *Yale Law Journal, 100,* 1545–1610.

Gutek, B. A. (1978). Strategies for studying client satisfaction. *Journal of Social Issues, 34*(4), 44–56.

Haynes, J. (1988). Power balancing. In J. Folberg & A. Milne (Eds.), *Divorce mediation: Theory and practice* (pp. 277–296). New York: Guilford Press.

Haynes, J. (1994). *The fundamentals of family mediation.* Albany: State University of New York Press.

Haynes, J., & Haynes, G. (1989). *Mediating divorce.* San Francisco: Jossey-Bass.

Haynes, J. M. (1981). *Divorce mediation: A practical guide for therapists and counselors.* New York: Springer.

Haynes, J. M., & Charlesworth, S. (1996). *The fundamentals of family mediation.* Sidney, Australia: Federation Press.

Heatherington, E. M. (1993). An overview of the Virginia longitudinal study of divorce and remarriage with a focus on early adolescence. *Journal of Family Psychology, 7,* 39–56.

Heister, J. W. (1985). Sequential mediation: A necessary therapeutic intervention technique. *Mediation Quarterly, 9*, 57–61.

Henry, W. P., Strupp, H. H., Butler, S. F., Schacht, T. E., & Binder, J. L. (1993). Effects of training in time-limited dynamic psychotherapy: Changes in therapist behavior. *Journal of Consulting and Clinical Psychology, 61*, 434–440.

Hensler, D. (1986). What we know and don't know about court administered arbitration. *Judicature, 69*, 270–278.

Hensler, D., Lipson, A., & Rolph, E. (1981). *Judicial arbitration in California: The first year*. Santa Monica, CA: RAND Institute for Civil Justice.

Hill, R., & Hansen, D. (1960). The identification of conceptual frameworks utilized in family study. *Marriage and Family Living, 22*, 299–311.

Hollon, S. D. (1996). The efficacy and effectiveness of psychotherapy relative to medications. *American Psychologist, 51*, 1025–1030.

Hollon, S. D., & Beck, A. T. (1994). Cognitive and cognitive–behavioral therapies. In A. E. Bergin & S. L. Garfield (Eds.), *Handbook of psychotherapy and behavior change* (pp. 428–466). New York: Wiley.

Holtzworth-Munroe, A., Smutzler, N., & Stuart, G. L. (1998). Demand and withdraw communication among couples experiencing husband violence. *Journal of Consulting and Clinical Psychology, 66*, 731–743.

House, E. R. (1980). *Evaluating with validity*. Beverly Hills, CA: Sage.

Howard, K., Kopta, S., Krause, M., & Orlinsky, D. (1986). The dose–effect relationship in psychotherapy. *American Psychologist, 41*, 159–164.

Illinois (1999). Chapter 750, Part IV (750 ILCS 5/404).

Irving, H. H., & Benjamin, M. (1983). Outcome effectiveness of conciliation counseling: An empirical study. *Conciliation Courts Review, 21*, 61–70.

Irving, H. H., & Benjamin, M. (1989). Therapeutic family mediation: Fitting the service to the interactional diversity of client couples. *Mediation Quarterly, 7*, 115–131.

Irving, H. H., & Benjamin, M. (1992). An evaluation of process and outcome in a private family mediation service. *Mediation Quarterly, 10*, 35–55.

Irving, H. H., & Benjamin, M. (1995). *Family mediation: Contemporary issues*. Thousand Oaks, CA: Sage.

Irving, H. H., Benjamin, M., Bohm, P. E., & Macdonald, G. (1981). A study of conciliation counseling in the Family Court of Toronto: Implications for socio-legal practice. In H. H. Irving (Ed.), *Family law: An interdisciplinary perspective* (pp. 41–70). Toronto, Canada: The Carswell Company, Ltd.

Irving, H. H., Bohm, P., Macdonald, G., & Benjamin, M. (1979). *A comparative analysis of two family court services: An exploratory study of conciliation counseling*. Toronto, Ontario, Canada: Welfare Grants Directorate, Department of National Health and Welfare, and the Ontario Ministry of the Attorney General.

Irving, H. H., & Irving, B. G. (1974). Conciliation counseling in divorce litigation. *Reports of Family Law, 16*, 257–266.

Isaacs, M. B., Montalvo, B., & Abelsohn, D. (1986). *The difficult divorce: Therapy for children and families.* New York: Basic Books.

Jacobson, N. S., & Addis, M. E. (1993). Research on couples and couple therapy: What do we know? Where are we going? *Journal of Consulting and Clinical Psychology, 61,* 85–93.

Jacobson, N. S., & Christensen, A. (1996). Studying the effectiveness of psychotherapy: How well can clinical trials do the job? *American Psychologist, 51,* 1031–1039.

Jacobson, N. S., Schmaling, K. B., & Holtzworth-Munroe, A. (1987). Component analysis of behavioral marital therapy: Two-year followup and prediction of relapse. *Journal of Marital and Family Therapy, 13,* 187–195.

Johnson, M. P. (1995). Patriarchal terrorism and common couple violence: Two forms of violence against women. *Journal of Marriage and the Family, 57,* 283–294.

Johnston, J. R., & Campbell, L. E. (1987). On-going postdivorce conflict and child disturbance. *Journal of Abnormal Child Psychology, 15,* 493–509.

Johnston, J. R., & Campbell, L. E. (1988). *Impasses of divorce: The dynamics and resolution of family conflict.* New York: Free Press.

Johnston, J. R., Campbell, L. E. G., & Tall, M. C. (1985). Impasses to the resolution of custody and visitation disputes. *Journal of Orthopsychiatry, 55,* 112–129.

Jones, T. S. (1985). "Breaking up is hard to do": An exploratory investigation of communication behaviors and phases in child-custody divorce mediation: Vol. I (Doctoral dissertation, Ohio State University, 1985). *Dissertation Abstracts International, 46*(12-A, Pt. 1), 3533.

Jones, T. S. (1988). Phase structures in agreement and no-agreement mediation. *Communication Research, 15,* 470–495.

Jones, T. S. (1994). A dialectical reframing of the mediation process. In J. P. Folger & T. S. Jones (Eds.), *New directions in mediation: Communication research and perspectives* (pp. 26–47). Thousand Oaks, CA: Sage.

Judd, C. M., Drake, R. A., Downing, J. W., & Krosnick, J. A. (1991). Some dynamic properties of attitude structures: Context-induced response facilitation and polarization. *Journal of Personality and Social Psychology, 60,* 193–202.

Jung, J. (1971). *The experimenters' dilemma.* New York: Harper & Row.

Kallner, R. (1977). Boundaries of the divorce lawyer's role. *Family Law Quarterly, 10,* 289–398.

Kandel, R. F. (1994). Power plays: A sociolinguistic study of inequality in child custody mediation and a hearsay analog solution. *Arizona Law Review, 36,* 879–972.

Kansas. (1999). Chapter 23, Article 6 (K.S.A. Sec. 23–601–607; Sec. 23–605 as amended by Kan. HB 2150, 1999).

Kazdin, A. E. (1994). Methodology, design, and evaluation in psychotherapy research. In A. E. Bergin & S. L. Garfield (Eds.), *Handbook of psychotherapy and behavior change* (4th ed., pp. 19–71). New York: Wiley.

Kazdin, A. E. (1998). *Methodological issues and strategies in clinical research* (2nd ed.). Washington, DC: American Psychological Association.

Keilitz, S. L., Daley, H. W. K., & Hanson, R. A. (1992). *Multi-state assessment of divorce mediation and traditional court processing* (Paper prepared for the National Center for State Courts). Alexandria, VA: State Justice Institute.

Kelly, J. B. (1983). Mediation and psychotherapy: Distinguishing the differences. *Mediation Quarterly, 1,* 33–44.

Kelly, J. B. (1989). Mediated and adversarial divorce: Respondents' perceptions of their processes and outcomes. *Mediation Quarterly, 24,* 71–88.

Kelly, J. B. (1990a). Is mediation less expensive? Comparison of mediated and adversarial divorce costs. *Mediation Quarterly, 8,* 15–25.

Kelly, J. B. (1990b). *Mediated and adversarial divorce resolution processes: An analysis of post-divorce outcomes* (Final report prepared for the Fund for Research in Dispute Resolution). Washington, DC: Fund for Research in Dispute Resolution.

Kelly, J. B. (1991). Parent interaction after divorce: Comparison of mediated and adversarial divorce processes. *Behavioral Sciences and the Law, 9,* 387–398.

Kelly, J. B. (1993). Current research on children's postdivorce adjustment: No simple answers. *Family and Conciliation Courts Review, 31,* 29–49.

Kelly, J. B. (1995). Power imbalance in divorce and interpersonal mediation: Assessment and intervention. *Mediation Quarterly, 13,* 83–98.

Kelly, J. B. (1996). A decade of divorce mediation research: Some answers and questions. *Family and Conciliation Courts Review, 34,* 373–385.

Kelly, J. B., & Duryee, M. A. (1992). Women's and men's views of mediation in voluntary and mandatory mediation settings. *Family and Conciliation Courts Review, 30,* 34–49.

Kelly, J. B., & Gigy, L. L. (1989). Divorce mediation: Characteristics of clients and outcomes. In K. Kressel, D. G. Pruitt, & Associates (Eds.), *Mediation research* (pp. 263–283). San Francisco: Jossey-Bass.

Kelly, J. B., Gigy, L., & Hausman, S. (1988). Mediated and adversarial divorce: Initial findings from a longitudinal study. In J. Folberg & A. Milne (Eds.), *Divorce mediation: Theory and practice* (pp. 453–474). New York: Guilford Press.

Kelly, J. B., Zlatchin, C., & Shawn, J. (1985). Divorce mediation: Process, prospects, and professional issues. In C. P. Ewing (Ed.), *Psychology, psychiatry, and the law: A clinical and forensic handbook* (pp. 243–279). Sarasota, FL: Professional Resource Exchange.

Kendall, P. C. (1998). Empirically supported psychological therapies. *Journal of Consulting and Clinical Psychology, 66,* 3–6.

Kendall, P. C., & Chambless, D. L. (Eds.). (1998). Empirically supported psychological therapies [Special issue]. *Journal of Consulting and Clinical Psychology, 66*(1).

Kenney, L. M., & Vigil, D. (1998). A lawyer's guide to therapeutic interventions in domestic relations court. *Arizona State Law Journal, 28,* 629–671.

Kerbeshian, L. A. (1994). ADR: To be or . . .? *North Dakota Law Review, 70,* 381–434.

Kidder, L. H., Judd, C. M., & Smith, E. R. (1986). *Research methods in social relations* (5th ed.). New York: Holt, Rinehart & Winston.

Kitzmann, K. M., & Emery, R. E. (1993). Procedural justice and parents' satisfaction in a field study of child custody dispute resolution. *Law and Human Behavior, 17,* 553–567.

Kitzmann, K. M., & Emery, R. E. (1994). Child and family coping one year after mediated and litigated child custody disputes. *Journal of Family Psychology, 8,* 150–159.

Klein, D. M., & Jurich, J. A. (1993). Metatheory and family studies. In P. G. Boss, W. J. Doherty, R. LaRossa, W. R. Schumm, & S. K. Steinmetz (Eds.), *Sourcebook of family theories and methods: A contextual approach* (pp. 31–66). New York: Plenum.

Klein, D. M., & White, J. M. (1996). *Family theories: An introduction.* Thousand Oaks, CA: Sage.

Kolb, D. M. (1995, October). The love for three oranges or: What did we miss about Ms. Follett in the library? *Negotiation Journal,* 339–348.

Kolb, D. M., & Kressel, K. (1994). Practical realities in making talk work. In D. M. Kolb (Ed.), *When talk works: Profiles of working mediators* (pp. 459–493). San Francisco: Jossey-Bass.

Kovach, K. K. (1994). *Mediation: Principles and practice.* St. Paul, MN: West.

Kramer, R. M. (1994, October). Integrative complexity and conflict theory: Evidence of an emerging paradigm [Review of the books: *Hidden conflict in organizations: Uncovering behind-the-scenes disputes, Negotiation in social conflict,* and *Organizational justice: The search for fairness in the workplace*]. *Negotiation Journal,* 347–357.

Kraus, S. J. (1995). Attitudes and the prediction of behavior: A meta-analysis of the empirical literature. *Personality and Social Psychology Bulletin, 21,* 58–75.

Krauss, D. A., & Sales, B. D. (2000). The best interest of the child standard and the role of psychologists in the resolution of contested child custody cases. *Psychology, Public Policy, and Law, 6.*

Kressel, K. (1985). *The process of divorce: How professionals and couples negotiate settlements.* New York: Basic Books.

Kressel, K., Frontera, E. A., Florenza, S., Butler, F., & Fish, L. (1994). The settlement-orientation vs. the problem-solving style in custody mediation. *Journal of Social Issues, 50,* 67–84.

Kressel, K., & Hochberg, A. M. (1987). Divorce attorneys: Assessment of a typology and attitudes towards legal reform. *Journal of Divorce, 10*(3/4), 1–14.

Kressel, K., Jaffee, N., Tuchman, B., Watson, C., & Deutsch, M. (1980). A typology of divorcing couples: Implications for mediation and the divorce process. *Family Process, 19,* 101–116.

Kressel, K., Pruitt, D. G., & Associates. (Eds.). (1989). *Mediation research: The process and effectiveness of third-party intervention*. San Francisco: Jossey-Bass.

Krokoff, L. J., Gottman, J. M., & Haas, S. D. (1989). Validation of a global rapid couples interaction scoring system. *Behavioral Assessment, 11*, 65–79.

Kubler-Ross, E. (1969). *On death and dying*. New York: Macmillan.

Landau, B. (1995). The Toronto Forum on Women Abuse: The process and the outcome. *Family and Conciliation Courts Review, 33*(1), 63–78.

Lasagna, L., & von Felsinger, J. M. (1954). The volunteer subject in research. *Science, 120*, 359–461.

Lavee, Y. (1993). Seven types of marriage: Empirical typology based on ENRICH. *Journal of Marital and Family Therapy, 19*, 325–340.

Lawyers see rise in anger of parties in domestic disputes. (1996, May 8). *Los Angeles Daily Journal*, p. 1.

Leick, C. (1989). Guidelines for mediator/attorney cooperation. *Mediation Quarterly, 23*, 37–52.

Leitch, M. L. (1986/1987). The politics of compromise: A feminist perspective on mediation. *Mediation Quarterly, 14/15*, 163–175.

Lemon, J. A. (1985). *Family mediation practice*. New York: Free Press.

Lerman, L. G. (1984). Mediation of wife abuse cases: The adverse impact of informal dispute resolution on women. *Harvard Women's Law Review, 7*, 57–113.

Levinger, G., & Rubin, J. Z. (1994, July). Bridges and barriers to a more general theory of conflict. *Negotiation Journal*, 201–215.

Levy, R. J. (1984). Comment on the Pearson–Thoennes study and on mediation. *Family Law Quarterly, XVII*, 525–533.

Lind, E. A., & Tyler, T. R. (1988). *The social psychology of procedural justice*. New York: Plenum.

Little, M., Thoennes, N., Pearson, J., & Appleford, R. (1985). A case study: The custody mediation services of the Los Angeles Conciliation Court. *Conciliation Courts Review, 23*(2), 1–13.

Lloyd, S. A. (1990). Conflict types and strategies in violent marriages. *Journal of Family Violence, 5*, 269–284.

Louisiana. (1999). Title 9, Code Book I, Code Title V, Chapter 1, Part IV (La. R.S. 9:363).

Lowry, K. (1993). Evaluation of community-justice programs. In S. E. Merry & N. Milner (Eds.), *The possibility of popular justice: A case study of community mediation in the United States* (pp. 89–122). Ann Arbor: University of Michigan Press.

Luban, D. (1989). The quality of justice. *Denver University Law Review, 66*, 381–417.

Lyon, M., Thoennes, N., Pearson, J., & Appleford, R. (1985). A case study: The custody mediation services of the Family Division, Connecticut Superior Court. *Conciliation Courts Review, 23*(2), 15–26.

Maccoby, E. E., Buchanan, C. M., Mnookin, R. H., & Dornbusch, S. M. (1993). Postdivorce roles of mothers and fathers in the lives of their children. *Journal of Family Psychology, 7,* 24–38.

MacCoun, R. J., Lind, E. A., Hensler, D. R., Bryant, D. L., & Ebener, P. A. (1988). *Alternative adjudication: An evaluation of the New Jersey Automobile Arbitration Program.* Santa Monica, CA: Rand.

MacCoun, R. J., Lind, E. A., & Tyler, T. R. (1992). Alternative dispute resolution in trial and appellate courts. In D. K. Kagehiro & W. S. Laufer (Eds.), *Handbook of psychology and law* (pp. 95–118). New York: Springer-Verlag.

Magana, H. A., & Taylor, N. (1993). 1992 Meyer Elkin Essay Contest Winner: Child custody mediation and spouse abuse: A descriptive study of a protocol. *Family and Conciliation Courts Review, 31,* 50–64.

Mahoney, M. R. (1991). Legal images of battered women: Redefining the issue of separation. *Michigan Law Review, 90,* 1–94.

Maine (1994). Title 19, Section 752. Repealed.

Maine (1998). Title 19-A, Part 1, Chapter 3 (19-A.M.R.S. Sec. 251).

Margolin, F. M. (1973). *An approach to resolution of visitation disputes post-divorce: Short-term counseling* (Doctoral dissertation, United States International University, 1973). *Dissertation Abstracts International, 34*(4-B), 1754.

Marlow, L., & Sauber, S. (1990). *The handbook of divorce mediation.* New York: Plenum.

Marthaler, D. (1989). Successful mediation with abusive couples. *Mediation Quarterly, 23,* 53–66.

Marx, H. H. (1963). *Theories in contemporary psychology.* New York: Macmillan.

Maslow, A. H., & Sakoda, J. M. (1952). Volunteer error in the Kinsey study. *Journal of Abnormal Social Psychology, 47,* 259–262.

Mathis, R. D., & Yingling, L. C. (1990). Recommendations for divorce mediation with chaotically adaptable family systems. *Mediation Quarterly, 8,* 125–136.

Maxwell, N. G. (1992). The feminist dilemma in mediation. *International Review of Comparative Public Policy, 4,* 67–84.

Mayo, E. (1933). *The human problems of an industrial civilization.* Cambridge, MA: Harvard University Press.

McCrory, J. (1987). Legal and practical issues in divorce mediation: An American perspective. In J. McCrory (Ed.), *The role of mediation in divorce proceedings: A comparative perspective [United States, Canada and Great Britain]* (pp. 144–165). Burlington: University of Vermont, Vermont Law School.

McEwen, C. A., Mather, L., & Maiman, R. J. (1994). Lawyers, mediation and the management of divorce practice. *Law & Society Review, 28,* 149–187.

McEwen, C. A., Rogers, N. H., & Maiman, R. J. (1995). Bring in the lawyers: Challenging the dominant approaches to ensuring fairness in divorce mediation. *Minnesota Law Review, 79,* 1317–1411.

McGillicuddy, N. B., Welton, G. L., & Pruitt, D. G. (1987). Third party intervention: A field experiment comparing three different models. *Journal of Personality and Social Psychology, 53,* 104–112.

McIntyre, J. (1994, March 18). Practice research network: Pilot stage. *Psychiatric News.*

McIsaac, H. (1981). Mandatory conciliation custody/visitation matters; California's bold stroke. *Conciliation Courts Review, 19*(2), 73–81.

McIsaac, H. (1983). Court-connected mediation. *Conciliation Courts Review, 21*(2), 49–56.

McIsaac, H. (1987). Toward a classification of child custody disputes: An application of family systems theory. *Mediation Quarterly, 14–15,* 39–50.

McLaughlin, J. M. (1987). An extension of the right of access: The pro se litigant's right to notification of the requirements of the summary judgment rule. *Fordham Law Review, 55,* 1109–1137.

Meierding, N. R. (1993). Does mediation work? A survey of long-term satisfaction and durability rates for privately mediated agreements. *Mediation Quarterly, 11,* 157–170.

Melamed, J. (1989). Attorneys and mediation: From threat to opportunity. *Mediation Quarterly, 23,* 13–22.

Mellema, A., & Bassili, J. N. (1995). On the relationship between attitudes and values: Exploring the moderating effects of self-monitoring and self-monitoring schematicity. *Personality and Social Psychology Bulletin, 21,* 885–892.

Menkel-Meadow, C. (1984). Toward another view of legal negotiation: The structure of problem-solving. *UCLA Law Review, 31,* 754–842.

Menkel-Meadow, C. (1993). Commentary: Professional responsibility for third-party neutrals. *Alternatives, 11,* 129–131.

Menkel-Meadow, C. (1995, July). The many ways of mediation: The transformation of traditions, ideologies, paradigms, and practices [Review of the books: *The promise of mediation: Responding to conflict through empowerment and recognition, When talk works: Profiles of mediators,* and *The possibility of popular justice: A case study of American community justice*]. *Negotiation Journal,* 217–242.

Merry, S. E., & Silbey, S. S. (1984). What do plaintiffs want? Reexamining the concept of dispute. *The Justice System Journal, 9,* 151–178.

Michigan (1999). Title 25, Chapter 245, (M.C.L. 552.513); (M.S.A. 25,176(13); (M.C.R. 3.216(B)(1–4)).

Milne, A. (1978). Custody of children in a divorce process: A family self-determination model. *Conciliation Courts Review, 16*(2), 1–10.

Milne, A., & Folberg, J. (1988). The theory and practice of divorce mediation: An overview. In J. Folberg & A. Milne (Eds.), *Divorce mediation: Theory and practice* (pp. 3–25). New York: Guilford Press.

Minnesota. (1999a). Chapter 518 (Minn. Stat. Sec. 518.619).

Minnesota. (1999b). Minnesota General Rules of Practice, Rule 310, Part C (Minn. Gen. Prac. Rule 310.01; 114.01).

Minuchin, S. (1974). *Families and family therapy.* Cambridge, MA: Harvard University Press.

Mischel, W. (1968). *Personality and assessment.* New York: Wiley.

Mississippi Court Rules, Uniform Chancery Court Administrative Order, 1998.

Mitchell, F. (1998). The dispute resolution continuum: A diversity of new ideas. *Diversity Update, 4*(3), 2–3.

Mnookin, R. H. (1975). Child-custody adjudication: Judicial functions in the fact of indeterminacy. *Law and Contemporary Problems, 39,* 226–292.

Mnookin, R. H. (1984). Divorce bargaining: The limits on private ordering. In J. M. Eekelaar & S. N. Katz (Eds.), *The resolution of family conflict: Comparative legal perspectives* (pp. 364–383). Toronto, Ontario, Canada: Butterworths.

Mnookin, R. (1993, Summer/Fall). Why negotiations fail: An exploration of barriers to the resolution of conflict. *National Institute for Dispute Resolution (NIDR) Forum,* 21–32.

Mnookin, R., & Kornhauser, L. (1979). Bargaining in the shadow of the law: The case of divorce. *Yale Law Review, 88,* 950–997.

Model Standards of Practice for Divorce and Family Mediators. (2000). Symposium on standards of practice, October 1998. *Family and Conciliation Courts Review, 38*(1), 110–122.

Montana Code Annotated. (1998). Title 40, Chapter 4 Part 3 (Mont. Code Anno. Sec. 40-4-301 through 40-4-308).

Morrill, C. (in press). Institutional change through interstitial emergence: The growth of alternative dispute resolution in American law, 1965–1995. In W. W. Powell & D. L. Jones (Eds.), *How institutions change.* Chicago: University of Chicago Press.

Morrill, C., & Facciola, P. C. (1992). The power of language in adjudication and mediation: Institutional contexts as predictors of social evaluation. *Law & Social Inquiry, 17,* 191–212.

Mosten, F. S. (1997). *A complete guide to mediation: The cutting-edge approach to family law practice.* Chicago: American Bar Association.

Myers, D. G. (1996). *Social psychology* (5th ed.). New York: McGraw-Hill.

Myers, S., Gallas, B., Hanson, R., & Keilitz, S. (1988). Divorce mediation in the States: Institutionalization, use and assessment. *State Court Journal, 12*(4), 17–25.

Nader, L. (1990). *Harmony ideology: Justice and control in a Zapotec mountain village.* Stanford, CA: Stanford University Press.

New Hampshire. (1999). Title XLIII, Chapter 458 (RSA 458:15-a); Title XXX, Chapter 328-C (RSA 328-C:9).

Newmark, L., Harrell, A., & Salem, P. (1995). Domestic violence and empowerment in custody and visitation cases. *Family and Conciliation Courts Review, 33*(1), 30–62.

Norcross, J. C. (1994). *Prescriptive eclectic therapy* [Video]. Washington, DC: American Psychological Association.

Norcross, J. C., & Beutler, L. E. (1997). Determining the therapeutic relationship of choice in brief therapy. In J. N. Butcher (Ed.), *Personality assessment in managed health care* (pp. 42–60). New York: Oxford University Press.

North Carolina. (1999). Chapter 50, Article 1 (N.C. Gen. Stat. Section 50-13.1).

Nye, F. I., & Berardo, F. M. (Eds.). (1981). *Emerging conceptual frameworks in family analysis* (Rev. ed.). New York: Prager. (Original work published 1966)

Ogus, A., McCarthy, P., & Wray, S. (1987). Court-annexed mediation programs in England and Wales. In J. McCrory (Ed.), *The role of mediation in divorce proceedings: A comparative perspective [United States, Canada, and Great Britain]* (p. 63). Burlington: University of Vermont, Vermont Law School.

O'Leary, K. D. (1993). Through a psychological lens: Personality traits, personality disorders, and levels of violence. In R. J. Gelles & D. Loeske (Eds.), *Current controversies regarding psychological explanations of family violence* (pp. 7–30). Newbury Park, CA: Sage.

O'Leary, K. D., Vivian, D., & Malone, J. (1991, November). *Assessment of physical aggression in marriage.* Paper presented at the annual meeting of the Association for the Advancement of Behavior Therapy, San Francisco.

Oregon Revised Statutes. (1997). Title 11, Chapter 107 (O.R.S. 107.55).

Pearson, J. (1981). Child custody: Why not let the parents decide? *Judges Journal, 20*(1), 4–10, 12.

Pearson, J. (1991). The equity of mediated divorce agreements. *Mediation Quarterly, 9,* 179–197.

Pearson, J. (1993). Ten myths about family law. *Family Law Quarterly, 27,* 279–299.

Pearson, J. (1994, October). Family mediation. In S. Keilitz (Ed.), *A report on current research findings—Implications for courts and future research needs* (National symposium on court-connected dispute resolution research). Washington, DC: State Justice Institute.

Pearson, J., Ring, J. L., & Milne, A. (1983). A portrait of divorce mediation services in the public and private sector. *Conciliation Courts Review, 21,* 1–24.

Pearson, J., & Thoennes, N. (1982). The mediation and adjudication of divorce disputes: The benefits outweigh the costs. *The Family Advocate, 4,* 26–32.

Pearson, J., & Thoennes, N. (1984a). Dialogue: A reply to professor Levy's comment. *Family Law Quarterly, 17,* 535–538.

Pearson, J., & Thoennes, N. (1984b). Mediating and litigating custody disputes: A longitudinal evaluation. *Family Law Quarterly, 17,* 497–524.

Pearson, J., & Thoennes, N. (1985a). Mediation versus the courts in child custody cases. *Negotiation Journal, 1,* 235–244.

Pearson, J., & Thoennes, N. (1985b). A preliminary portrait of client reactions to three court mediation programs. *Conciliation Courts Review, 23*(1), 1–14.

Pearson, J., & Thoennes, N. (1986). Mediation in custody disputes. *Behavioral Sciences and the Law, 4,* 203–216.

Pearson, J., & Thoennes, N. (1988a). Divorce mediation: An American picture. In R. Dingwall & J. Eekelaar (Eds.), *Divorce mediation and the legal process* (pp. 71–91). Oxford, England: Clarendon.

Pearson, J., & Thoennes, N. (1988b). Divorce mediation research results. In J. Folberg & A. Milne (Eds.), *Divorce mediation: Theory and practice* (pp. 429–452). New York: Guilford Press.

Pearson, J., & Thoennes, N. (1988c). Supporting children after divorce: The influence of custody on support levels and payments. *Family Law Quarterly, 22,* 319–339.

Pearson, J., & Thoennes, N. (1989). Divorce mediation: Reflections on a decade of research. In K. Kressel, D. G. Pruitt, & Associates (Eds.), *Mediation research: The process and effectiveness of third-party intervention* (pp. 9–30). San Francisco: Jossey-Bass.

Pearson, J., Thoennes, N., & Vanderkooi, L. (1982). The decision to mediate: Profiles of individuals who accept and reject the opportunity to mediate contested custody and visitation issues. *Journal of Divorce, 6,* 17–35.

Perluss, D., & Prochnau, K. (1993). *Washington State Courthouse Facilitator Pilot Project: A one year project of the legal services programs of Washington.* Paper presented to the American Bar Association Committee on the Delivery of Legal Services, Seattle, WA.

Persons, J. B. (1991). Psychotherapy outcome studies do not accurately represent current models of psychotherapy: A proposed remedy. *American Psychologist, 46,* 99–106.

Persons, J. B., & Silberschatz, G. (1998). Are results of randomized controlled trials useful to psychotherapists? *Journal of Consulting and Clinical Psychology, 66,* 126–135.

Pilkonis, P. (1999, Spring). Empirically supported treatment task force approach. *Clinical Science, 1,* 3.

Popper, K. R. (1992a). *Conjectures and refutations: The growth of scientific knowledge* (5th ed.). New York: Routledge.

Popper, K. R. (1992b). *Logic of scientific discovery.* New York: Routledge.

Prochaska, J. O., & DiClemente, C. C. (1992). The transtheoretical approach. In J. C. Norcross & M. R. Goldfried (Eds.), *Handbook of psychotherapy integration* (pp. 300–334). New York: Basic Books.

Pruitt, D. G. (1971). Indirect communication and the search for agreement in negotiation. *Journal of Applied Social Psychology, 1,* 205–239.

Pruitt, D. G. (1981). *Negotiation behavior.* New York: Academic Press.

Pruitt, D. G. (1995, October). Process and outcome in community mediation. *Negotiation Journal,* 365–377.

Pruitt, D. G., & Carnevale, P. J. (1982). The development of integrative agreements in social conflict. In V. J. Derlega & J. Grzelak (Eds.), *Living with other people* (pp. 151–181). New York: Academic Press.

Pruitt, D. G., & Carnevale, P. J. (1993). *Negotiation in social conflict.* Pacific Grove, CA: Brooks/Cole.

Pruitt, D. G., & Drews, J. L. (1969). The effect of time pressure, time elapsed, and the opponent's concession rate of behavior in negotiation. *Journal of Experimental Social Psychology, 5*, 43–60.

Pruitt, D. G., & Johnson, D. F. (1970). Mediation as an aid to face saving in negotiation. *Journal of Personality and Social Psychology, 14*, 239–246.

Putnam, L. L. (1994, October). Challenging the assumptions of traditional approaches to negotiation. *Negotiation Journal,* 337–346.

Putnam, L. L., & Folger, J. P. (1988). Communication, conflict and dispute resolution: The study of interaction and the development of conflict theory. *Communication Research, 15*, 349–359.

Putnam, L. L., & Holmer, M. (1992). Framing, reframing and issue development. In L. L. Putnam & M. E. Roloff (Eds.), *Communication and negotiation* (pp. 128–155). Newbury Park, CA: Sage.

Putnam, L. L., & Roloff, M. E. (Eds.). (1992). *Communication and negotiation.* Newbury Park, CA: Sage.

Reber, A. S. (1985). *Dictionary of psychology.* London: Penguin.

Regehr, C. (1994). The use of empowerment in child custody mediation: A feminist critique. *Mediation Quarterly, 11*, 361–371.

Reynolds, P. D. (1971). *A primer in theory construction.* Indianapolis, IN: Bobbs-Merrill.

Ricci, I. (1980). *Mom's house, dad's house.* New York: Macmillian.

Ricci, I. (1989). Mediation, joint custody and legal agreements: A time to review, revise, and refine. *Family and Conciliation Courts Review, 27*, 47–55.

Ricci, I., Depner, C. E., & Cannata, K. V. (1991). Profile: Child custody mediation services in California Superior Courts. *Family and Conciliation Courts Review, 30*, 229–242.

Rice, L. N., & Greenberg, L. S. (1984). *Patterns of change: Intensive analysis of psychotherapy process.* New York: Guilford Press.

Rich, W. (1980). The role of lawyers: Beyond advocacy. *Brigham Young University Law Review, 1980*, 767–784.

Rifkin, J. (1994). The practitioner's dilemma. In J. P. Folger & T. S. Jones (Eds.), *New directions in mediation: Communication research and perspectives* (pp. 204–208). Thousand Oaks, CA: Sage

Rifkin, J., Millen J., & Cobb, S. (1991). Toward a new discourse for mediation: A critique of neutrality. *Mediation Quarterly, 9*, 151–164.

Riggio, R. E., & Porter, L. W. (1990). *Introduction to industrial/organizational psychology.* Glenview, IL: Scott, Foreman.

Robinson, L. A., Berman, J. S., & Neimeyer, R. A. (1990). Psychotherapy for the treatment of depression: A comprehensive review of controlled outcome research. *Psychological Bulletin, 108*, 30–49.

Roehl, J. A., & Cook, R. F. (1985). Issues in mediation: Rhetoric and reality revisited. *Journal of Social Issues, 41*, 161–178.

Rogers, N., & McEwen, C. (1994). *Mediation: Law, policy and practice* (2nd ed.,

Vol. 1–2, 1996 Cumulative Supplements and Revised Appendix B; 1998 Cumulative Supplement). Deerfield, IL: Clark, Boardman & Callahan.

Rohrbaugh, M., Shoham, V., Spungen, C., & Steinglass, P. (1995). Family systems therapy in practice: A systemic couples therapy for problem drinking. In B. Bongar & L. E. Beutler (Eds.), *Comprehensive textbook of psychotherapy: Theory and practice* (pp. 228–253). New York: Oxford University Press.

Rosenthal, R., & Rosnow, R. L. (1991). *Essentials of behavioral research: Methods and data analysis* (2nd ed.). New York: McGraw-Hill.

Roth, A., & Fonagy, P. (1996). *What works for whom? A critical review of psychotherapy research.* New York: Guilford Press.

Rubin, J. Z. (1971). The nature and success of influence attempts in a four-party bargaining relationship. *Journal of Experimental Social Psychology, 7,* 17–35.

Rubin, J. Z. (1980). Experimental research on third-party intervention in conflict: Toward some generalizations. *Psychological Bulletin, 87,* 379–391.

Rubin, J. Z. (1985). Third party intervention in family conflict. *Negotiation Journal, 1,* 269–281.

Rubin, J. Z. (1994). Models of conflict management. *Journal of Social Issues, 50*(1), 33–45.

Rubin, J. Z., & Brown, B. R. (1975). *The social psychology of bargaining and negotiation.* New York: Academic Press.

Rubin, J. Z., & Levinger, G. (1995). Levels of analysis: In search of generalizable knowledge. In B. B. Bunker & J. Z. Rubin (Eds.), *Conflict, cooperation, and justice* (pp. 13–38). San Francisco: Jossey-Bass.

Rubin, J. Z., Pruitt, D. G., & Kim, S. H. (1994). *Social conflict: Escalation, stalemate and settlement* (2nd ed.). New York: McGraw-Hill.

Rush, A. J., Beck, A. T., Kovacs, M., & Hollon, S. (1977). Comparative efficacy of cognitive therapy and pharmacotherapy in the treatment of depressed patients. *Cognitive Therapy and Research, 1,* 17–37.

Sales, B. D. (1983). The legal regulation of psychology: Scientific and professional interactions. In J. Scheirer & B. L. Hammonds (Eds.), *The master lecture series: Vol. 2. Psychology and the law* (pp. 9–25). Washington, DC: American Psychological Association.

Sales, B. D., Beck, C. J., & Haan, R. K. (1993a). Is self-representation a reasonable alternative to attorney representation in divorce cases? *Saint Louis University Law Journal, 37,* 553–605.

Sales, B., Beck, C. J., & Haan, R. E. (1993b). *Self-representation in divorce cases.* Chicago: American Bar Association.

Salius, A. J., & Maruzo, S. D. (1988). Mediation of child-custody and visitation disputes in a court setting. In J. Folberg & A. Milne (Eds.), *Divorce mediation: Theory and practice* (pp. 163–190). New York: Guilford Press.

Sander, F. E. A. (1976). Varieties of dispute processing, The Pound Conference. *Federal Rules Decisions, 70,* 111–134.

Santa Clara County, California. (1997). Code of Civil Procedure, Sec. 638–641, Waiver of Rule of Court 244.1(C).

Saposnek, D. T. (1983). *Mediating child custody disputes: A systematic guide for family therapists, court counselors, attorneys, and judges.* San Francisco: Jossey-Bass.

Saposnek, D. T., Hamburg, J., Delano, C. D., & Michaelsen, H. (1984). How has mandatory mediation fared?: Research findings of the first year's follow-up. *Conciliation Courts Review, 22*(2), 7–19.

Sarat, A., & Felstiner, W. L. F. (1986). Law and strategy in the divorce lawyer's office. *Law & Society Review, 20,* 93–134.

Sarat, A., & Felstiner, W. L. F. (1989). Lawyers and legal consciousness: Law talk in the divorce lawyer's office. *Yale Law Journal, 98,* 1663–1688.

Sarat, A., & Felstiner, W. L. F. (1995). *Divorce lawyers and their clients.* New York: Oxford University Press.

Schlissel, S. W. (1992). A proposal for final and binding arbitration of initial custody determinations. *Family Law Quarterly, XXVI,* 71–84.

Schulte, D., Kunzel, R., Pepping, G., & Schulte-Bahrenberg, T. (1992). Tailor-made versus standardized therapy of phobic patients. *Advances in Behaviour Research and Therapy, 14,* 67–92.

Schwebel, A. I., Gately, D. W., Milburn, T. W., & Renner, M. A. (1993). PMI-DM: A divorce mediation approach that first addresses interpersonal issues. *Journal of Family Psychotherapy, 4*(2), 69–90.

Schwebel, A. I., Gately, D. W., Renner, M. A., & Milburn, T. W. (1994). Divorce mediation: Four models and their assumptions about change in parties' positions. *Mediation Quarterly, 11,* 211–227.

Schwebel, R., & Schwebel, A. I. (1985). The psychological/mediation intervention model. *Professional Psychology, 16,* 86–97.

Scott, E. (1992). Pluralism, parental preference, and child custody. *California Law Review, 80,* 615–672.

Sechrest, L., McKnight, P., & McKnight, K. (1996). Calibration of measures for psychotherapy outcome studies. *American Psychologist, 51,* 1065–1071.

Seligman, M. (1994). *What you can change and what you can't: The complete guide to successful self-improvement.* New York: Knopf.

Seligman, M. (1995). The effectiveness of psychotherapy: The Consumer Reports survey. *American Psychologist, 50,* 965–974.

Selvini-Palazzoli, M., Boscolo, L., Ceechin, G., & Prata, G. (1980). Hypothesizing circularity-neutrality. *Family Process, 19,* 73–85.

Shadish, W. R., & Ragsdale, K. (1996). Random versus nonrandom assignment in controlled experiments: Do you get the same answer? *Journal of Consulting and Clinical Psychology, 64,* 1290–1305.

Shepard, A. (1990). Divorce, interspousal torts, and res judicata. *Family Law Quarterly, 24,* 127–155.

Shepard, A. (2000, Winter). AFCC hosts symposium on model standards of practice for mediators. *AFCC Newsletter, 19*(1), 10.

Shoham, V., & Rohrbaugh, M. (1996). Promises and perils of empirically supported psychotherapy integration. *Journal of Psychotherapy Integration, 6*, 191–206.

Shoham, V., & Rohrbaugh, M. (1997). Interrupting ironic processes. *Psychological Science, 8*, 151–153.

Shoham, V., Rohrbaugh, M., Stickle, T., & Jacob, T. (1998). Demand–withdraw couple interaction moderate retention in cognitive-behavioral vs. family-systems treatments for alcoholism. *Journal of Family Psychology, 12*(4), 1–21.

Shoham-Salomon, V. (1991). Introduction to special section on client–therapy interaction research. *Journal of Consulting and Clinical Psychology, 59*, 203–204.

Shoham-Salomon, V., & Hannah, M. T. (1991). Client–treatment interaction in the study of differential change process. *Journal of Clinical and Consulting Psychology, 59*, 217–225.

Shoham-Salomon, V., & Rosenthal, D. (1987). Paradoxical interventions: A meta-analysis. *Journal of Consulting and Clinical Psychology, 55*, 22–28.

Silbey, S. S. (1993, October). Mediation mythology. *Negotiation Journal*, 349–353.

Silbey, S. S., & Merry, S. E. (1986). Mediator settlement strategies. *Law & Policy, 8*(1), 7–32.

Simon, L., Sales, B., & Sechrest, L. (1992). Licensure of functions. In D. K. Kagehiro & W. S. Laufer (Eds.), *Handbook of psychology and law* (pp. 542–564). New York: Springer-Verlag.

Singer, J. (1992). The privatization of family law. *Wisconsin Law Review, 1992*, 1443–1567.

Slaikeu, K. A., Culler, R., Pearson, J., & Thoennes, N. (1985). Process and outcome in divorce mediation. *Mediation Quarterly, 10*, 55–74.

Slaikeu, K. A., Pearson, J., Luckett, J., & Myers, F. C. (1985). Mediation process analysis: A descriptive coding system. *Mediation Quarterly, 10*, 25–53.

Smith, B., & Sechrest, L. (1991). Treatment of Aptitude × Treatment interactions. *Journal of Consulting and Clinical Psychology, 59*, 233–244.

Smoron, K. A. (1998). Conflicting roles in child custody mediation: Impartiality/neutrality and the best interests of the child [Co-winning essay: 1997 Law School Essay Contest]. *Family and Conciliation Courts Review, 36*, 258–280.

Somary, K., & Emery, R. E. (1991). Emotional anger and grief in divorce mediation. *Mediation Quarterly, 8*, 185–197.

South Dakota. (1999). Title 25, Chapter 25-4 (S.D. Codified Laws Sec. 25-4-59; 25-4-60).

Spanier, G. B., & Anderson, E. A. (1979). The impact of the legal system on adjustment to marital separation. *Journal of Marriage and the Family, 41*, 605–613.

Spencer, J. M., & Zammit, J. D. (1976). Mediation–arbitration: A proposal for private resolution of disputes between divorced or separated parents. *Duke Law Journal*, 911–939.

Stanton, M. D. (1981). Strategic approaches to family therapy. In A. S. Gurman

& D. P. Kniskern (Eds.), *Handbook of family therapy* (pp. 361–402). New York: Bruner/Mazel.

The State Bar of Michigan v. Virginia Cramer, 249 NW2d.1.

Stiles, W. B., Shapiro, D. A., & Elliott, R. (1986). Are all psychotherapies equivalent? *American Psychologist, 41*, 165–180.

Straus, M. A., & Gelles, R. J. (1990). Societal change and change in family violence from 1975 to 1985 as revealed by two national surveys. In M. A. Straus & R. J. Gelles (Eds.), *Physical violence in American families: Risk factors and adaptations to violence in 8,154 families* (pp. 113–132). New Brunswick, NJ: Transaction.

Taylor, A. (1988). A general theory of divorce mediation. In. J. Folberg & A. Milne (Eds.), *Divorce mediation: Theory and practice* (pp. 61–82). New York: Guilford Press.

Taylor, A. (1997). Concepts of neutrality in family mediation: Contexts, ethics, influence, and transformative process. *Mediation Quarterly, 14*, 215–236.

Taylor, S. E., Peplau, L. A., & Sears, D. O. (1997). *Social psychology.* Upper Saddle River, NJ: Prentice Hall.

Texas (1994). Texas Family Code, Sections 3.522, 153.0071, 202.002.

Thoennes, N., & Pearson, J. (1985). Predicting outcomes in divorce mediation: The influence of people and process. *Journal of Social Issues, 41*, 115–126.

Thoennes, N., Pearson, J., & Bell, J. (1991). *Evaluation of the use of mandatory divorce mediation.* Unpublished manuscript prepared for the State Justice Institute, Williamsburg, VA.

Thoennes, N., Salem, P., & Pearson, J. (1995). Mediation and domestic violence: Current policies and practices. *Family and Conciliation Courts Review, 33*(1), 6–29.

Tjosvold, D., & van de Vliert, E. (1994). Applying cooperative and competitive conflict theory to mediation. *Mediation Quarterly, 11*, 303–311.

Tomm, K. (1987). Interventive interviewing: Part II. *Family Process, 26*, 126–183.

Treadway, D. C. (1989). *Before it's too late: Working with substance abuse in the family.* New York: Norton.

Treuthart, M. P. (1993). In harm's way? Family mediation and the role of the attorney advocate. *Golden Gate University Law Review, 23*, 717–779.

Trost, M. R., & Braver, S. L. (1987). *Mandatory divorce mediation: Two evaluation studies* (Final report presented to the conciliation court of the Superior Court of the State of Arizona, Maricopa County, February 1987). Phoenix: Arizona State University.

Trost, M. R., Braver, S. L., & Schoeneman, R. (1988). Mandatory mediation: Encouraging results for the court system. *Conciliation Courts Review, 26*(2), 59–65.

Tyler, T. R. (1989). The quality of dispute resolution processes and outcomes: Measurement problems and possibilities. *Denver University Law Review, 66*, 419–436.

Tyler, T. R. (1990). *Why people obey the law.* New Haven, CT: Yale University Press.

Tyler, T. R. (1997). Citizen discontent with legal procedures: A social science perspective on civil procedure reform. *American Journal of Comparative Law, 45,* 871–904.

VandenBos, G. R. (1996). Outcome assessment of psychotherapy. *American Psychologist, 51,* 1005–1006.

Varela, F. (1979). *Principles of biological autonomy.* New York: Elsevier North-Holland.

Vincent, M. (1995). Mandatory mediation of custody disputes: Criticism, legislation and support. *Vermont Law Review, 20,* 255–297.

Waldron, J. A., Roth, C. P., Fair, P. H., Mann, E. M., & McDermott, J. F. (1984). A therapeutic mediation model for child custody dispute resolution. *Mediation Quarterly, 3,* 5–20.

Walker, J. A. (1986). Assessment in divorce conciliation: Issues and practice. *Mediation Quarterly, 11,* 43–56.

Walker, J. A. (1989). Family conciliation in Great Britain: From research to practice to research. *Mediation Quarterly, 24,* 29–54.

Walker, L. E. (1984). *The battered woman syndrome.* New York: Springer.

Wallerstein, J. S., & Lewis, J. (1998). The long-term impact of divorce on children: A first report from a 25-year study. *Family and Conciliation Courts Review, 36,* 368–383.

Watzlawick, P., Weakland, J., & Fisch, R. (1974). *Change.* New York: Norton.

Weakland, J. H., & Fisch, R. (1992). Brief therapy—MIR style. In S. H. Budman, M. F. Hoyt, & S. Friedman (Eds.), *The first session in brief therapy* (pp. 306–323). New York: Guilford.

Weakland, J. H., Watzlawick, P., Fisch, R., & Bodin, A. (1974). Brief therapy: Focused problem resolution. *Family Process, 13,* 141–168.

Webster's New World Dictionary, 2nd College Edition. (1984). New York: Simon & Schuster.

Weis, D. L. (1998). The use of theory in sexuality research. *Journal of Sex Research, 35*(1), 1–9.

Weiss, R. L., & Summers, K. J. (1983). Marital interaction coding system—III. In E. Filsinger (Ed.), *Marriage and family assessment* (pp. 85–115). Beverly Hills, CA: Sage.

Weiss, W. W., & Collada, H. B. (1977, October). Conciliation counseling: The court's effective mechanism for resolving visitation and custody disputes. *Family Coordinator,* 444–446.

Weissman, M. M., & Markowitz, J. C. (1994). Interpersonal psychotherapy: Current status. *Archives of General Psychiatry, 51,* 599–606.

Weitzman, L. J. (1985). *The divorce revolution.* New York: Free Press.

Wheeler, D. (1985). Rethinking family therapy education and supervision: A feminist model. *Journal of Psychotherapy and the Family, 1,* 53–71.

White, M., & Epston, D. (1990). *Narrative means to therapeutic ends*. New York: Norton.

Winslade, J., & Cotter, A. (1997). Moving from problem solving to narrative approaches in mediation. In G. Monk, J. Winslade, K. Crocket, & D. Epston (Eds.), *Narrative therapy in practice: The archaeology of hope* (pp. 252–274). San Francisco: Jossey-Bass.

Winslade, J., Monk, G., & Cotter, A. (1998, January). A narrative approach to the practice of mediation. *Negotiation Journal*, 21–41.

Wisconsin Statutes. (1998). Chapter 767 (Wis. Stat. Sec.767.11).

Yeaton, W. H., & Sechrest, L. (1981). Critical dimensions in the choice and maintenance of successful interventions: Strength, integrity, and effectiveness. *Journal of Consulting & Clinical Psychology, 49*, 156–167.

Yellott, A. W. (1990). Mediation and domestic violence: A call for collaboration. *Mediation Quarterly, 8*, 39–50.

Zanna, M. P., & Rempel, J. K. (1988). Attitudes: A new look at an old concept. In D. Bar-Tal & A. W. Kruglanski (Eds.), *The social psychology of knowledge* (pp. 315–334). Cambridge, England: Cambridge University Press.

TABLE OF AUTHORITIES

AUTHOR INDEX

SUBJECT INDEX

individual-level variables in success of, 37–38

and non-communicating relationships, 32–33

Gender
and communication patterns, 50
and satisfaction with mediation procedures/outcomes, 88–90, 182
Good faith effort, 13
Gottman, J. M., 64–65
Gray, B., 174–175

Haynes, J. M., 10, 49–50
Health maintenance organizations (HMOs), 149, 151
Hearings, number of litigation, 102
Hennepin County (Minnesota), 6, 112, 118
HMOs. See Health maintenance organizations
Hopkins Symptom Checklist—90, 75
"Hostile" couples, 65–66
"Hostile/detached" couples, 65
Hybrid mediation models and programs, 12, 163–164

IDP (interpersonally dysfunctional parent), 37
Illinois, 12
Impartiality (of mediator), 41–45
Individual psychological functioning, effect of adversarialness on, 73–75
Informality, maintaining, 51
Information, mediator's perception vs. use of, 42
Interdependence, 186
Interpersonally dysfunctional parent (IDP), 37
Intervention research, 169–172
Intimidation, abuse by, 29

Joffee, W., 11–12
Judges
frustration of, with litigation, 3–4
and mediation research, 23

Justice (in divorce litigation), 196–197

Kansas, 13, 14
Kelly, J. B., 68–69, 182–183
Kressel, K., 46

Labor management model of mediation, 10
Lawyers. See Attorneys
Least detrimental alternative, 4
Legal fees, 99–102
Legal model of mediation, 9–10
Legal system
difficulties of performing research within, 23–24
efficiency of, 194–195, 198–204
Litigation process, 66–73
adversarialness in, 61–62
dissatisfaction with, 81
growth of mediation and frustration with, 3–5
justice in, 196–197
lack of research on improvements to, 22
satisfaction with, 78–82
variables in, 200–202
Los Angeles, 112, 113
Louisiana, 12, 14

Maine, 13, 62
Manuals, treatment, 139–140, 144, 150–151
Massachusetts, 7
Mediation
ambivalence toward, 32–33, 38
assumptions about cost benefits of, 115–120
benefits of, 16–17
communication and information model of, 11–12
and compliance with court orders, 91–97
confidentiality of, 13
costs of, 100
definition of, 3
evolution of, in United States, 5–9
flexibility of, 52

Mediation (*continued*)
goals of, 190, 197–198
good faith requirement for, 13
growth of, in United States, 15–16
hybrid models of, 12
issues addressed in, 13
labor management model of, 10
lawyer involvement in, 14
legal model of, 9–10
mandated, 7, 12
perceived need for, 3–5
referral of cases to, 12
similarities among various types of, 14–1514
therapeutic model of, 10–11
waiver from, 12–13
Mediation research
effects of, on current mediation theory, 167–177
mediation theory as basis for, 181–183
methodological limits in, 21–24
and psychotherapy research, 125–126
Mediation theory
as basis for mediation research, 181–183
and conceptual critiques of mediation, 174–177
conflict stories, Cobb's theory of, 184–189
current, 167–179
and definitions of theory, 183–184
evaluation of, 184
evolution of, 168–169
future of, 193–204
and goals of mediation, 197–198
and justice in divorce litigation, 196–197
for narrative-based intervention, 189–190
and outcome-based evaluations, 172–174
in process and intervention research, 169–172
quasitherapy, mediation as, 195–196
and system efficiency, 194–195, 198–204
transformative approach, 168–169, 190–192
Mediator(s). *See also* Neutral third party
attitudes of, 42–45
bias in, 42

choice of, 151–152
function of, 80
male-female mediator team, 15
qualifications of, 14
Mental health practitioners, frustration of, 4–5
Methodological problems in mediation research, 21–24
Michigan, 12
Minnesota, 14
Mississippi, 14
Models, mediation, 9–12
communication and information model, 11–12
hybrid models, 12
labor management model, 10
legal model, 9–10
problem-solving model, 46–47
therapeutic model, 10–11
Model Standards, 7–8
Montana, 12, 14
Multiple impact therapy, 6

Narrative-based intervention, 189–190
National Association for Community Mediation, 7
National Center for State Courts, 15
National Conference on Peacemaking and Conflict Resolution, 7
Neutral third party (as mediator), 41–55
accountability of, 51–54
equidistancing by, 47–51
impartiality of, 41–45
problem-solving approach by, 46–47
New Hampshire, 12, 13
No-fault-based divorce system, 5–6
North Carolina, 13

Oregon, 113
Outcome-based evaluation, 172–174
Overhead costs, 113–114

Parents
conflict between, 64–66
emotionality of, 4
frustration of, with litigation, 3
Patriarchal terrorism, 29

ABOUT THE AUTHORS

Connie J. A. Beck, PhD, is an assistant professor of psychology in The Psychology, Policy and Law Program at the University of Arizona, Tucson. Her work focuses on how the legal system creates or exacerbates psychological distress and how it can be adjusted or restructured to minimize that distress. She considers both the effects on legal professionals of working in legal settings and the effects of legal processes on those people who have disputes and attempt to resolve them using the legal system. She and Bruce D. Sales are currently writing a sequel to this book, tentatively titled *Theory in Divorce Mediation*.

Bruce D. Sales, PhD, JD, is director of The Psychology, Policy and Law Program at the University of Arizona, Tucson, where he is also a professor of psychology, psychiatry, sociology, and law. His most recent books are *Accommodating Abused Children in the Courtroom: Forensic Assessment and Testimony* (with Susan Hall; American Psychological Association [APA], in press), *Treating Adult and Juvenile Offenders With Special Needs* (coedited with José B. Ashford and William H. Reid; APA, 2001), and *Ethics in Research with Human Participants* (coedited with Susan Folkman; APA, 2000). Professor Sales is the editor for two APA book series: *Law and Mental Health Professionals*, and *Law and Public Policy: Psychology and the Social Sciences*; is a Fellow of the APA and the American Psychological Society; is a recipient of the APA Award for Distinguished Professional Contributions to Public Service and the Distinguished Contributions Award from the American Psychology–Law Society; and is an elected member of the American Law Institute. In 1999, he was awarded an Honorary Doctorate of Science from the City University of New York for being the founding father of forensic psychology as an academic discipline.

About the Authors

Connie J. A. Beck, PhD, is an assistant professor of psychology in The Psychology, Policy and Law Program at the University of Arizona, Tucson. Her work focuses on how the legal system creates or exacerbates psychological distress and  how it can be adjusted or restructured to minimize that distress. She considers both the effects on legal professionals of working in legal settings and the effects of legal processes on those people who have disputes and attempt to resolve them using the legal system. She and Bruce D. Sales are currently writing a sequel to this book, tentatively titled *Theory in Divorce Mediation.*

Bruce D. Sales, PhD, JD, is director of The Psychology, Policy and Law Program at the University of Arizona, Tucson, where he is also a professor of psychology, psychiatry, sociology, and law. His most recent  books are *Accommodating Abused Children in the Courtroom: Forensic Assessment and Testimony* (with Susan Hall; American Psychological Association [APA], in press), *Treating Adult and Juvenile Offenders With Special Needs* (coedited with José B. Ashford and William H. Reid; APA, 2001), and *Ethics in Research With Human Participants* (coedited with Susan Folkman; APA, 2000). Professor Sales is the editor for two APA book series: *Law and Mental Health Professionals* and *Law and Public Policy: Psychology and the Social Sciences;* is a Fellow of the APA and the American Psychological Society; is a recipient of the APA Award for Distinguished Professional Contributions to Public Service and the Distinguished Contributions Award from the American Psychology–Law Society; and is an elected member of the American Law Institute. In 1999, he was awarded an Honorary Doctorate of Science from the City University of New York for being the founding father of forensic psychology as an academic discipline.